Conten

First published in 2003 by Green Books Ltd.
Reprinted 2004, 2005, 2006, 2007, 2008, 2009, 2010.
Foxhole, Dartington, Totnes, Devon TQ9 6EB
Text & illustrations © Nicky Scott and Bob Gale
Design by Rick Lawrence. Printed by Kingfisher Print & Design, Totnes, Devon, UK
ISBN 978 1 903998 23 6   All rights reserved

Introduction

Once people start composting, they get hooked! It is a very simple and satisfying process: not only will your dustbin be lighter, but it won't smell so disgusting—and nor will your compost heap, if you follow the simple instructions in this booklet.

Even where people do not have gardens, they often have access to communal green spaces which they either can manage themselves or in partnership with the local council; and green spaces need compost! I've been taken on a tour of housing estates in London, where green spaces are not much in evidence, and there's plenty of composting going on, with the finished compost being used in window boxes, hanging baskets and on open community spaces (see page 20 for more on this).

Some people who do have gardens have extremely small ones, but fortunately you can compost in a very small space.

Many people have been offered cut-price composting bins by their Local Authority, but all too often there has been little information or support to go with these bins, with the result that many bins have later been found discarded unused, or used for other purposes. Other Local Authorities have had remarkably successful campaigns in which every single bin sale is accompanied by a thorough training session, and further supported by a compost 'hot line' and regular get-togethers, so that people can share experiences and get further help.

Composting has become a hot political issue. Under European law, Britain must reduce the amount of 'waste' going to landfill, particularly waste which can be composted. To do this, we have to massively increase the amount of recycling and composting. A hierarchy has been introduced, which puts disposal of waste by incineration and land-filling as the worst options, and home composting as the very best option since it reduces the amount of material to be disposed of.

With the enormous problems that face the world, it may seem that our individual efforts are going to be completely insignificant, but many problems we confront are created by individual actions, and we do have enormous powers. We can all choose to shop ethically and environmentally. With composting, we can address more than one issue at once. Not only can we stop buying peat-based compost, but also we can make peat-free compost ourselves from materials we commonly put in the dustbin. Up to two-thirds of the average dustbin contents can be composted. One third is organic matter, largely food waste. Another third is paper and cardboard, which can also be composted. Not only is this a good way to significantly reduce the amount that you are putting in your dustbin, but you now have a much better mix to add to either a composting system or a wormery system.

Of course, paper (magazines and newspapers) can go for recycling, and some councils also take flat-packed cardboard, but we all have plenty of cardboard packaging, toilet roll centres, egg boxes, kitchen paper, cereal boxes and cardboard boxes that can be composted.

For many years I have been on the Committee of the Community Composting Network. We have as our mission statement, 'Everyone composting!' We feel that just about sums it all up. If everybody were composting, then the environment we all live in, from the local level right up to the whole planet, would be in a far better state. This booklet will give you all the information you need for successful composting.

Nicky Scott

Acknowledgements

Special thanks to Bob Gale for all the wonderful illustrations; John Elford for his faith in commissioning the book; all my colleagues at the Community Composting Network for their comments, especially Richard Gomme, Nick McAllister, Hugh Baker, Pauline Pears, Jerry Ash, Tom Roberts, Steve Tinling, Louise Halestrap, Judith Thornton and Holly Tiffen; last but not least, all my other colleagues tirelessly working to promote composting and recycling in Government—and eating far too few biscuits in the process!

What is Composting?

Everything that lived recently could be composted

Natural products that were once part of a living organism, such as wood and wool, are not only food for a host of insects and other creatures but will slowly rot if the conditions are right. Composting is a way of accelerating this process by creating the ideal conditions for a variety of small organisms, most of which are only visible through a microscope.

Getting the mix right

Composting depends on bringing together the materials that you want to compost, in roughly the right proportions. There are basically two types:

- 'Greens': the wet, soft, green materials (high in nitrogen), and
- 'Browns': dry, harder, absorbent materials (high in carbon)

Bread and cheese

An analogy I like comes from the Centre for Alternative Technology (CAT): they refer to bread (dry, hard, 'brown', carbon) and cheese (soft, wet, 'green', nitrogen). This analogy also gives you an idea of the relative volumes that you need: for example a bucket of kitchen waste needs to be mixed with at least a bucket of scrunched up paper and cardboard or other 'browns', such as garden shreddings. In fact you can add a lot more paper and cardboard than this—just put it all in your kitchen bin together!

- If you get the proportions roughly right everything composts readily.
- If it's too wet it stagnates and goes smelly.
- If it's too dry—it just doesn't do anything.
- Material for composting needs to be wet, but also with plenty of air spaces, much like good soil. If soil is healthy it will have a good structure with plenty of air spaces and damp like a wrung out sponge. The same conditions are ideal for compost making.
- So if you create the right conditions, the bacteria, fungi, and countless other micro- and macro-organisms responsible for composting, will thrive.

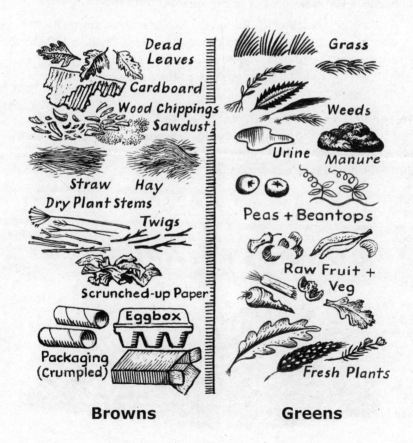

Browns

Greens

You can always add more micro-organisms by adding a light sprinkling of healthy topsoil, or even better, inoculate with some of the previous batch of compost (also see section on *Activators* on page 27).

Conclusion

- Get the mixture right from the start and Compost Happens!
- The most important thing to do is to mix dry, absorbent materials into wet sloppy stuff. Otherwise it starts to smell really unpleasant!
- The aerobic bacteria, which do most of the work breaking down the raw materials into compost, need both air and water. (See opposite for more on *Life in the Heap*).
- A pile of dry carbon-rich materials, like branches, sawdust, woodchip etc, is not going to cause a problem. It could be left as a long-term heap or a wildlife refuge, or it could be used to mix with green, soft, smelly materials as they arise.

Remember: even if you disregard all the above information, and just dump and run, eventually everything will get eaten by something or other, and converted into a dark crumbly substance that will positively enhance your soil.

COMPOST HAPPENS!

Life in the Heap

The whole secret of compost making is to set up the ideal environment for the bacteria, fungi and other creatures that are concerned with the decomposition process. They thrive in a moist but not waterlogged environment, with plenty of air: ideally everything is coated with water but there are air spaces between.

What is astonishing is the amount of life that a compost heap supports. A gram of healthy soil (roughly a teaspoon) contains about a billion microscopic organisms: predominantly bacteria and fungi, but literally thousands of different species. Then in the top nine inches of soil there are other larger fauna: mites, springtails, spiders, ants, beetles, centipedes, millipedes, slugs and snails 10,000–100,000 per square metre (and that's just in the top 9 inches!). And of course earthworms (30–300 per sq. metre)— these are not the same as the worms found in compost heaps. Now that's a staggering amount of soil life in each gram, in each square metre, and in each acre.

And compost heaps are richer than soils

Given the right conditions, colonies of bacteria can double every hour. A compost heap provides those conditions. The hundred thousand million or so bacteria in a teaspoonful will double in an hour— and keep on doubling, reaching astronomical numbers. It is primarily this phenomenal rise in the numbers of bacteria, all respiring, consuming and reproducing, converting the energy stored in the materials in the heap, which gives rise to the heat.

It's not just the bacteria that multiply in the heap, although the thermophilic (heat-loving) bacteria are the ones that really thrive in the heat. As the heap cools, there's plenty of food to go around for everyone. Compost heaps become a magnet for all kinds of creatures, including some bigger ones. Predatory beetles move in on larvae and smaller creatures; frogs and toads do likewise, as do slow worms and grass snakes, which love the warmth in a heap. Birds will visit to pick off insects and larvae, and bats will even visit at night. For wildlife value alone, it's worth making compost.

Questions & Answers

Here are some brief answers to questions that people often ask about composting. The subjects are discussed in more detail later in the book.

Why should I compost?

A third of the average dustbin is taken up with potentially compostable materials—two thirds, if you include paper and cardboard. Your dustbin could be considerably lighter and instead of filling up landfill sites you could be improving your garden soil (see page 26).

What can I compost?

Anything that recently lived *could* be composted, but you need to be careful with certain materials such as meat and fish (page 15), and animal faeces (page 31). However you can compost all your fruit and vegetable trimmings, food waste, grass cuttings, old plants, prunings, hedge clippings, hair, paper, used tissues, cardboard, the dusty contents of your Hoover bag and so on.

Are there different methods of composting?

Yes, composting means controlling the decomposition process: basically, speeding it up. You can speed it up by hot composting (page 12) or more slowly by cool composting (page 10). Or you can use other systems such as wormeries (page 21), fermentation (page 17) or in-vessel composting (page 19).

Will composting attract pests and diseases?

Cooked food, and even some raw fruit and vegetable trimmings can attract a variety of pests—mice, rats, foxes etc. To be really sure of excluding these pests, compost them in a container, especially during the winter months: see freezer system (page 19), fermentation (page 17), and feeding to worms (page 21). To minimise the number of flies, cover fruit waste with a layer of compost or soil.

If you grow your own vegetables you can end up with masses of trimmings—most of these are fine in an open composting system, without being totally enclosed.

What's the best method for a small garden?

You obviously need a compact container. The plastic composter bins that councils promote are fine for garden composting, but you may want to have a pest-proof container as well—see above.

Will my compost heap smell?

A compost heap should not smell unpleasant—if it does, then it is lacking air. It needs aerating, and/or something dry and airy mixed with it. The easiest solution is to always add plenty of scrunched up paper and cardboard as you go—it's a great way of getting rid of all that packaging, cereal boxes, envelopes, toilet roll centres, egg boxes and so on (page 4). Having a small shredder can be a boon (page 13).

Can I compost diseased plant materials?

You can, but there is a risk involved. When you become a confident 'hot composter' (page 12), the hot composting process will kill off plant diseases. Some experts say that adding compost helps to prevent and cure some plant diseases (page 29).

What can I do if I produce more compost than I can use?

Serious gardeners never have enough compost: they mulch their gardens, treat the lawn, feed houseplants, make hanging baskets, fill tubs etc. So if you can't use it, give it to gardening friends.

I live in a city flat, and only have a balcony. How can I compost?

It can be done. Some people even keep worms inside—I've seen them in a cunningly designed window seat! A wormery will not take up much space on a balcony—or you could ask the council if they could help start a community scheme (page 19).

Where can I buy composting bins?

You can buy them at garden centres and hardware stores—any many local councils offer subsidised bins.

Cool Composting

The compost bin that most people are familiar with is the plastic 'Dalek'-type bin, promoted by many Local Authorities. There is some variation in size and colour, and whether or not an access hatch is provided.

Because they have a small capacity (less than a cubic metre), they do not hold the heat well and are only suitable for cool composting. Most people will be cool composting most of the time, whether in a plastic bin or in a larger heap, as hot composting only works when you have large quantities at one time.

Mix and dump

You will generally be adding a fairly small amount at a time. Even so, you want to make sure that each time something is added to the heap, particularly if it is wet and smelly, it is mixed with something dry and absorbent. You can either keep a separate bin for autumn leaves, paper, card, or even part-rotted woodchip or sawdust etc, next to your compost bin so that you can mix as you go along, or just mix it into your kitchen bucket in the same way.

The 'Dalek' type of bin is fine for this kind of 'cool' composting. A cool compost system will soon have plenty of worms in it working away from the bottom upwards. In fact, without even trying you will be operating a kind of hybrid system, with some composting going on at the top and a wormery at the bottom.

Lifting the lid

You may well find that you get masses of tiny flies that fly up when you lift the lid. These will mostly be harmless fruit flies, which are particularly attracted by—well, fruit, as it happens! One way to control them is to leave the lid off the bin (or half off) for a while. This allows access to larger predatory beetles, which will set up home in your bin and will soon be feasting on fruit fly larvae. You can also wrap fruit waste in paper, or bury it in the heap—don't be tempted to use fly spray!

Siting the bin

A compost heap is best sited on soil, but will even work on concrete, as long as you put in the right mixture of materials and add light sprinklings of healthy soil to introduce soil micro-organisms, or a large dollop of compost or well rotted manure. Worms will even find their way across tarmac and concrete to colonise your heap! They will like it even more if you have a good bedding layer for them to colonise: moist, scrunched-up cardboard is ideal. Putting the bin in the sun will speed up the process, but it will still work in the shade. Put it anywhere that's convenient, but not too close to the house.

High-fibre compost

The real key to successful cool composting is the inclusion of plenty of high fibre. Paper and card are derived from the cellulose in wood, and provide the carbon that the process needs. Make sure paper is not in flat sheets, and is scrunched up. Add plant matter too (dry stems will create airways), and fresh fruit and vegetable trimmings are ideal. Keen composters add shredded harder woody material—one way to shred them is to run a mower over them. Pernicious weeds need to be killed off before being included (see page 28). Cooked foods, bread, oil, fat, cheese and meat etc are more problematic (see page 16), and are best left out of your compost heap until you are composting successfully.

Hot Composting

When all the conditions are right, a compost heap can get really hot. However, unless the heap is big enough (or very well insulated), this heat will rapidly dissipate (see page 31).

It isn't really necessary to make a hot heap unless you want to cook weed seeds and roots, or to rapidly kill any potential diseases or pathogens.

Making a hot heap

• To make a hot heap, first gather all your materials together.

• The best time is when the growing season is in full swing, when you can go and gather plant material to bulk up your heap.

• Nettles and other weeds can always be found somewhere— neighbours might be happy to help you with materials.

• You might be able to get hold of some strawy manure; your local hairdresser will happily give you hair; the greengrocer, spoiled fruit and veg; the brewery will give you hop waste, and so on.

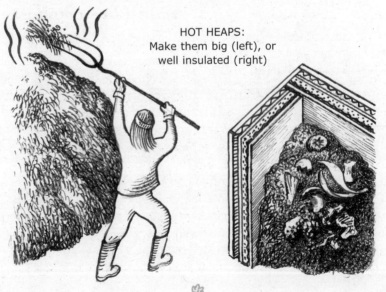

HOT HEAPS:
Make them big (left), or
well insulated (right)

Very small shredders, like this one, run very quietly and some crush rather than chip, which many composters prefer

- You could have bags of leaves saved from the autumn, or a nice pile of partly rotten wood chip.

- A shredder can be really useful for the tough and bigger stuff!

- Don't forget to add your cardboard and paper. Choose a time when you can add hedge prunings and grass cuttings.

- In short, assemble as much as you can. It should be enough to completely fill a four-foot (1.2 metres) square bin to a similar depth or more. It can be smaller than this, but if so you will really need to insulate the bin first.

- The 'Rolls-Royce' design for this type of heap is the New Zealand box (see below), but you can make a cheap simple version out of old pallets. These can simply be tied together, and you can easily insulate them if desired and line the inside with cardboard sheets to cover up the gaps.

- Start with a layer of material high in carbon (i.e. the tougher, drier stuff): not too thick — just a few inches.

The New Zealand Box ⌒

- Follow with a thinner layer, high in nitrogen — e.g. grass cuttings.
- Add water as you go, if the materials are on the dry side.
- Adding small amounts from a previous heap will 'inoculate' the heap with countless micro-organisms. So if you have it, put in the uncomposted top layer of a previous heap.

When the heap is built, cover it with some plastic sacks or sheet to keep in the water vapour which will be given off, and some old carpet which will help to keep the heat in.

Troubleshooting

After a day or so, the heap should be very hot: when you take the covers off you should be able to see the steam rising. If not, the mixture wasn't right:

- **It could be too dense and wet**: If wet, it needs opening up. Re-mix, adding something to absorb the water, to let the air in and to add carbon.
- **Or too light and airy**: If dry, it needs watering, or remixing with something green and sappy. Do not turn large musty dusty heaps. Wet them down first; otherwise, to avoid breathing in the fungal spores, wear a dust mask.

Monitoring and Turning

A large heap made in one go will rapidly heat up in a few days, then start to cool down. Keen composters have a thermometer on a probe, so that they can monitor when the temperature drops. At this point they turn the heap. The advantage of doing this is that you can mix all the ingredients: you can move the materials which were on the outside towards the middle, and vice versa. You can also check the moisture content etc, and adjust if necessary. After turning, the heap should re-heat and again it can be turned, to accelerate composting.

How Long Does it Take?

Cool composting will take six months to a year, or longer for dense clumps or unshredded woody material. Pre-shredding or chopping plant matter up with a sharp spade will speed up the process, as will turning a cool heap. Follow the stage drawings below, and make sure that when you put materials back in, that you mix it all up with some finished compost as a 'starter', and some fresh matter to balance its wetness or dryness. (See *What is composting?* at the beginning of the booklet.)

Hot compost can be made extremely quickly. After two or three turns, all the weeds and roots should have been cooked up. All this can happen in less than a month. The compost can be used at this stage as a mulch, but it is best left to 'simmer' and then gradually cool down and mature. As it cools, the worms and other small creatures move in to finish off the process. They will gradually turn the entire mass into a rich dark material resembling sticky chocolate cake! This will take a further six months to a year, depending on the season. When it's too cold, worms and other organisms just slow right down or stop.

1. Lift up the entire compost bin

2. The uncomposted top section can go back in

3. The compost can be harvested

4. Either bag it to use later, or use straight away

Many people will opt for a second composter. However it is easy to lift the whole bin, scoop the top section off—which will only be partially composted—and harvest the finished layer at the bottom.

What do I do with Kitchen waste?

Every household generates masses of material which can easily be composted. Even if you don't have a garden you can make compost for use in tubs, hanging baskets or to be used on some communal space (see *City composting* on page 19).

Food wastes need to be composted with more thought and care. Cooked food, dairy produce, bread, raw meat, potato peelings, root vegetables and whole fruits are food to a variety of creatures you don't want. They are really best dealt with in some kind of enclosed system: see *Worms* (page 21) and *City Composting* (page 19). However, the rest—fresh, raw vegetable tops and tails (leek trimmings, carrot tops, etc), fruit peel, onion skins, dead flowers, tea leaves, tea bags, coffee grounds and so on—can be added to the compost heap, although they still tend to be rather wet and smelly (they're high in nitrogen and water). The easiest thing to do is to mix them half-and-half with paper and cardboard (high in carbon and air, and absorbent of water), as this gives a good carbon to nitrogen ratio C:N. Save up all cardboard tubes, egg boxes, envelopes without their windows, Hoover dust, used tissues and so on. The paper and cardboard is an ideal way to soak up the liquids from the kitchen scraps. Line your kitchen bin with plenty of newspaper and/or cardboard and it will help keep it clean too.

A Green Cone composter

You can add the above to a garden composting system, or just mix it up with the trickier materials (still not forgetting the cardboard and scrunched paper, though) and deal with it in an enclosed system.

How to deal with meat and fish

The most obvious thing is to produce as little food waste as possible! Many people, of course, have a dog that will eat much of their left-overs. I never put meat or fish on my compost heap. Any bones get boiled up for stock, then dried out thoroughly and crushed. Finally they go into the compost or wormery.

Some food can be suitable for feeding to wild birds, especially in the winter, which is the time when all animals and birds are most desperate for food and when the compost heap slows right down. You can mix fats with breadcrumbs, seeds etc to put out for the birds. A half-coconut (or other container) can be filled with a hot fat mixture, for this purpose. When it has cooled and solidified hang it outside.

However, the ultimate pets for transforming waste are worms! See page 21.

The 'green cone' composter (see drawing opposite) consists of a basket like a washing basket, which is buried in the ground with a double skin cone, which is all that is visible above ground. This makes it difficult for rats to get in. The material breaks down and is pulled into the surrounding soil by worms. Since kitchen waste is largely liquid, much of this also goes into the soil where the nearby plants can take it up. This is more of a waste disposal option though, as you don't harvest the compost.

Fermentation A yet more advanced (but still remarkably simple) system uses fermentation. The Effective Micro-organism 'E.M. Bokashi' system uses bacteria, which thrive without air to convert the material. Unlike most airless systems, E.M. Bokashi does this without unpleasant smells. Many foods are preserved using fermentation processes, such as sourdough bread, beer, and sauerkraut. With E.M. Bokashi you generally have two sets of buckets. Each set is a pair of buckets, which fit together (see drawing on next page). The one on top has holes drilled in the bottom, so that liquids can collect underneath in the second bucket.

The E. M. Bokashi airless system

Every time material is added a little sprinkling of the micro-organisms is added, and the material is pushed firmly down and resealed. When the top bucket is full another set of buckets is started, and when that set is full the first set is emptied. You can either bury the contents, which very rapidly break down in the soil, or add them to your compost heap where they are no longer attractive to rats. For more information on Bokashi, see *www.livingsoil.co.uk*.

Burying Many gardeners bury kitchen scraps, particularly in the winter in a trench, which will become the site for runner beans in the following season. Don't do this with woody materials, though, as it causes 'nitrogen robbery'(i.e. it takes the nitrogen away from the growing plants).

City composting—See page 19.

Incorporating into a hot heap—This is most likely to happen in the summer, when you can quite easily bury kitchen scraps and cover them with abundantly available fresh material.

City Composting

We have to reduce the amount of compostable material going into landfill sites. The trouble is that composting food waste in the open air attracts flies, birds and other animals: the potential to spread disease is obvious. But if we can do the first, hot phase of composting in the extremely controlled conditions inside specialised composting containers, we can guarantee the temperature required to kill all the potential pathogens. The commercial composting sector utilises a variety of high tech, extremely expensive in-vessel composting units.

A Simple Low-Tech Solution

You don't have to go to all the expense of the commercial sector to make an in-vessel composter. All you need is a container which is sealed and well insulated, but which can also let air flow through it. A simple solution is to use an old de-gassed chest freezer. All over the country people are clubbing together to make compost (see the Community Composting Network in the Resource section), and you too could share a freezer system between a few households—see below.

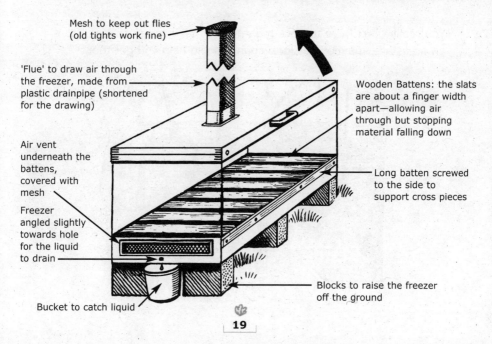

Mesh to keep out flies (old tights work fine)

'Flue' to draw air through the freezer, made from plastic drainpipe (shortened for the drawing)

Wooden Battens: the slats are about a finger width apart—allowing air through but stopping material falling down

Air vent underneath the battens, covered with mesh

Long batten screwed to the side to support cross pieces

Freezer angled slightly towards hole for the liquid to drain

Blocks to raise the freezer off the ground

Bucket to catch liquid

Composting without Gardens

I saw a more refined-looking version than the freezer (see previous page) on a housing estate in London. There was a small communal garden over the road, but the estate itself was just tarmac. The composting unit was housed in a smart stainless steel box, which contained two composting sections. A grid on the bottom allowed any liquid to drain off into a pipe, which in this case led to the sewer. When the box was opened it was easy to see the finished black compost at the bottom and the layer thick with worms just under the fresh food layer. The worms had found their own way to the composting unit and managed to squeeze in! This was in the middle of a sea of tarmac and concrete. This system was really a sealed 'hybrid' system. The top section was hot composting but because relatively small amounts were being added all the time and it wasn't an insulated container, the environment was perfect for worms, which could get away from the heat by burrowing down, if they needed to.

The local council had helped them set it all up and had helped them with window boxes and hanging baskets as well as planning the communal garden over the road.

Another high-rise estate has installed a mechanised in-vessel composter called the 'Webbs Rocket', to deal with the estate's food waste.

You really don't have to have a garden to make compost! If you live on an estate, maybe your local council could help you out too.

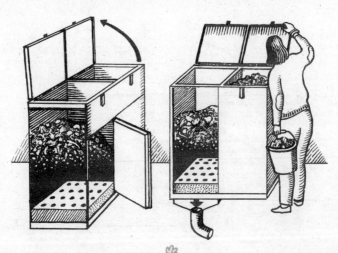

Worms and wormeries

I prefer the term worm farming to worm composting. It reminds you constantly that what you are doing is keeping livestock, and you are responsible for their welfare.

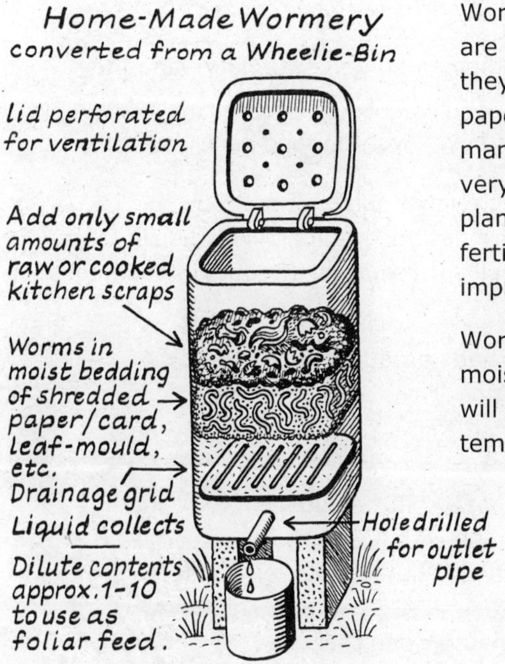

Home-Made Wormery
converted from a Wheelie-Bin

lid perforated
for ventilation

Add only small
amounts of
raw or cooked
kitchen scraps

Worms in
moist bedding
of shredded →
paper/card,
leaf-mould,
etc.
Drainage grid
Liquid collects

Dilute contents
approx.1–10
to use as
foliar feed.

Hole drilled
for outlet
pipe

Worms eat rotting matter, and are particularly useful because they will eat your food waste, paper and cardboard. Their manure, called 'worm casts', is very beneficial for all soils and plants. It is used more as a fertiliser than as a bulky soil improver.

Worms like it to be cool and moist, but not too cold. They will not be very active at low temperatures, and if it gets too hot, they will climb out if they can. If they get too wet, they may drown or migrate.

Starting off with worm farming

• When you are starting from scratch, as with any animal, you have to provide a suitable living environment.

• Containers can be home-made or bought, but whichever kind you use you must start the worms off with a generous bedding layer.

• This can be leafmould, finished compost (preferably sieved), shredded-up newspaper and/or cardboard, well rotted sawdust or woodchip, or a mixture of any or all of these.

• Whatever it is, it must be thoroughly wetted—especially paper and cardboard, as worms will die if they dry out.

- After you introduce the worms into the container, let them settle down for a day or two. They will be quite happy eating what's in there.

- Only feed them small amounts at a time: they don't want a great pile of stuff dumped on them as it can compost and generate heat—and they like it cool!

- Worms can eat about their own weight in food each day.

Wormeries should ideally have a large surface area, but unfortunately most of them are designed to look like wheelie bins (see drawing) with a very small surface area. The main advantages of these bins are that:

- You can tap off the liquid that's produced to water down as a liquid feed for plants, and

- They take up less space.

However, if you don't regularly tap off the liquid, the container will gradually fill up with it and drown all your worms—and knock you out with the odour!

If you separate out your materials so that fresh vegetable trimmings mostly go in your compost heap and the kitchen scraps go in the wormery, then you won't create masses of liquid.

Many large containers (such as old dustbins and barrels) can be adapted to become worm bins. If they have a hole in the bottom, you can easily plug this with some chicken wire doubled over. A good lid is vital to keep rats out. It doesn't have to seal completely—a small gap allows beneficial beetles in, which will keep the small fruit fly larvae in check. You can also buy, or make wooden wormeries. These give a larger surface area and are easier to manage, although they do take up more space. There are also stacking wormeries, such as the 'Can o'Worms'.

Harvesting

Wormeries take a long time to fill up with worm casts. When they are getting pretty full, the best thing to do is to remove the freshest material plus the layer immediately underneath. This will contain most of the worms; put the whole lot to one side. It can all go back into your wormery when you have harvested the worm casts.

If you want to harvest every last worm:

• Tip the rest of the material in the bin out on to a sheet of plastic or tarpaulin laid out on the ground.

• Make little piles of the compost all over the sheet and the worms will go to the bottom.

• By the time you've had a tea break the worms should be in position for harvesting.

• Pick the tops off all the piles—put the compost in a bucket as you go, the worms will be at the bottom against the plastic sheet.

• If you really want to increase the population, you can pick through the compost carefully looking for the egg cases, which look a bit like rather large grape pips.

Using Worm Casts

Worm casts are the crème de la crème of composts, and are best used by the handful rather than the wheelbarrow load. Think of worm casts as fertiliser, not compost: a little goes a long way. Give all your pot plants, window boxes, hanging baskets a top dressing. Water them thoroughly first, and then top dress with a handful or so of worm casts. You can do the same with any garden plants.

Leafmould and Grass

Making leafmould is ridiculously easy: you just gather up leaves and put them somewhere to stop blowing around! In a large garden, the common solution is to build a wire enclosure to be filled up with leaves. The only additions you need are water, and time. The leaves are broken down by being gradually consumed by fungi. Some take several years to fully break down, so you need to keep collecting them each year. If you only have a small garden, you may prefer to fill plastic bags with leaves instead. Make sure the leaves aren't bone dry—there must be enough water for the fungi to decompose them.

Fast leafmould (composting leaves)

You can speed up leafmould production by picking them off grassy areas using a lawnmower. This chops up the leaves and mixes them with grass, which is high in nitrogen. The grass is also mostly water, so you end up with the magic mixture of carbon and air (in the leaves), nitrogen and water (in the grass cuttings), and micro-organisms (on both). If you make a decent pile of these, they will heat up!

Cardboard mould

You can also layer cardboard with grass cuttings to make a wonderful leafmould/peat substitute. Just make a layered stack of thin layers of grass with flat cardboard sheet between.

Peat substitute

Whatever method you use, you will end up with leafmould. This resembles peat, and can be used in much the same way, but unlike peat, it is a renewable resource. Leafmould is an invaluable ingredient in seed and potting mixes (see *Using Your Compost* on page 26), so don't let those leaves go to waste! If you only have very small amounts of leaves, they can just be added to the compost heap, wormery etc.

Grasscuttings—leave them on the lawn!

Although grass cuttings are really useful in composting systems, they can also be a headache, especially in large quantities. You have to incorporate them into a heap in very thin layers, and you really have to do it as soon as they are generated. (This is where the stack of cardboard sheets comes in handy) So why not just leave them on the lawn instead? As long as the grass is not too long it will not form a thatch on the top. Besides, continually removing grass cuttings impoverishes the soil. This is great for wild flower meadows, but not for lush lawns.

Using Your Compost

All kinds of compost mixtures can be made for plants. We need one mix for seed raising, and a stronger mix for pricking out and growing on. Plants need to have mixes which both hold water and allow drainage. Most of the materials for compost mixes can come from the garden: principally sieved compost, leafmould and even molehills or good sieved soil. Many growers steam-sterilise soil for mixes to kill weed seeds, and some even use the heat from the composting process to achieve the same end.

Sometimes it is enough to just have sieved compost as the sole ingredient for growing plants on. More usually though the compost is 'opened up' by the addition of sharp sand, vermiculite, or something similar.

Recipes

Recipes don't have to be slavishly copied in either cookery or gardening: for one thing, the raw materials vary. Use your senses, feel the mix, squeeze it, smell it, put some in a pot and water it, and see what it does. Try a 'mix' for potting which is just pure sieved compost. For seeds, try compost made from composted leaves and grass or cardboard and grass. With other mixes, try leafmould and soil, plus some sharp sand (not builders' sand) or grit: e.g. two parts (buckets) compost, one leafmould, one soil and one sand.

Activators

Compost made correctly doesn't need an activator. Commercially available activators are generally either chemical nitrogen, which can have a detrimental effect on the micro-organisms in the heap, or a bacterial culture, which is unnecessary given the ideal conditions in the heap for the rapid growth of bacteria colonies. If you want to introduce more bacteria, the easiest way is to always inoculate each heap with a proportion of the previous heap. Also the odd light sprinkling of soil will introduce countless millions of bacteria.

Nevertheless, some people swear by activators:

- Urine is probably the cheapest and best (dilute 1:4).
- Seaweed (either freshly harvested, as liquid concentrate, or as a dried meal).
- Biodynamic gardeners and farmers, who follow the teachings of Rudolph Steiner, always put special herbal preparations into their heap. These can be bought from the Biodynamic Association (see *Resources* section).
- Maye E. Bruce formulated a simplified version consisting of the main herbs used in the biodynamic preparations in the 1930s. This can still be obtained through the Henry Doubleday Research Association and is called QR, which stands for quick return. The

main herbs in QR are camomile, dandelion, valerian, yarrow, nettle, and powdered oak bark. (Be careful adding these plants, as some are quite pernicious weeds, and small bits of root not properly composted could take hold and thrive in your compost.)

- Nettles compost extremely well, and are a valuable addition to any compost heap.

Dealing with weeds

Unless you are confident that you have a really hot heap, which will cook pernicious weeds, it's probably best to exclude them from your compost heap. But weed roots contain lots of valuable minerals, so it's a great shame to waste them: they can be dried out in the sun for a few days before composting, but watch they don't go to seed. One option is particularly useful for very earthy weed clumps like couch grass. You make a neat stack of the earthy clods, and then cover up the whole heap with thick black plastic to exclude all light. This needs to be left for about two years to be sure that all the weeds have died, and the result is a lovely rich loam. Smaller amounts can be treated in light-proof bags.

Another option is to drown the weeds to release their minerals. They can either be put in a hessian sack and weighed down in a barrel of water, or simply stuffed into a barrel of water and a cover put on. After a few weeks, the whole lot will rot and smell awful—so do it well away from human habitation! The smelly water can be used on plants (the smell will go away very quickly), and the plant remains can now be safely composted.

- Plants die without light
- Most plants will 'drown' in water.

Fly tipping is illegal, and has doubtless caused the spread of invasive weeds.

Japanese Knotweed

Japanese knotweed is extremely pernicious and difficult to kill. You can be prosecuted for taking it to centralised composting sites or fly tipping it. Although the tops, or canes, can be composted, even the tiniest piece of the crown will regenerate. If you have it on your property, you could try cutting the fresh green top growth off regularly. (Beware mowing it, as it can spread the plant further afield unless done with care.) This will have to be done at least once a month for several years. The green tops can be composted—but make sure that you don't have any of the crown with it! Once you have weakened the

plant, you can then dig over the ground and remove as much root and crown as you can. These are best burnt, as composting is too risky. Don't plant anything where the knotweed was, because more is bound to come up and you must remove all the re-growth! Knotweed will come up through tarmac and concrete, and even treatments with herbicides take several years to kill off the plant. For more advice on knotweed, look at www.ex.ac.uk/knotweed or contact your local environment agency.

Compost 'teas'

Composting gardeners have always maintained that compost has healing and disease-suppressing qualities. Now the anecdotes are being confirmed by scientific evidence.

Many plant diseases, including clubroot, which affects the cabbage family, white rot, which affects the onion family, brown rot, which affects potatoes, and many field crop diseases can be suppressed by the application of compost. Compost is the key to building and maintaining healthy soils. As we've seen, the life in the heap mirrors the life in the soil. It is the complex relationships of (principally) fungi and plants which is so important. Making your own compost and adding it to your soil is one of the best things—if not the single most important one—that we can all undertake to benefit the planet.

Some authorities are now claiming that 'compost teas' are also beneficial. You can make a brew by putting a sack of compost in a barrel of water for a few days: then remove the sack, squeezing most water out, strain, dilute 1:10, and use as a foliar feed on your plants (a similarly useful 'juice' is the liquid you can tap from a worm bin or a 'freezer' system). Undoubtedly more research is needed in this area, but one thing is for sure—it's not going to do any harm and could be very beneficial. Don't spray plants in full sun, and for maximum effect add a drop of liquid soap and aim to coat leaves both above and below. N.B.: It's for the plants—not to replace your own cuppa!

What can't I compost?

You can't compost materials that never lived—like glass, plastic, metal, stone. Large pieces of wood will take an awfully long time—unless they have been chipped up, which vastly increases their surface area. Often large pieces of wood are better used as firewood or as wildlife refuges—many beetles depend on this kind of habitat. Some, like the stag's horn beetle, have become very rare because of people being over zealous in cleaning up their gardens of rotting lumps of wood. Newts and toads spend lots of time under rotting piles of wood, so find a place to make a wildlife pile, instead of trying to compost it all.

High Risk Materials

Dog and cat faeces These can contain parasitic worms which can cause blindness, and therefore it is generally not recommended that they are composted, especially when there are children around. Personally I think they are better composted than left lying around: a carefully made hot compost will destroy these pathogens. Composting is incredible in the way that it purifies diseased matter, but you must treat it with respect. Wash your hands carefully after handling compost—especially if you have been more adventurous with what you do compost. Some commercial cat litter is now compostable.

Nappies Disposable nappies are an environmental time bomb, as well as being unpleasant and hazardous items in the dustbin. Buried in landfill sites they are said to take centuries to break down. Where possible, it is best to use re-useable nappies. You either buy and wash them yourself, or use a nappy laundry service. There are also nappies now made with bio-degradable plastic. These can be composted: urine is safe enough, but faeces need to be composted carefully, with plenty of other material to make a suitable mix. If you don't want to compost the faeces, soiled liners can be flushed down the toilet, and the rest of the nappy composted.

Coal Ash Although coal was formed from living organisms, it was at a time when our atmosphere was different: coal ash contains high levels of sulphur. Very small amounts are not going to be a problem, but too much will poison the soil. (Wood and charcoal ash, however, are fine for composting.)

Pernicious Weeds Be very careful when composting persistent weeds—see page 28.

Diseased Plants Composting is an amazing process: an astonishing number and variety of organisms are involved, and the heat generated can easily reach 60–70°C. Plant and animal pathogens as well as weeds are destroyed by the heat generated, and the hotter it gets the more quickly they die.

Weed seeds and human and plant pathogens are killed during the first few days of hot composting when the temperature is above 55°C. But even above just 40°C, few will have survived after a month or so. To ensure complete pathogen removal, it's important to mature your compost. The warm, post-hot composting phase produces the 'hygienisers', i.e. the organisms that attack pathogens, including those that produce antibiotics. You need a well managed, regularly turned, hot system to tackle diseased plants (which is why most gardening experts will tell you to burn them), but the bacterial 'fire' of the compost heap is just as effective!

Meat, fish and cooked foods Special care needs to be taken with these materials. See *What can I do with kitchen waste?* (page 16), *City Composting* (page 19) and *Worm Farming* (page 21).

General advice If you can confidently compost these materials, do it!

Waste not —compost!

Resources

Books

Composting: an easy household guide by Nicky Scott (Green Books)

All about Composting by Pauline Pears (HDRA/Search Press)

The Rodale Book of Composting (Rodale Press, USA)

Magazine

The Growing Heap, the magazine of the Community Composting Network

Organisations

The Community Composting Network

67 Alexandra Road,
Sheffield S2 3EE
Tel 0114 2580 483
ccn@gn.apc.org
www.othas.org.uk/ccn

The Composting Association

Avon House, Tithe Barn Road,
Wellingborough, Northants,
NN8 1DH *www.compost.org.uk*

Biodynamic Agricultural Association

Painswick Inn, Stroud, Glos.
Tel/Fax: 01453 759501
www.anth.org.uk/biodynamic

Green Books

Foxhole, Dartington, Totnes
Devon TQ9 6EB
Tel 01803 863260
sales@greenbooks.co.uk
www.greenbooks.co.uk

HDRA—The Organic Organisation

Ryton-on-Dunsmore
Coventry CV8 3LG
Tel 02476 303517
www.hdra.org.uk

Mucking In: A Guide to Community Composting:
A pack produced by HDRA and the Wildlife Trust. Available from The Community Composting Network.

50 Walks in

THE COTSWOLDS

First published 2002
Researched and written by Christopher Knowles, Nicholas Reynolds,
Nick Channer, Ann F Stonehouse and David Hancock
Introduction by Chris Bagshaw

Produced by AA Publishing
© Automobile Association Developments Limited 2002
Illustrations © Automobile Association Developments Limited 2002

Published by AA Publishing (a trading name of Automobile
Association Developments Limited, whose registered office is
Millstream, Maidenhead, Windsor, SL4 5GD;
registered number 1878835)

Ordnance Survey This product includes mapping data licensed from
Ordnance Survey® with the permission of the
Controller of Her Majesty's Stationery Office.
© Crown copyright 2002. All rights reserved. Licence number 399221

ISBN 0 7495 3511 3

A1230

A CIP catalogue record for this book is available
from the British Library.

The contents of this book are believed correct at the time of printing.
Nevertheless, the publishers cannot be held responsible for any errors
or omissions or for changes in the details given in this book or for
the consequences of any reliance on the information it provides. We
have tried to ensure accuracy in this book, but things do change and
we would be grateful if readers would advise us of any inaccuracies
they may encounter.

We have taken all reasonable steps to ensure that these walks are
safe and achievable by walkers with a realistic level of fitness.
However, all outdoor activities involve a degree of risk and the
publishers accept no responsibility for any injuries caused to
readers whilst following these walks. For more advice on walking
safely see page 8. The mileage range shown on the front cover is for
guidance only – some walks may exceed or be less than these
distances.

Some of these routes may appear in other AA walks books.

Visit the AA Publishing website at www.theAA.com

Paste-up and editorial by Outcrop Publishing Services Ltd, Cumbria
for AA Publishing

Colour reproduction by LC Repro
Printed in Italy by G Canale & C SPA, Torino, Italy

Legend

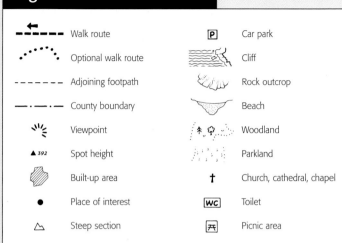

← - - - - -	Walk route	P	Car park
⋯⋯	Optional walk route	≈	Cliff
- - - - - -	Adjoining footpath		Rock outcrop
— · — · —	County boundary		Beach
⧉	Viewpoint	🌳	Woodland
▲ 392	Spot height		Parkland
	Built-up area	†	Church, cathedral, chapel
●	Place of interest	WC	Toilet
△	Steep section	�	Picnic area

The Cotswolds locator map

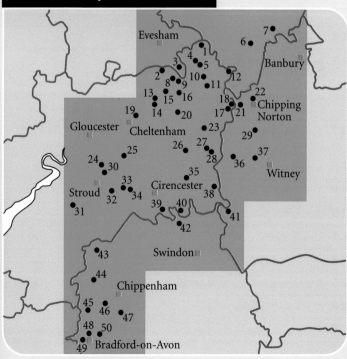

Contents

Contents

Rating: Each walk is rated for its relative difficulty compared to the other walks in this book. Walks marked 🚶🚶🚶 are likely to be shorter and easier with little total ascent. The hardest walks are marked 🚶🚶🚶 .

Walking in Safety: For advice and safety tips ➤ 8.

Introducing The Cotswolds

For many people the Cotswolds epitomise a vision of rural England. Here are pretty golden-stone villages, huddled in tranquil wooded valleys, bisected by sparkling brooks and surrounded by evergreen farmland. But for many too, this vision is unrealised. The crowds that throng around Broadway and Bourton-on-the-Water, buying their ice creams and enjoying the various tourist 'attractions' are surely missing something. Take a bit more time to explore this region and you will see that sometimes the myth and the reality can be reconciled, especially if you are prepared to step out of your car and get your boots muddy.

Protected

The whole region is protected by the Cotswolds Area of Outstanding Natural Beauty (AONB), at 790 square miles (2038sq km) the largest area in the country to be designated in this way. In the east, these 'official' Cotswolds reach surprisingly deep into Oxfordshire, to the north they point green fingers into both Warwickshire and Worcestershire, in the south, Wiltshire and North East Somerset claim their portions, but the lion's share of this beautiful landscape falls in Gloucestershire, and you will find this is where the majority of the walks in this guide are too.

Changing Scenery

Approaching the Cotswolds from the north east, you'll notice the scenery begins to change in subtle ways. The half-timber and thatch of 'Shakespeare Country' begins to give way to a honey-coloured stone which defines the borders of the region. This is the oolitic limestone that tilts down from west to east. In the east the gradually rising profile is virtually indistinguishable. One is only vaguely aware that the surrounding countryside is gaining in altitude. This is open, arable farming country, punctuated by dark stands of trees and rivers flanked by water-meadows. Here you will find the source of the mighty Thames. Although the watershed is hardly apparent, the presence of two great east–west canals hints that it may have once presented a formidable obstacle to transport. These waterways – the Thames and Severn and the Kennet and Avon canals – provide some of the best level walking in the southern Cotswolds and cut through the very heart of the suddenly dramatic valleys that emerge on the western side.

Idyllic

But it is the idyllic stone-built villages that attract visitors to all parts of the Cotswolds, and on these walks you will find out why. In Snowshill, Bibury, Castle Combe and Stanton, the impossibly lovely buildings will take your breath away. And in Chipping Campden, you'll feel you have found the epicentre of this vernacular wealth. The townscapes are sublime too, as you'll find at Bradford-on-Avon, Corsham and Burford. There is an intimacy about these warm buildings which never fails to thrill and inspire locals and visitors alike. You will not be the first to experience the uplifting charm of the Cotswolds. Thousands of years ago ancient peoples were moved to commemorate the burial of their dead on these undulating hills. At Belas Knap, you'll find one of the best preserved remnants of such burials, and at the Rollright Stones you may wonder at what insights these early folk possessed when they lined up their megalithic arrays with the midsummer moon.

Fine Buildings
Vernacular architecture in the Cotswolds undoubtedly provides many of the stars of the built environment, but there are some grand houses too. There's nothing

Using this Book

Information Panels
An information panel for each walk shows its relative difficulty (➤ 5), the distance and total amount of ascent (that is how much ascent you will accumulate throughout the walk). An indication of the gradients you will encounter is shown by the rating ▲▲▲ (fairly flat ground with no steep slopes) to **▲▲▲** (undulating terrain with several very steep slopes).

Minimum Time
The minimum time suggested is for approximate guidance only. It assumes reasonably fit walkers and doesn't allow for stops.

Suggested Maps
Each walk has a suggested map. This will usually be a 1:25,000 scale Ordnance Survey Explorer map. Laminated aqua3 versions of these maps are longer lasting and water resistant.

Start Points
The start of each walk is given as a six-figure grid reference prefixed by two letters indicating which 100km square of the National Grid it refers to. You'll find more information on grid references on most Ordnance Survey maps.

Dogs
We have tried to give dog owners useful advice about how dog friendly each walk is. Please respect other countryside users. Keep your dog under control at all times, especially around livestock, and obey local bylaws and other dog control notices. Remember it is against the law to let your dog foul in many public areas, especially in villages and towns.

Car Parking
Many of the car parks suggested are public, but occasionally you may find you have to park on the roadside or in a lay-by. Please be considerate when you leave your car, ensuring that access roads or gates are not blocked and that other vehicles can pass safely. Remember that pub car parks are private and should not be used unless you have the owner's permission.

Maps
Each walk is accompanied by a sketch map drawn from the Ordnance Survey map and appended with the author's local observations. The scale of these maps varies from walk to walk. Some routes have a suggested option in the same area with a brief outline of the possible route. You will need a current Ordnance Survey map to make the most of these suggestions.

here on the scale of Longleat or Blenheim, but you'll find Sezincote and Compton Wynyates delightful nevertheless. Church buildings are also an impressive part of this legacy. The romantic remains of Hailes Abbey sit quietly at the foot of the escarpment and are best seen from the footpath near Beckbury Camp, where Thomas Cromwell surveyed their destruction for Henry VIII. Among the outstanding churches, Chipping Camden is a tribute to the wealth of the medieval wool trade and the twin churches at Eastleach Turville and Eastleach Martin eye each other across the River Leach.

Hill Country

Buildings and villages are not for everyone though and, at its western edge, the Cotswold escarpment can hold its own for lovers of wide views. From Dover's Hill down to Uley Bury, you'll see faraway Wales, the Forest of Dean and the Malvern Hills, as well as catching some fine panoramas of the Cotswolds themselves rising up from

Walking in Safety

All these walks are suitable for any reasonably fit person, but less experienced walkers should try the easier walks first. Route finding is usually straightforward, but you will find that an Ordnance Survey map is a useful addition to the route maps and descriptions.

Risks

Although each walk here has been researched with a view to minimising the risks to the walkers who follow its route, no walk in the countryside can be considered to be completely free from risk. Walking in the outdoors will always require a degree of common sense and judgement to ensure that it is as safe as possible.

- Be particularly careful on cliff paths and in upland terrain, where the consequences of a slip can be very serious.

- Remember to check tidal conditions before walking on the seashore.

- Some sections of route are by, or cross, busy roads. Take care and remember traffic is a danger even on minor country lanes.

- Be careful around farmyard machinery and livestock, especially if you have children with you.

- Be aware of the consequences of changes in the weather and check the forecast before you set out. Carry spare clothing and a torch if you are walking in the winter months. Remember the weather can change very quickly at any time of the year and, in moorland and heathland areas, mist and fog can make route finding much harder. Don't set out in these conditions unless you are confident of your navigation skills in poor visibility. In summer remember to take account of the heat and sun; wear a hat and carry spare water.

- On walks away from centres of population you should carry a whistle and survival bag. If you do have an accident requiring the emergency services, make a note of your position as accurately as possible and dial 999.

PUBLIC TRANSPORT ⓘ

There are good rail links to many of the towns which surround the Cotswolds and the Cotswold Line from London to Worcester and Hereford cuts through the northern part with several stops connecting to dedicated bus links. In the south, the railway line down the Avon Valley has some very convenient halts for walkers on the Kennet and Avon Canal. You can get train times from the national rail enquiry line on 08457 48 49 50. Outside these favoured places, travel by public transport can be a hit and miss affair with no through ticketing and some very poor connections. There is a bewildering array of operators and getting home again after a walk which finishes later than six o'clock in the evening can be difficult. For timetable information you should call the various county travel information lines. In Oxfordshire call 01865 810405, in Gloucestershire call 01452 425543 (24 hours), in Wiltshire call 08457 090899, in Warwickshire call 01926 414140. For other areas call Traveline on 0870 608 2 608 (24 hours). You can also find details on the internet at www.pti.org.uk.

the Severn Plain and Vale of Evesham. The Cotswold Way National Trail follows this edge for much of its 101-mile (163km) route.

Historic Landscape

This is the land where Laurie Lee grew up, made famous by his evocative childhood memories in *Cider with Rosie*. Here Arts and Crafts pioneers rediscovered pre-industrial values in design and created everything from glassware to revolutionary gardens. A century before, the Industrial Revolution transformed the local woollen industry, bringing great mills to the Stroud Valley and poverty to the old weaving villages. Much of the Cotswolds' history is tied to the fortunes of wool. At one time this was the wool capital of Europe. The elaborate medieval churches are testimonies to the wealth of their merchant patrons. But you'll find precious few sheep on the hills now. Agricultural changes over the last century almost brought the local 'Cotswold Lion' breed to extinction. Now your only glimpse of these fine beasts might be in one of the rare breeds centres. Whilst the stone walls and tight fields of pastoral farming survive on the poorer soils, arable dominates the Cotswold landscape.

Off the Beaten Path

Walk through this ever-changing landscape and see how little has actually changed over the centuries. The woods, the villages, the hidden valleys and surprising elevations remain. This apparent contradiction reflects the region's historical ability to reinvent itself and is why new generations of visitors will always discover the region for themselves. This selection of 50 walks introduces the themes and characters that created this living, beautiful landscape. It won't take you long to appreciate that the only way to enjoy the Cotswolds to the full is to step off the beaten path.

Walk 1

Gloucestershire's Gardens Around Mickleton

A walk that takes you past Kiftsgate Court and Hidcote Manor Garden, two early 20th-century creations of international repute.

•DISTANCE•	5½ miles (8.8km)
•MINIMUM TIME•	2hrs 30min
•ASCENT / GRADIENT•	625ft (190m) ▲▲▲
•LEVEL OF DIFFICULTY•	🚶🚶 🚶🚶 🚶🚶
•PATHS•	Fields, firm tracks, some possibly muddy woodland, 12 stiles
•LANDSCAPE•	Woodland, open hills and villages
•SUGGESTED MAP•	aqua3 OS Explorer 205 Stratford-upon-Avon & Evesham
•START / FINISH•	Grid reference: SP 162434
•DOG FRIENDLINESS•	On leads in livestock fields, good open stretches elsewhere
•PARKING•	Free car park at church
•PUBLIC TOILETS•	None on route
•CONTRIBUTOR•	Christopher Knowles

BACKGROUND TO THE WALK

This walk takes you within striking distance of two of the finest planned gardens in the country. The first, Kiftsgate Court, is the lesser known of the two but nonetheless demands a visit. The house itself is primarily Victorian, whilst the garden was created immediately after World War One by Heather Muir, who was a close friend of Major Johnston, the creator of the nearby Hidcote Manor Garden. Kiftsgate's gardens are designed around a steep hillside overlooking Mickleton and the Vale of Evesham, with terraces, paths, flowerbeds and shrubs. The layout is in the form of rooms and the emphasis is more on the plants themselves, rather than on the overall design. The steeper part of the garden is almost a cliff. It's clad in pine trees and boasts wonderful views across the vale below.

Major Johnson's Rooms

The second horticultural treat is Hidcote Manor Garden, part of the little hamlet of Hidcote Bartrim. This garden is the fruit of over 40 years of work by Major Lawrence Johnson, an East Coast American who purchased the 17th-century manor house in 1907 and gave it to the National Trust in 1948. Many people consider it be one of the greatest of English gardens, and certainly it is one of the most influential. Hidcote grew from almost nothing – when Major Johnson first arrived there was a just a cedar tree and a handful of beeches on 11 acres (4.5ha) of open wold. To some extent it reconciles the formal and informal schools of garden design. Hidcote is not one garden but several. Like Kiftsgate it is laid out in a series of 'outdoor rooms', as they have been described, with walls of stone and of hornbeam, yew and box hedge. These rooms are themed, having names such the White Garden and the Fuchsia Garden, for example. There is also a wild garden growing around a stream, as well as lawns and carefully placed garden ornaments that help to create a bridge between the order within and the disorder without.

Walk 1

Have a Butchers

This walk begins in Mickleton, at the foot of the Cotswold escarpment, below these two fine gardens. Clearly a Cotswold village, notwithstanding its mixture of stone, thatch and timber, the parish church at the village edge, lurks behind a striking house in the so-called Cotswold Queen Anne style. It has a 14th-century tower and an interesting monument to the 18th-century quarry owner from Chipping Campden, Thomas Woodward. Near the hotel in the village centre is a Victorian memorial fountain designed by William Burges, the architect behind Cardiff Castle. There is also a fine butcher's shop here, a sight to behold, especially in autumn, when it's festooned with locally shot pheasant. As if to further enhance the village's Cotswold credentials, this was also the birthplace of Endymion Porter, a patron of the Cotswold Olimpick Games on Dover's Hill (➤ Walk 4).

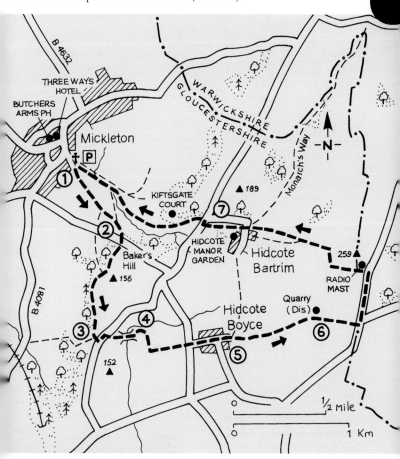

Walk 1 **Directions**

① With the **church** to your left, turn right up a bank to a gate. Cross a field on a left diagonal to a gate at a thicket. Follow a path through the trees. Emerge into a field and follow its left margin to a gate at the end.

② In the next field go half right to a gate in the corner. Cross a road and go up some steps to a stile. Turn right to walk around the edge

> ### WHILE YOU'RE THERE
> It would be a shame to miss the two fine gardens. **Kiftsgate Court** is open 2–6 on Wednesday, Thursday, Sunday and public holidays during April, May, August and September. In June and July it is open 12–6 on Wednesday, Thursday, Saturday and Sunday. Home-made teas are available but dogs are not welcome. Just up the road, **Hidcote Manor Garden** is owned by the National Trust and is open daily, 10:30–6:30. Closed Thursday and Friday, March–November, except June and July, when it's closed Friday only. It can get crowded, but there is a good restaurant and plant sales centre.

of the field as it bears left. After 250yds (229m), take a path among trees, a steep bank eventually appearing down to the right. The path brings you to a field and then to a barn.

③ At the barn turn left on to a track. Just about opposite, keep left of a hedge, following the edge of a field to the bottom corner. Go through a gap to a bridge across a stream and turn left.

> ### WHAT TO LOOK FOR
> In **Hidcote Boyce** some of the houses, though built of stone broadly in the Cotswold style, are unusually tall. There doesn't seem to be any good reason for this, but the style is almost unique to the village. Climbing the hill out of Hidcote Bartrim, you will find yourself in an area of bumps and hillocks – these are the remains of an old stone quarry.

④ Follow the margin of the field as it goes right and then right again. Continue until you come to a gate on the left. Go through this and walk until you reach another gate at a road. Walk ahead through **Hidcote Boyce**. Where the road goes right, stay ahead to pass through a farmyard.

⑤ Beyond a gate take a rising track for just over ¼ mile (400m). Where this track appears to fork, stay to the left to enter a field. Bear left and then right around a hedge and head for a gate. In an area of grassy

mounds stay to the left of a barn and head for a gate visible in the top left corner.

⑥ Follow the next field edge to a road. Turn sharp left to follow the lesser road. Immediately before a radio transmission mast turn left on to a track and follow this all the way down to pass to the right of **Hidcote Manor Garden**. After passing the garden's main entrance go left through a gate into shrubland and turn right. Follow the path to a field and cross it to a gate on the far side.

⑦ At the road turn right and then, before **Kiftsgate Court**, turn left through a gate and descend through a field. Pass through some trees and follow the left-hand side of the next field until you come to a gate on the left. Go through this and cross to another gate. Follow the edge of the next field. Where the field opens up head just to the left of **Mickleton church**. Go through a gate leading between the two cemeteries to return to the start.

> ### WHERE TO EAT AND DRINK
> In Mickleton the **Butchers Arms** serves good pub food, and the **Three Ways Hotel** is recommended for its puddings in particular. It's the home of the famous 'Pudding Club', where you can taste the finest in traditional English desserts. There is also a restaurant at **Hidcote Manor Garden** and a tea room at **Kiftsgate Court**

Around Dumbleton Hill

Several centuries of church-building can be seen around Dumbleton Hill.

•DISTANCE•	8 miles (12.9km)
•MINIMUM TIME•	3hrs 15min
•ASCENT / GRADIENT•	427ft (130m) ▲ ▲ ▲
•LEVEL OF DIFFICULTY•	🚶 🚶 🚶
•PATHS•	Mostly good paths, field tracks and village roads, 6 stiles
•LANDSCAPE•	Gentle farmland and quiet villages
•SUGGESTED MAP•	aqua3 OS Explorer OL45 The Cotswolds
•START / FINISH•	Grid reference: SP 039363
•DOG FRIENDLINESS•	Mixed farming area, so off lead with discretion
•PARKING•	On street near church in Wormington
•PUBLIC TOILETS•	None on route
•CONTRIBUTOR•	Nicholas Reynolds

BACKGROUND TO THE WALK

Wormington sits quietly away from the B4078, perhaps less busy now than in its first recorded mention in 1297. Today a hexagonal bench, ringing a splendid specimen tree, invites you to sit whilst donning your walking boots. Tucked behind this tiny green stands St Katherine's Church, a small, almost petite, building of 14th-century origin. It boasts a 9th-century stone crucifix, dug up in nearby Wormington Grange and said to have been salvaged from Winchcombe Abbey, and a stunning, 400-year-old brass depicting a mother and child in the lady's bed chamber.

Family Funded

Whereas St Katherine's is spire-less, having just a short bell-turret, the 200ft (61m) Victorian Gothic spire of St Andrew's Church in Toddington is visible from afar. On an ancient site amongst yew trees, the honey-stone building is largely the work of masons in the 17th, 18th and 19th centuries, funded by the Tracy family. The Tracy family also built the 17th-century Toddington House, all but demolished in living memory. The 2nd Baron Sudeley gave his name to the side chapel; this is his last resting place, with his wife, in a marble tomb. An inscription shows that the 6th Baron Sudeley was killed in action in 1941.

Gatehouse Remains

What remains of Toddington House is part of the gatehouse, and that is little more than a façade. You can see the remnants over the churchyard wall, to the left. Walk a little further round for sight of the magnificent Toddington Manor. Something approaching a 'cloak of secrecy' hangs over it at present – a sometime college for foreign students, it is owned by a Middle Eastern family that is never seen. Beside the road at Toddington you may still see evidence of 21st-century pipe laying – this is to carry water from Tewkesbury to Stanton.

Dumbleton's history goes back to Saxon times, although the oldest features apparent today are at St Peter's Church, primarily its arched north doorway. The church has undergone several additions and changes; some have suggested that the purpose of the 15th-century south aisle was to provide a place for masses for the victims of the Black

Death. Also of note in the church are two piscinas (stone basins), over 600 years old. A hall was first built in Dumbleton in the 16th century. However, that was demolished and the present-day Dumbleton Hall is the 1830 creation of G S Repton. He was commissioned by Edward Holland, the owner of the estate and founder of the Royal Agricultural College in Cirencester. Dumbleton Hall has a landscaped lake and, from the footpath, a variety of trees seemingly worthy of a small arboretum. The hall is now a 42-bedroomed hotel.

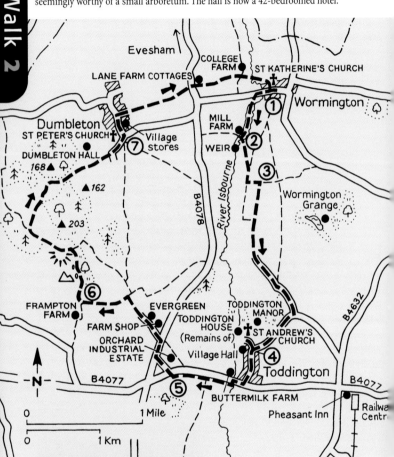

Walk 2 Directions

① Walk westwards, on the road, to some power lines. Just after these take the footpath on the left. Pass through a gate, maintaining this line for a further 450yds (412m).

② Turn away from **Mill Farm** (view the water wheel first), to cross the **River Isbourne**. Cross a narrow field, noting the mill's weir to your right. Go diagonally across another field, under power lines again, turning right beside a fence that soon becomes hedgerow. In about 120yds (110m) turn left through a gate to walk along the right-hand field edge. Within 200yds (183m) turn right.

③ Follow this mud track – later a green lane and finally tarmac – for

WHAT TO LOOK FOR ⓘ

Early in the walk, at Mill Farm, only a few paces off-route, are the remnants of an overshot **watermill** on the River Isbourne. The water still flows over the mill race on to fragments of the wheel, spokes of wood and rims and paddles of metal. The mill was in active use, grinding corn, well into the 20th century.

nearly 1¼ miles (2km), to a road junction. Turn right, passing the unwelcoming entrance to **Toddington Manor**, to a junction.

④ Here a sign points to Toddington's church. Visit the church and view the ruin of **Toddington House**. Retrace your steps, then walk through Toddington village. Now turn right. Just after the pavement gives out (before the piggy **Buttermilk Farm**), cross over to a fingerpost and stile. Walk behind a screen of trees for 760yds (695m). The ground here is being reinstated after laying water pipelines.

WHERE TO EAT AND DRINK ⓘ

The only source of refreshments on the route is the **village store** in Dumbleton (closed all-day Sunday, Saturday and Monday afternoons). At Toddington is the **Pheasant Inn**, and at the station the **Flag & Whistle Tearoom** is open when the steam railway is operating.

⑤ Re-cross the road to take the minor road past **Orchard Industrial Estate**. At the T-junction turn right. Go left, before the farm shop, up the driveway, passing the incongruous, black-and-white effect farmhouse called '**Evergreen**'. At the next T-junction turn left along a pitted, grassy tarmac way, contouring the hill. Reach a single, broken tree just before the track bends left to **Frampton Farm**.

⑥ Go ahead for about 30 paces, then turn hard right, uphill, heading for a gate near trees. Once through this, the way soon steepens. On the brow join a stony track coming in from the right. There are good views back. Now on the level, continue for about 600yds (549m) to signposts at a junction of tracks. Follow 'Public Bridleway Dumbleton 1¼ miles', soon into a big, open field. A good track now leads all the way down to a minor road, then the driveway to **Dumbleton Hall** (a hotel).

⑦ Cross to the crucifix-style war memorial and turn left. Visit the church. About 30yds (27m) beyond **Dairy Lane** on the left, turn right along a residential cul-de-sac and then enter a field to skirt two field edges. Cross the **B4078** and, when the drive to **Lane Farm Cottages** bends left, go forward to find a field path, crossing two fields. Cross the service road to **College Farm**. Go over the small **River Isbourne** on a concrete bridge with corrugated iron sides. Pass under power lines and over a stile into pasture, then walk to the end of a breeze block barn wall. Turn right to a gate, rejoining the road in **Wormington**.

WHILE YOU'RE THERE ⓘ

At Toddington's **Gloucestershire and Warwickshire Railway** you'll see not just steam trains but assorted rolling stock and lovingly preserved diesels too. The station yard seems to be a magnet for old vehicles in general – there are several fire engines, ambulances and buses on display as well. Trains currently run for 6½ miles (10.4km), to the west of Gotherington, extending another 3 miles (4.8km) to Cheltenham racecourse station in 2003. On the same site is the North Gloucestershire Narrow Gauge Railway, which operates a more limited timetable.

William Morris's Broadway

A haunt of the Arts and Crafts pioneer towers above this Worcestershire village.

•DISTANCE•	5 miles (8km)
•MINIMUM TIME•	2hrs 30min
•ASCENT / GRADIENT•	755ft (230m) ▲▲▲
•LEVEL OF DIFFICULTY•	🏃 🏃 🏃
•PATHS•	Pasture, rough, tree-root path, pavements, 8 stiles
•LANDSCAPE•	Flat vale rising to escarpment
•SUGGESTED MAP•	aqua3 OS Explorer OL45 The Cotswolds
•START / FINISH•	Grid reference: SP 094374
•DOG FRIENDLINESS•	Sheep-grazing country (some cattle and horses too) so only off lead in empty fields; some stiles may be tricky
•PARKING•	Pay-and-display, short stay, 4hrs maximum in Church Close, Broadway; longer stay options well-signposted
•PUBLIC TOILETS•	At Church Close car park and at country park
•CONTRIBUTOR•	Nicholas Reynolds

BACKGROUND TO THE WALK

If Caspar Wistar were alive today, a springtime visit to Broadway would give him much pleasure. Visitors come in swarms to this Worcestershire village which lies against the edge of the Cotswolds – understandably, for its one of the sweetest places in England. They buzz around a linear honeycomb, the honey-stone buildings stretching for the best part of a mile (1.6km). Horse chestnut trees flame with pinky-red candelabras and walls drip with the brilliant lilac flowers of wisteria. Caspar, the 18th-century American anatomist after whom the wisteria genus was named, would surely not miss this photo opportunity. (The fact that wisteria and pink horse chestnut are not 'authentic', as both were introduced to Britain centuries after Broadway's older buildings were constructed, doesn't seem to matter!) There are many buildings of note in Broadway, not least the partly 14th-century Lygon (pronounced 'Liggon') Arms. The Savoy Group bought it for £4.7 million in 1986. History has contributed to this price – in 1651 Oliver Cromwell stayed there on the night before the decisive clash in the Civil War, the Battle of Worcester.

Arts and Crafts

Less historic but more affordable is Broadway Tower. The 6th Earl of Coventry's four-storey folly (1799) has served as home to a printing press and a farmhouse, but is best known as a country retreat for William Morris (1834–96). Appropriately, in 1877 he founded the Society for the Protection of Ancient Buildings. Artistically, Morris empathised with the Pre-Raphaelite Brotherhood, a group, primarily of painters, founded in 1849 by William Holman Hunt. They believed that British art had taken a 'wrong turn' under the influence of Raphael, who, with Michelangelo and Leonardo da Vinci had made up the trio of most famous Renaissance artists. Raphael (1483–1520) was catapulted to fame and fortune in his late-twenties when commissioned to paint the stanze (Papal apartments) for Pope Julius II. The English Pre-Raphaelites challenged the teachings of the establishment, producing vividly coloured paintings, lit unconventionally, which had an almost flat appearance.

In 1859, the middle-class Morris married Jane, an 18-year-old, working-class model for Dante Gabriel Rossetti, his British-born mentor. Rossetti's wife committed suicide after two years of their marriage. Rossetti then proceeded to have an affair with Jane. Morris and some friends (including Rossetti!) set up a company producing crafted textile and stained-glass products. Morris was fascinated by pre-industrial techniques. Ironically, only the wealthy could afford to enjoy his essentially medieval art. Disillusioned by the Industrial Revolution, he was attracted to Socialism in the 1870s. He joined the Social Democratic Federation and became increasingly militant. He wrote extensively on Socialism and gave lectures, even on street corners. All the while he was writing prose and poetry and, when Tennyson died in 1892, Morris was invited to succeed him as poet laureate. He declined the invitation and died four years later.

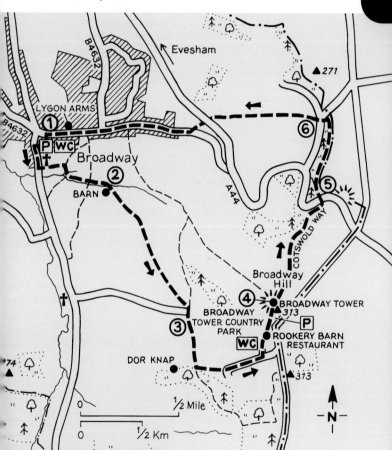

Walk 3 **Directions**

① Walk back down **Church Close** then turn left. At the far end of the church wall turn left, soon passing a tiny, narrow orchard. At a gate

before a strip of grass turn immediately right, to reach a simple log bridge over a rivulet. Turn half left, across uneven pasture. Go to the right-hand field corner. In 40yds (37m) reach a bridge of two railway sleepers beside a stone barn.

Walk 3

② Cross this to a waymarker through a boggy patch to two stiles. Maintain your line to reach a gate. Cross a large field, now scarcely gaining any height. On joining a vague, sunken lane bear right, to descend briefly to a gate (there's a water trough near by). A tree-lined, dirt track soon reaches another gate within 60yds (55m).

WHERE TO EAT AND DRINK ⓘ

Part-way round the route, the **Rookery Barn Restaurant** welcomes walkers (and chess players). Apart from teas and coffees, call in here for simple meals, including a vegetarian ratatouille lasagne. Dogs are welcome – above a bowl of water was chalked the sign 'Water 4 mutleys'. You can sit outside, by the adjacent children's play area. Otherwise, options abound in busy Broadway.

---

③ Slant uphill, passing in front of a stone building with, sadly, modern windows – Dor Knap (close by) is better. At the woodland ahead turn left. Join a tarmac road, steadily uphill. At the brow turn left, into **Broadway Tower Country Park**, and pass the **Rookery Barn Restaurant**. A tall kissing gate gives access to **Broadway Tower**.

④ Beyond the tower go through a similar gate, then take the little gate immediately on the right. Move down, left, 20yds (18m) to walk in a hollow, through pasture and scrubby hawthorns, to a gate in a dry-stone wall. Soon cross a tractor track and walk parallel to it in a similar hollow, guided by **Cotswold Way** acorn waymarkers. Aim for some bright metal gates amongst trees. Beyond these go straight ahead and in 45yds (41m), at the next marker, bear right, walking above the road. Soon cross it carefully, to footpath signs opposite.

⑤ Leave the Cotswold Way here. More care is needed in following these next instructions: descend, initially using wooden steps. Ignore a path on the left after 50yds (46m), then after another 50yds (46m) take the yellow arrow waymarker pointing up to the right, over more steps. About 25 paces beyond these steps use a wooden handrail to go down a few more steps. After another 50yds (46m) you'll see an orange **Badger Trail** disc. Go forward on this for just 10yds (9m). Here the orange disc points left, but take the yellow marker, straight ahead. Follow this narrow path (beware many exposed tree roots) near the top of this dense wood. Eventually take steps on the left, down to cross a road junction.

⑥ Take the field path signposted 'Broadway'. Descend sweetly through pastures. Swing left then right to pass under the new road, emerging near the top end of the old one. Turn right, on to the dead end of **Broadway**'s main street. In the centre, 50yds (46m) beyond three red telephone boxes, turn left, through an arcade, to **Church Close** car park.

WHILE YOU'RE THERE ⓘ

The four flights of stairs up the **Broadway Tower** add little to the already splendid view but inside it's crammed full of history (fee; closed Monday to Friday from November to March). Directly on the route is the **Wild Ridge Farm Park**, one of the country park's trinity of attractions. You don't have to be a child (or even with children!) to enjoy an hour in this modest, hands-on farm park, sited on slopes overlooking the Vale of Evesham. The larger animals include wallabies, llamas, and belted Galloway cattle (a breed distinguished by a wide stripe of white around the torso of its otherwise black body).

Olimpick Playground Near Chipping Campden

Walk out from the Cotswolds' most beautiful wool town to Dover's Hill, the spectacular site of centuries-old Whitsuntide festivities.

•DISTANCE•	5 miles (8km)
•MINIMUM TIME•	2hrs
•ASCENT / GRADIENT•	280ft (85m) ▲ ▲ ▲
•LEVEL OF DIFFICULTY•	🚶 🚶 🚶
•PATHS•	Fields, roads and tracks, 8 stiles
•LANDSCAPE•	Open hillside, woodland and village
•SUGGESTED MAP•	aqua3 OS Explorer OL45 The Cotswolds
•START / FINISH•	Grid reference: SP 151391
•DOG FRIENDLINESS•	Suitable in parts (particularly Dover's Hill) but livestock in some fields
•PARKING•	Chipping Campden High Street or main square
•PUBLIC TOILETS•	A short way down Sheep Street
•CONTRIBUTOR•	Christopher Knowles

BACKGROUND TO THE WALK

The Cotswold Olimpicks bear only a passing resemblance to their more famous international counterpart. What they lack in grandeur and razzmatazz, however, they make up for in picturesqueness and local passion. Far from being one of the multi-million dollar shrines to technology which seem so vital to the modern Olympics, the stadium is a natural amphitheatre – the summit of Dover's Hill, on the edge of the Cotswold escarpment. The hill, with spectacular views westwards over the Vale of Evesham, is an English version of the site of the Greek original.

Royal Assent

Dover's Hill is named after the founder of the Cotswold Olimpicks, Robert Dover. Established with the permission of James I, they were dubbed 'royal' games, and indeed have taken place during the reign of 14 monarchs. Dover was born in Norfolk in 1582. He was educated at Cambridge and then was called to the bar. His profession brought him to the Cotswolds but he had memories of the plays and spectacles that he had seen in the capital, for this was the era of Shakespeare.

The Main Event

It is generally accepted that the first games took place in 1612, but they may well have begun at an earlier date. It is also possible that Dover was simply reviving an existing ancient festivity. Initially, at least, the main events were horse-racing and hare-coursing, the prizes being, respectively, a silver castle ornament and a silver-studded collar. Other competitions in these early games were for running, jumping, throwing, wrestling and staff fighting. The area was festooned with yellow flags and ribbons and there were many dancing events as well as pavilions for chess and other similarly cerebral contests.

Annual Event

The Olimpicks soon became an indispensable part of the local Whitsuntide festivities, with mention of them even being made in Shakespeare's work. Robert Dover managed the games for 30 years and he died in 1652. The games continued in a variety of forms throughout the following centuries, surviving several attempts to suppress them when they became more rowdy and seemed to present a threat to public order and safety. They finally became an established annual event once again in 1966.

Nowadays, the games are a more like a cross between pantomime and carnival, but they have somehow retained their atmosphere of local showmanship. At the end of the evening's events all the spectators, holding flaming torches, file down the road back into Chipping Campden, where the festivities continue with dancing and music along the main street and in the square.

The Wool Town

It's worth lingering in Chipping Campden, before or after the walk. Possibly the most beautiful of all the Cotswold towns, it was once famous throughout Europe as the centre of the English wool trade. A leisurely stroll along its curving High Street of handsome stone houses should be an essential part of your visit. The church too is particularly fine and it's also worthwhile searching out the Ernest Wilson Memorial Garden, on the High Street.

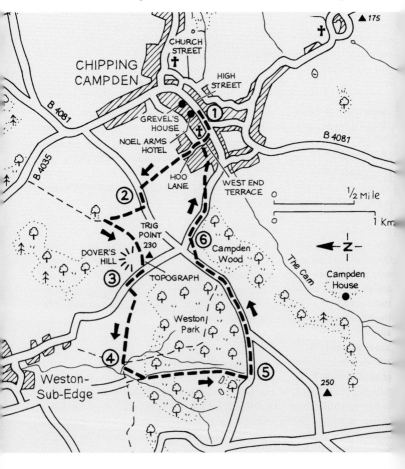

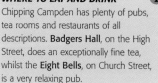

Walk 4 Directions

① Turn left from the **Noel Arms**, continue to the **Catholic church**, and turn right into **West End Terrace**. Where this bears right, go straight ahead on **Hoo Lane**. Follow this up to a right turn, with farm buildings on your left. Continue uphill over a stile to a path and keep going to a road.

② Turn left for a few paces and then right to cross to a path. Follow this along the field edge to a stile. Go over to **Dover's Hill** and follow the hedge to a stile with extensive views before you. Turn left along the escarpment edge, which drops away to your right. Pass a **trig point** and then a **topograph**. Now go right, down the slope, to a kissing gate on the left. Go through to a road and turn right.

> ### WHILE YOU'RE THERE ℹ
> **Broadway Tower**, with its associations with William Morris (▶ Walk 3), stands about 4 miles (6.4km) to the south west of Chipping Campden. A Gothic folly, built in Portland stone in 1799, it glowers across the Vale of Evesham. There is an interesting small museum inside and fine views across the vale from the top.

③ After 150yds (137m) turn left over a stile into a field. Cross this and find a gate in the bottom right-hand corner. Head straight down the next field. At a stile go into another field and, keeping to the left of a fence, continue to another stile. Head down the next field, cross a track and then find adjacent stiles in the bottom left corner.

④ Cross the first one and walk along the bottom of a field. Keep the stream and fence to your right

and look for a stile in the far corner. Go over, crossing the stream, and then turn left, following a rising woodland path alongside the stream. Enter a field through a gate and continue ahead to meet a track. Stay on this, passing through gateposts, until you come to a country lane and turn left.

> ### WHERE TO EAT AND DRINK ℹ
> Chipping Campden has plenty of pubs, tea rooms and restaurants of all descriptions. **Badgers Hall**, on the High Street, does an exceptionally fine tea, whilst the **Eight Bells**, on Church Street, is a very relaxing pub.

⑤ After 400yds (366m) reach a busier road and turn left for a further 450yds (411m). Shortly before the road curves left, drop to the right on to a field path parallel with the road. About 200yds (183m) before the next corner go half right down the field to a road.

⑥ Turn right, down the road. Shortly after a cottage on the right, go left into a field. Turn right over a stile and go half left to the corner. Pass through a kissing gate, cross a road among houses and continue ahead to meet **West End Terrace**. Turn right to return to the centre of **Chipping Campden**.

> ### WHAT TO LOOK FOR
> On reaching Dover's Hill, the route almost doubles back on itself – this is necessary in order to observe legal rights of way. Spend a little time poring over the **topograph** – on a clear day there is much to try to identify. In Campden, look out for the 14th-century **Grevel's House**, opposite Church Lane. William Grevel, called 'the flower of the wool merchants of all England', is thought to have been the inspiration for the merchant in *The Canterbury Tales*.

Walk 5

Arts and Crafts in the Campdens

A walk between Chipping and Broad Campden follows the rise and fall of the Guild of Handicraft.

•DISTANCE•	2½ miles (4km)
•MINIMUM TIME•	1hr 15min
•ASCENT / GRADIENT•	83ft (25m)
•LEVEL OF DIFFICULTY•	
•PATHS•	Fields, road and track, 8 stiles
•LANDSCAPE•	Farmland, hills, village
•SUGGESTED MAP•	aqua3 OS Explorer OL45 The Cotswolds
•START / FINISH•	Grid reference: SP 151391
•DOG FRIENDLINESS•	Suitable in parts but livestock in some fields
•PARKING•	Campden High Street or parking area on main square
•PUBLIC TOILETS•	Short way down Sheep Street
•CONTRIBUTOR•	Christopher Knowles

BACKGROUND TO THE WALK

This walk starts in Chipping Campden, perhaps the finest of all Cotswold villages and extends to Chipping Campden's near neighbour, Broad Campden. Broad Campden does not have a spectacular high street, nor even much of a church, but it does have some exceptionally pretty houses (several of which, unusually for the Cotswolds, are thatched), an attractive pub and a 17th-century Quaker Meeting House, all in a snug, overlooked fold of the Cotswold countryside. It was here, in this idyllic rural setting, that Charles Ashbee set up his Guild of Handicraft.

Charles Ashbee

Born in Isleworth in Surrey, in 1863, Ashbee received his art education at King's College, Cambridge and was apprenticed to Bodley and Garner, a company specialising in Gothic revival architecture. As a consequence he became involved with, and subsequently a leader of, the burgeoning Arts and Crafts Movement, the leading light of which was the poet and artist William Morris. In 1888 Ashbee founded the Guild and School of Handicraft. In its educational programme it laid great emphasis on training in the Arts and Crafts tradition with particular prominence on furniture design.

Guild of Handicraft

Ashbee's work shows in its sparseness and restraint all the typical elements of the Arts and Crafts Movement. He also drew public attention to the activities of other artists, notably he promoted the work of the Greene brothers and of Frank Lloyd Wright. In his essay *Should We Stop Teaching Art?* (1911) he discussed the changing nature of industrial patronage and organisation, reflecting his move towards reconciling the use of industrial methods.

The move to Chipping Campden in 1902 (and later to Broad Campden, where Ashbee converted a derelict Norman chapel into a place to live in 1905) was not an altogether successful one and by 1908 the Guild of Handicraft was no more – having fallen prey to competition from other cheaper producers like Liberty's. Ashbee died in 1942. However, the craft tradition he pioneered has not altogether died out. In Sheep Street in Chipping Campden, where the original Guild shops stood just off the High Street, the silversmiths at David Hart's continue to produce beautiful, handcrafted work in the way that Ashbee would have approved of.

Alec Miller, a guildsman who came to Campden from Glasgow, describes the effect that his first sight of the village had on him; and somehow expresses the guiding principles of the Guild of Handicraft. 'I walked up Campden's one long street entranced and happy – a mile-long street with hardly a mean house, and with many of great beauty and richness… I could not 'read' the history embodied in these stone-built houses, so rich, so substantial and of such beautiful stone.'

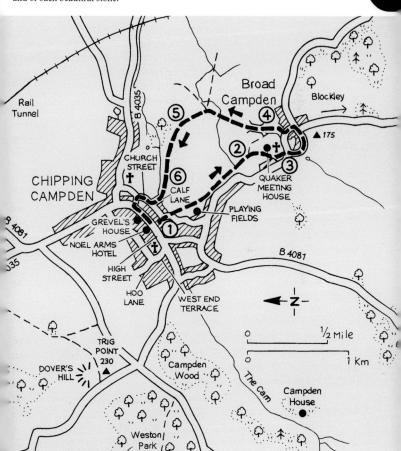

Walk 5 **Directions**

① From Chipping Campden **High Street**, walk through the arch next to the **Noel Arms Hotel** and continue ahead to join a path. Pass some playing fields and at a junction with a road go left into a field and then immediately right to follow the edge of the field parallel with the road.

Walk 5

② After 600yds (549m), fork right and come to a gate. Follow a drive, walk past a house and then leave the drive to walk ahead to a gate. Pass through into an alley and follow it to pass the **Quaker Meeting House**.

③ Emerge at the green with the church to your left. At a junction, continue ahead to walk through the village. The road bears left and straightens. After the turning for Blockley, go left down a road marked 'Unsuitable for Motors'. After 70yds (64m) turn right along the drive of '**Hollybush**'. Pass through a gate and then another and continue along the left, lower margin of an orchard.

④ Cross a stile, then a bridge and turn sharp right to walk along the right edge of a field, with the stream on the right. Go right to the end of the field to cross the stream and in the next field go straight across, bearing a little right, to a gap. Go up the next field to a stile and cross into a field.

⑤ Turn left and then go half right to pass to the right of a house. Cross a stile and then go half right to a gate. Go through and go quarter right down to another stile in the corner. In the next field go half right, with **Campden church** away to the right, to approach a stream near a stone arch.

⑥ Do not cross the stream but, 70yds (64m) after the arch, turn right through a gate and follow the path as it turns left to a drive. Turn right and follow the drive to a road (**Calf Lane**). At the road turn right and at the top turn left into **Church Street** (turn right to visit the church) to return to a junction with the main street.

Perfect Mansion at Compton Wynyates

Enjoy spectacular views of one of Warwickshire's finest houses on this scenic walk over high ground.

•**DISTANCE**•	6 miles (9.7km)
•**MINIMUM TIME**•	2hrs 30min
•**ASCENT / GRADIENT**•	298ft (90m) ▲▲▲
•**LEVEL OF DIFFICULTY**•	🚶🚶 🚶🚶 🚶
•**PATHS**•	Field paths, tracks and roads, 10 stiles
•**LANDSCAPE**•	Undulating countryside on edge of Cotswolds
•**SUGGESTED MAP**•	aqua3 OS Explorer 206 Edge Hill & Fenny Compton
•**START / FINISH**•	Grid reference: SP 338437
•**DOG FRIENDLINESS**•	On lead or under control across farmland
•**PARKING**•	Spaces in Tysoe
•**PUBLIC TOILETS**•	None on route
•**CONTRIBUTOR**•	Nick Channer

BACKGROUND TO THE WALK

Regarded as one of the most visually striking mansions in England and described by Pevsner as 'the most perfect picture-book house of the Early Tudor decades', Compton Wynyates is all that remains of the village of Compton-in-the-Hole, which was depopulated by Sir William Compton during the reign of Henry VIII. The reason was simple. Sir William wanted to create a spacious park around his new home, built in brick on the site of an earlier structure, and the village was in the way.

Compton Wynyates

Lying in a secluded fold of the hills, about 12 miles (19km) south east of Stratford-upon-Avon, Compton Wynyates first came into the possession of Philip de Compton in about 1204 and has been in the same family ever since. The original moated house was demolished and a new brick and stone building begun in about 1481 by Edmund de Compton, part of which still survives in the vicinity of the courtyard. The rebuilding of Compton Wynyates took about 40 years to complete.

The house passed to Edmund's son who, at the end of the 15th century, was a young page to Prince Henry. He was knighted by Henry VIII following the Battle of Tournai in 1512 and, as a gesture of thanks, the King also gifted him the old castle at Fulbroke, near Warwick. However, so keen was the Compton family to improve and enlarge Compton Wynyates that the castle was soon demolished to provide extra materials. Undoubtedly, the timber roof of the hall and the oriel window facing the courtyard came from Fulbroke. Many other distinguished features from that period include the battlemented towers and the great porch, which has the arms of Henry VIII and Catherine of Aragon above the door.

The variety of colour in the brickwork is breathtaking, with hardly two bricks being the same shade. As you look down the drive towards the house, you should catch a hint of pale rose, orange, dark red and blue. Henry VIII stayed here on several occasions, as did

Elizabeth I, James I and Charles I, but it was during the Civil War that Compton Wynyates experienced its darkest days. The house was besieged and finally captured by the Parliamentarians before eventually being returned to the Compton family. The church was completely demolished at the time and this period in Britain's history left deep scars on Compton Wynyates.

Secret Passages

Privately owned and sadly not open to the public, Compton Wynyates comprises a fascinating network of secret passages, hidden rooms and fine stairways. It is said there are almost 100 rooms and about 300 windows. The dining room has a fine Elizabethan, or perhaps early Jacobean, ceiling and there are many portraits in the house of Compton ancestors. Carved panels depicting the Battle of Tournai and a 16th-century tapestry of Cupid picking grapes are among many other historic features.

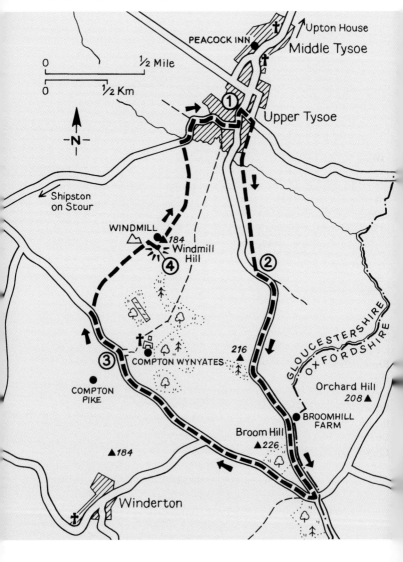

Walk 6 Directions

① Make for the southern end of **Upper Tysoe** and look for the turning signposted 'Shenington and Banbury'. Follow the road, keeping **Middleton Close** on the left, and turn right just before the speed de-restriction signs at a gate and footpath sign. Keep alongside the field boundary to a stile in the corner and continue ahead across the field to the next stile. Keep ahead in the next field, passing under power lines, and make for a plank bridge and stile in the boundary hedge ahead. Go straight on up the field slope and, on reaching the brow of the hill, look for a stile and plank bridge in the hedge by the road.

WHILE YOU'RE THERE

Visit nearby **Upton House**, now in the care of the National Trust. The house dates back to 1695 and was acquired and remodelled in 1927–29 by Walter Samuel, son of the founder of Shell. Upton has a fine collection of English and continental old master paintings, and outdoors is an impressive garden with terraces, herbaceous borders and an interesting 1930s water garden.

---

② Turn left and follow the road as it curves right and up the hill. Pass **Broomhill Farm** and continue ahead to the first crossroads. Turn right here, signposted 'Compton Wynyates', and pass a turning on the left to **Winderton**. Follow the lane along to the main entrance to **Compton Wynyates** on the right.

③ Keep walking ahead, passing a house on the left-hand side and, as the road begins to curve left, look for a galvanised gate and stile on the right. Join the green lane and

follow it to the next gate and stile. Continue ahead and, when the track curves to the left, go straight ahead over a stile and up the edge of the field. Pass a ruined stone-built barn and make for the top corner of the field. Take some steps up the bank before climbing steeply but briefly up to a stile. Keep a stone wall and a restored **windmill** on your left-hand side and look over to the right for a splendid view of Compton Wynyates house.

WHERE TO EAT AND DRINK

The **Peacock Inn**, a traditional village pub, is situated in the centre of Tysoe and offers a range of snacks and main meals. There is also a pleasant beer garden and restaurant.

---

④ Make for a stile a few paces ahead and then follow the path over the high ground, keeping to the right of the windmill. Make for a hedge corner ahead, pass through the gap and then descend the field slope, keeping the hedge on your right. Pass into the next field and keep close to the right-hand boundary. Aim a little to the left of the bottom right corner of the field and make for a stile leading out to the road. Turn right and return to the centre of **Tysoe**.

WHAT TO LOOK FOR

Tysoe church is a rare, Grade I listed building dating back to the 11th century at least. Among various treasures inside are a striking octagonal Perpendicular font, ancient brasses and window glass. **Compton Pike** can be seen across the fields as you approach the main entrance to Compton Wynyates. The pike, more a spire really, is a beacon thought to have been erected at the time of the Spanish Armada in 1588. It may also have been put up to indicate the position of the old village of Compton-in-the-Hole.

Edge Hill and a Theatre of War

Climb a spectacular wooded escarpment and enjoy fine views over a Civil War battleground.

•DISTANCE•	3½ miles (5.7km)
•MINIMUM TIME•	1hr 30min
•ASCENT / GRADIENT•	280ft (85m) ▲▲▲
•LEVEL OF DIFFICULTY•	🚶 🚶 🚶
•PATHS•	Field and woodland paths, country road, 6 stiles
•LANDSCAPE•	Edge Hill escarpment
•SUGGESTED MAP•	aqua3 OS Explorer 206 Edge Hill & Fenny Compton
•START / FINISH•	Grid reference: SP 370481
•DOG FRIENDLINESS•	On lead in Radway and Ratley, under close control on Centenary Way
•PARKING•	Radway village
•PUBLIC TOILETS•	None on route
•CONTRIBUTOR•	Nick Channer

BACKGROUND TO THE WALK

The scene may look peaceful now but just over 360 years ago the fields below the tree-lined escarpment known as Edge Hill were anything but quiet. This tranquil corner of south Warwickshire was the setting for the first major battle of the Civil War in 1642.

The Battle of Edge Hill

On the morning of Sunday 23 October Charles I's army departed from Cropredy Bridge, a few miles away in neighbouring Oxfordshire, arriving at Edge Hill, which was already occupied by Prince Rupert's army, at noon. A staggering 14,000 Royalist troops spread out across the entire hillside, from the Knowle to Sunrising Hill, and as many as 10,000 Parliamentarians, under the command of the Earl of Essex, were massed in the fields below.

Led by Prince Rupert, the cavalry of the King's right flank charged and routed the enemy, pursuing the men beyond the village of Kineton, several miles to the north west. They began to celebrate.

Driven Back

Elsewhere, the Royalists were not doing so well. Commanding the left flank, the Commissary-General attacked the enemy's right. At first, his efforts proved successful but on reaching a line of hedgerows and ditches near Little Kineton, he was driven back. At the same time the King advanced his centre, also with some success, until he, too, was forced to abandon further progress – his way blocked by trees and hedges. The Royalist army suffered many casualties.

Open to attack on both sides, the centre gave way and the Royal standard-bearer, Sir Edmund Verney, was killed. The standard was subsequently taken, though later recovered. Prince Rupert re-emerged from Kineton and relieved the King's centre, thus avoiding defeat.

The battle still raged as darkness descended over the escarpment and the Earl of Essex and his forces withdrew to Kineton for the night. The King slept in a nearby barn and then breakfasted in Radway the following morning. Neither side seemed keen to continue the battle and the King resumed his march to London unopposed while Essex withdrew to Warwick. Inconclusive though it was, the battle claimed the lives of over 4,000 men that day. 1,200 of them were buried by the vicar of Kineton.

There were to be several occasions during the Civil War when it looked as if Charles might win. But two factors ruined his chances. One was the spirit and military genius of Oliver Cromwell, whose successes at Marston Moor (1644) and Naseby (1645) earned him a reputation as the foremost cavalry leader of his day, and the other was the intervention of the Scots. The first Civil War finally ended in 1646, four years after the Battle of Edge Hill.

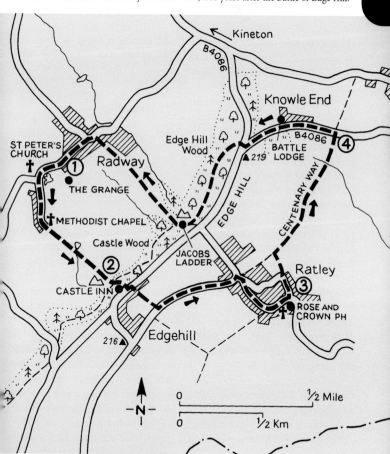

Walk 7 Directions

① Walk through the village of **Radway** to the church. Veer left here into **West End** and pass alongside the grounds of **The Grange** on your left. Curve left by a pond and some thatched cottages. The 19th-century Methodist chapel can be seen here. Follow the lane as it becomes a stony track and go through a kissing gate into a field. Walk ahead to a stile and continue ahead across

Walk 7

WHERE TO EAT AND DRINK
The octagonal Radway Tower, now the **Castle Inn**, was erected by Sanderson Miller to mark the centenary of the first battle in the Civil War. It's certainly an unusual venue for a public house and worth closer investigation. The Castle is open all day for food and drink at the weekend and there is a popular beer garden. The historic **Rose and Crown** at Ratley is a useful watering hole midway round the walk.

the sloping field towards Radway Tower, now the **Castle Inn**. Look for a gap in the hedge by an inspection cover and maintain the same direction, climbing steeply towards the wooded escarpment.

② Make for a stile and enter the wood. Continue straight over the junction and follow the markers for the Macmillan Way up the slope to the road. With the Castle Inn on your right, turn left for several paces to a right-hand path running between **Cavalier Cottage** and **Rupert House**. Make for a stile, turn left at the road and walk along to **Ratley**. When the road bends left by a copper beech tree, turn right to a fork. Veer right and follow the High Street down and round to the left. Pass the church and keep left at the triangular junction.

③ With the **Rose and Crown** over to your right, follow **Chapel Lane** and, when it bends left, go straight ahead up some steps to a stile. Keep the fence on the left initially before striking out across the field to a stone stile in the boundary hedge. Turn right and follow the **Centenary Way** across the field to a line of trees. Swing left and now skirt the field to a gap in the corner. Follow the path down to a galvanised kissing gate, cut across the field to a footbridge and then head up the slope to a gap in the field boundary.

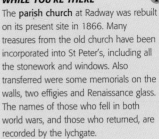

WHILE YOU'RE THERE
The **parish church** at Radway was rebuilt on its present site in 1866. Many treasures from the old church have been incorporated into St Peter's, including all the stonework and windows. Also transferred were some memorials on the walls, two effigies and Renaissance glass. The names of those who fell in both world wars, and those who returned, are recorded by the lychgate.

④ Turn left and follow the road past some bungalows. Pass **Battle Lodge** and make for the junction. Cross over and join a woodland path running along the top of the escarpment. On reaching some steps on the left, turn right and descend steeply via a staircase known as **Jacobs Ladder**. Drop down to a gate and then follow the path straight down the field to a stile at the bottom. Go through a kissing gate beyond it and then pass alongside a private garden to reach a drive. Follow it to the road and turn left for the centre of **Radway**.

WHAT TO LOOK FOR
The **Grange** in Radway was once owned by Walter Light, whose daughter married Robert Washington in 1564. The couple were the great-great-great grandparents of George Washington, the first President of the USA. The house was later owned by the architect Sanderson Miller who built the nearby tower. One of Miller's friends was the writer Henry Fielding who is said to have read his manuscript of *The History of Tom Jones* (1749) in the dining room here. Earl Haig, Commander-in-Chief of the British Forces during World War One, also rented The Grange for a time.

Stanton, Laverton and Buckland

A walk through three radiant Cotswold villages, two of which have strong connections with Methodism.

•DISTANCE•	2¾ miles (4.4km)
•MINIMUM TIME•	1hr 30min
•ASCENT / GRADIENT•	150ft (46m) ▲▲▲
•LEVEL OF DIFFICULTY•	🚶🚶 🚶🚶 🚶🚶
•PATHS•	Track, grassland, pavement, 8 stiles
•LANDSCAPE•	Grassland, wold, wide ranging views, villages
•SUGGESTED MAP•	aqua3 OS Explorer OL45 The Cotswolds
•START / FINISH•	Grid reference: SP 067344
•DOG FRIENDLINESS•	Livestock in most parts of walk
•PARKING•	Car park in Stanton village
•PUBLIC TOILETS•	None on route
•CONTRIBUTOR•	Christopher Knowles

BACKGROUND TO THE WALK

Laverton is a large hamlet with many fine examples of Cotswold vernacular stone architecture. Buckland, though smaller, is a village with two particularly interesting buildings. The 15th-century rectory is the oldest medieval parsonage in Gloucestershire still in use. Although it can be admired only from the street, it has some fine stained glass and a timbered great hall. In the 18th century it was often used as a base by the founder of Methodism, John Wesley. Handsome Buckland Manor is now a hotel, whilst the neighbouring church contains medieval glass restored by William Morris, and a painted panel originally in Hailes Abbey, 5 miles (8km) to the south.

Stanton Court

Stanton was rescued from oblivion in 1906 by the architect Sir Philip Stott, who bought and restored Stanton Court, as well as many of the village's 16th-century houses. The church, located along a lane leading from the market cross, has two pulpits – one dating from the 14th century, the other Jacobean – and a west gallery added by the Victorian restorer Sir Ninian Comper. John Wesley declaimed his message here in 1733. Stanton, in particular, is regularly used in period dramas for television and the cinema.

Spreading the Word

Methodism, the largest of the Protestant free Churches of Britain, originated among a group of devout 18th-century Oxford students under the influence of two brothers, John and Charles Wesley. As the name suggests, it is a radical and earnest creed, which arose out of dissatisfaction with the inadequacies of the established Church. The disillusionment of, in particular, John Wesley, was fostered by a missionary voyage to the American colonies in 1738. From then on he believed that he was destined to spread his beliefs – based on the idea of self-regeneration through faith, prayer and doing good works – across Britain.

He travelled about the country preaching in churches; and then, as bishops and churchmen became uneasy and banned him from the pulpit, he spoke at large, outdoor gatherings. His direct and 'methodical' approach clearly met with the approval of many a despairing congregation and in 1795 the movement, popular especially among the marginalised, lower ranks of society, was strong enough to secede from the Church of England. Needless to say, this was not enough for some and the Methodist movement itself fragmented into several splinters of varying degrees of moderation or severity.

By 1932, however, most branches had rejoined the fold and the modern Methodist Church has about half a million members. In some ways the number of adherents does not reflect the level of shock and concern that the movement engendered among the Establishment of 18th-century Britain. And yet, even today, it is not unusual to find some still remote corner of countryside commemorated locally as a place where Wesley spoke.

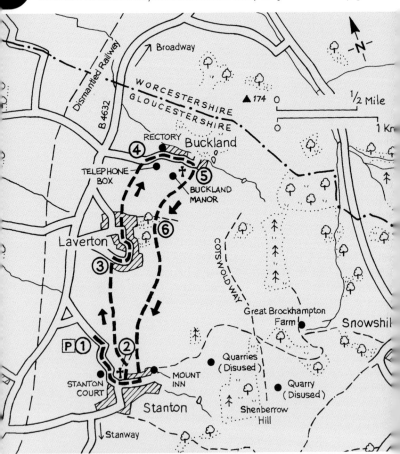

Walk 8 Directions

① From the car park turn right and then left into the village. Turn left at Stanton **war memorial** and head

for the churchyard. Pass to the right of the church and in the corner, turn right along an alley.

② At the end turn left and follow a path to a gate. Cross a plank bridge

Walk 8

to a field and bear left, heading towards a stile in a gap. Cross the stile and turn right. At the next corner cross a bridge stile and continue to another stile. Walk ahead, go over a stile just to the left of the field corner and continue towards **Laverton**.

WHAT TO LOOK FOR ⓘ
In Stanton, look for the dates and initials carved on the walls of some of the cottages, indicating the time of their construction and the stonemason responsible. Look too for **Stanton Court**, a beautiful Jacobean house that was owned and lived in by Sir Philip Stott, saviour of the village.

③ Aim to the left of a house and, at the road, turn right. Follow the road through Laverton as it goes left, then left again and right. At a junction, beside a tree with a seat, cross over to enter a firm bridle path and follow this to the main street of **Buckland**.

④ Turn right and walk through the village, passing the rectory on your left-hand side (shortly after a telephone box and a public footpath sign) and the church to the right. At the top, where the road

WHILE YOU'RE THERE ⓘ
Snowshill Manor, in the neighbouring village of Snowshill (▶ Walk 9) is filled with Japanese armour, musical instruments, farm implements, clocks and toys, and is definitely worth a visit. **Stanway House**, in the nearby village of Stanway, is the centre of a large estate owned by Lord Neidpath. The most striking feature of Stanway is the magnificent gatehouse to Stanway House, a gem of Cotswold architecture built in c1630 by Timothy Strong of Barrington. Stanway House itself, is an outstanding example of a Jacobean manor house.

curves left, go straight on to come to a kissing gate.

⑤ Go through to a field and turn right. Pass **Buckland Manor** on the right and go through another two kissing gates.

⑥ Go through a bridle gate and continue straight on. Pass through some trees to a gate. Continue on the same line and pass through a series of gates and stiles. This will bring you to a large field on the flank of the hill. Follow the prominent waymarkers and, after ¼ mile (400m), cross a stile beside a gate. Continue until the footpath appears to divide after a string of trees. Take the higher footpath and walk on a wide path between trees and bushes. Go over a stile and walk straight ahead until you come to a stile at the edge of **Stanton**. Go through this and walk on into the centre of the village.

Stanton and Stanway from Snowshill

Discovering three of Gloucestershire's finest villages, which were saved from decline and decay.

•DISTANCE•	6¼ miles (10.1km)
•MINIMUM TIME•	2hrs 45min
•ASCENT / GRADIENT•	625ft (190m) ▲▲▲
•LEVEL OF DIFFICULTY•	🚶🚶 🚶🚶 🚶
•PATHS•	Tracks, estate grassland and pavement
•LANDSCAPE•	High grassland, open wold, wide-ranging views and villages
•SUGGESTED MAP•	aqua3 OS Explorer OL45 The Cotswolds
•START / FINISH•	Grid reference: SP 096337
•DOG FRIENDLINESS•	On leads – livestock on most parts of walk
•PARKING•	Snowshill village
•PUBLIC TOILETS•	None on route
•CONTRIBUTOR•	Christopher Knowles

BACKGROUND TO THE WALK

The villages of the Cotswolds are radiant examples of English vernacular architecture, but they have not always been the prosperous places they are today. Many, like Stanton and Snowshill, were once owned by the great abbeys. With the dissolution of the monasteries they became the property of private landlords. Subsistence farmers were edged out by the introduction of short leases and enclosure of the open fields. Villagers who had farmed their own strips of land became labourers. The number of small farmers decreased dramatically and, with the innovations of the Industrial Revolution, so too did the demand for labour. Cheaper food flooded in from overseas and several catastrophic harvests compounded the problem.

To the Cities

People left the countryside in droves to work in the industrial towns and cities. Cotswold villages, once at the core of the most important woollen industry in medieval Europe, gradually became impoverished backwaters. But the villages themselves resisted decay. Unlike villages in many other parts of Britain, their buildings were made of stone. Enlightened landlords, who cherished their innate beauty, turned them into huge restoration projects.

Enlightened Landlords

The three villages encountered on this walk are living reminders of this process. Snowshill, together with Stanton, was once owned by Winchcombe Abbey. In 1539 it became the property of Henry VIII's sixth wife, Catherine Parr. The manor house was transformed into the estate's administrative centre and remained in the Parr family until 1919. Then the estate was bought by Charles Wade, a sugar plantation owner. He restored the house and devoted his time to amassing an extraordinary collection of art and artefacts, which he subsequently bequeathed to the National Trust. Now forming the basis of a museum, his collection, from Japanese armour to farm machinery, is of enormous appeal. Next on this walk comes Stanway, a small hamlet at the centre of a large estate owned by Lord Neidpath. The most striking feature here is the magnificent gatehouse to the Jacobean Stanway House, a gem of Cotswold architecture built around 1630.

Restored Houses

The village of Stanton comes last on this walk. It was rescued from decay and oblivion in 1906 by the architect Sir Philip Stott. He bought and restored Stanton Court and many of the village's 16th-century houses. The peaceful parish church is located along a lane leading from the market cross. It has two pulpits (one dating from the 14th-century, the other Jacobean) and a west gallery added by the Victorian restorer Sir Ninian Comper. The founder of Methodism, John Wesley, preached here in 1733 (➤ Walk 8).

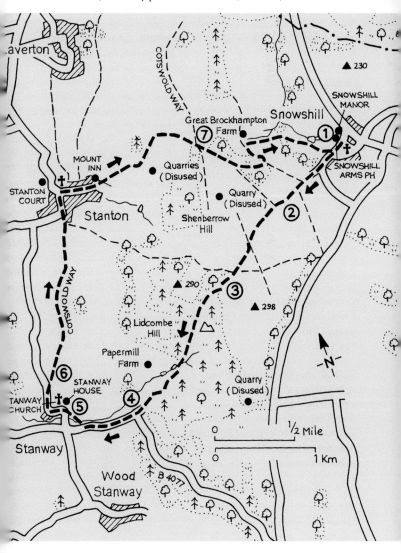

Walk 9

Walk 9 **Directions**

① Walk out of Snowshill village with the **church** on your left. After ¼ mile (400m) turn right, down a lane. After another ¼ mile (400m), at a corner, turn left up to a gate and enter a field.

② Go quarter left to a gate. In the next field go half right to the far corner and left along a track. Take the second footpath on the right through a gate into a field and walk across to another field. Cross this to a track.

WHAT TO LOOK FOR ⓘ

As you pass through Stanway, look to the left before you mount the stile. You'll see the cricket pitch and, overlooking it, a **thatched pavilion**. This was presented to Stanway at the beginning of the 20th century by J M Barrie, creator of Peter Pan, a keen cricketer and a regular visitor to Stanway House.

---

③ Walk down the track. After 275yds (251m) turn right on to a stony track, descending steeply through **Lidcombe Wood**. Where it flattens out a farm will come into view across fields to the right, after which the track bears left. Continue straight on along a narrow footpath to a road.

④ Walk along the pavement and, after 500yds (457m), turn right over a stile into a small **orchard**. Walk across this, bearing slightly right, to arrive at a gate. Go through this and walk with a high wall to your right, to reach a road.

⑤ Turn right and pass the impressive entrance to **Stanway House** and **Stanway church**. Follow the road as it goes right. Shortly after another entrance turn right over a stile. Go half left to another stile and in the next large field go half right.

⑥ Now walk all the way into **Stanton**, following the regular and clear waymarkers of the Cotswold Way. After 1 mile (1.6km) you will arrive at a stile at the edge of Stanton. Turn left along a track to a junction. Turn right here and walk through the village. Where the road goes left, walk straight on, passing the stone cross and then another footpath. Climb up to pass the **Mount Inn**. Behind it walk up a steep, shaded path to a gate. Then walk straight up the hill (ignoring a path to the right after a few paces). Climb all the way to the top to meet a lane.

⑦ Walk down the lane for 250yds (229m) then turn left over a stile into woodland. Follow the path, going left at a fork. At the bottom cross a stile on to a lane and turn left. Walk along here for 200yds (183m). Before a cottage turn right over a stile into a scrubby field. Cross to the far side and turn right through a gate. Continue to a stile on your right, cross it and turn left. Follow the margin of this grassy area to a gate and then follow the path back into **Snowshill**.

WHILE YOU'RE THERE ⓘ

Even those who usually shun museums should make an exception for the one at **Snowshill Manor**, which is more like a fantastical toyshop than a museum. Although the manor is near the heart of the village, the entrance is outside it, on the Broadway road. **Stanway House** has restricted opening hours but is similarly worth a visit – anything less like the conventional picture of a stately home is hard to imagine.

Blockley, Batsford and the Arboretum

The exotic legacy of a 19th-century diplomat adorns this part of the Cotswold escarpment.

•DISTANCE•	4½ miles (7.2km)
•MINIMUM TIME•	2hrs
•ASCENT / GRADIENT•	410ft (125m)
•LEVEL OF DIFFICULTY•	
•PATHS•	Lanes, tracks and fields, 8 stiles
•LANDSCAPE•	Woodland, hills with good views and villages
•SUGGESTED MAP•	aqua3 OS Explorer OL45 The Cotswolds
•START / FINISH•	Grid reference: SP 165348
•DOG FRIENDLINESS•	Some good lengthy stretches without livestock
•PARKING•	On B4479 below Blockley church
•PUBLIC TOILETS•	On edge of churchyard, just off main street in Blockley
•CONTRIBUTOR•	Christopher Knowles

BACKGROUND TO THE WALK

England seems to be a country of trees – it is a feature that visitors often remark on. Walking through Gloucestershire you are surrounded by many native species but, when you visit Batsford Arboretum, you will encounter 50 acres (20.3ha) of woodland containing over 1,000 species of trees and shrubs from all over the world, particularly from China, Japan and North America.

The Japanese Connection

The arboretum was originally a garden created in the 1880s by the traveller and diplomat, Bertie Mitford, 1st Lord Redesdale, grandfather to the renowned Mitford sisters. Posted as an attaché to the British Embassy in Tokyo, he became deeply influenced by the Far East. Throughout the park there are bronze statues, brought from Japan by Bertie Mitford, and a wide range of bamboos. After the 1st Lord Dulverton purchased Batsford in 1920, his son transformed the garden into the arboretum we see today, with its 90 species of magnolia, maples, cherry trees and conifers, all in a beautiful setting on the Cotswold escarpment. Batsford village is comparatively recent, having grown up at the gates of Batsford Park, a neo-Tudor house built between 1888 and 1892 by Ernest George. He built it for Lord Redesdale to replace an earlier, Georgian house. (It is not open to the public but is clearly visible from the arboretum.) Batsford church was constructed a little before the house, in 1862, in a neo-Norman style. It has several monuments to the Mitford family and a fine work by the sculptor Joseph Nollekens from 1808.

Silky Blockley

This walk starts in the unspoilt village of Blockley. It was originally owned by the bishops of Worcester but it didn't really begin to prosper until the 19th century. At one time no fewer than six silk mills, with over 500 employees, were driven by Blockley's fast-flowing stream.

Their silks went mostly to Coventry for the production of ribbon. Blockley's history is both enlightened and superstitious. It was one of the first villages in the world to have electric light: in the 1880s Dovedale House was illuminated through Lord Edward Spencer-Churchill's use of water to run a dynamo. In the early part of that same century the millenarian prophetess, Joanna Southcott, lived in the village until her death in 1814. The tower of Blockley's substantial church predates the silk boom by only 100 years or so, but inside the church are several imposing monuments to the owners of the local mansion, Northwick Park. At least two of these are by the eminent 18th-century sculptor, John Michael Rysbrack (1694–1770).

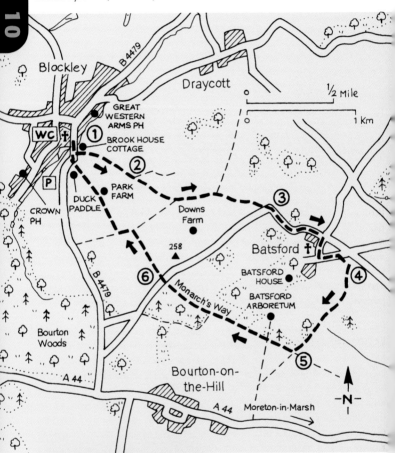

Walk 10 Directions

① Walk along the road with the church above you to your right. Continue ahead, pass **Brook House Cottage**, then turn left immediately, up a lane. Follow this as it ascends for ¼ mile (400m) until it bears left.

② Continue ahead to pass to the right-hand side of a barn. Pass through a gate and in the next field follow its right-hand boundary to another gate. Pass through this to stay on the left side of the next field. Pass into yet another field and then go half right to a gate leading out to a road.

> ### WHILE YOU'RE THERE ⓘ
> A short distance to the west of Blockley is **Upton**, the site of a medieval village that has since disappeared. Although the village was recorded in the Domesday Book in 1086, it is likely that Upton's inhabitants were forced out by the bishops of Worcester who sequestered the land for use as sheep pastures. Whilst there isn't a great deal to see on the ground, this is one of the few abandoned villages to have been excavated by archaeologists.

③ Turn left and follow the road down to a crossroads. Turn right to pass through **Batsford** village to a junction (from where you can visit the church on the right). Bear left, and, at the next junction, turn right.

④ After a few paces turn right on to a footpath and follow this through a succession of fields, negotiating stiles and gates where they arise. **Batsford House** will be visible above you to the right.

> ### WHERE TO EAT AND DRINK ⓘ
> Blockley is one of those rare creatures in the Cotswolds, a village with both a pub and a shop. The pub, the **Crown**, is also a hotel and it serves excellent lunches of all descriptions. There is also the **Great Western Arms**, on Station Road, named after the railway service, which in fact came no closer than Paxford.

⑤ Finally, go through a gate into a ribbed field and turn right to a stile just left of a house at a drive. Cross this (the entrance to **Batsford Arboretum**), pass through a gate and follow the path up the field to a stile. Cross and continue to a track. Follow this up until where it bears left. Turn right on to a path and almost immediately left at a wall, to continue the ascent. Keep going until you reach a road.

⑥ Cross the road to go through a gate and pass through two fields until you come to a path among trees. Turn left, go through another gate, and, after a few paces, turn right over a stile into a field with **Blockley** below you. Continue down to a stile at the bottom. Cross into the next field and pass beneath **Park Farm** on your right. Bear gently left, crossing stiles, along the **Duck Paddle**, until you come to a road. Turn right and return to your starting point in the village.

> ### WHAT TO LOOK FOR ⓘ
> An unusual feature of Blockley is its **raised footpaths**, running along the main street. It was noted in the 19th century that 'many dangerous accidents were occurring'. A parish waywarden of the day, Richard Belcher, added iron posts and railings, 'setting the unemployed to work in January and February'. At the south western end of the High Street is **Rock Cottage** where the prophetess, Joanna Southcott, lived.

The Nabob of Sezincote and Bourton-on-the-Hill

Discovering the influences of India through the Cotswold home of Sir Charles Cockerell.

•DISTANCE•	3 miles (4.8km)
•MINIMUM TIME•	1hr 15min
•ASCENT / GRADIENT•	85ft (25m)
•LEVEL OF DIFFICULTY•	
•PATHS•	Tracks, fields and lanes, 7 stiles
•LANDSCAPE•	Hedges, field and spinney on lower part of escarpment
•SUGGESTED MAP•	aqua3 OS Explorer OL45 The Cotswolds
•START / FINISH•	Grid reference: SP 175324
•DOG FRIENDLINESS•	Under close control – likely to be a lot of livestock
•PARKING•	Street below Bourton-on-the-Hill church, parallel with main road
•PUBLIC TOILETS•	None on route
•CONTRIBUTOR•	Christopher Knowles

BACKGROUND TO THE WALK

For anyone with a fixed idea of the English country house, Sezincote will come as a surprise. It is, as the poet John Betjeman said, 'a good joke, but a good house, too'. Built on the plan of a typical large country house of the era, in every other respect it is thoroughly unconventional. A large copper onion dome crowns the house, whilst at each corner of the roof are finials in the form of miniature minarets. The walls are of Cotswold stone, but the Regency windows, and much of the decoration, owe a lot to Eastern influence.

Hindu Architecture

Sezincote is a reflection of the fashions of the early 19th century. Just as engravings brought back from Athens had been the inspiration for 18th-century Classicism, so the colourful aqua-tints brought to England from India by returning artists, such as William and Thomas Daniell, were a profound influence on architects and designers. Sezincote was one of the first results of this fashion and the first example of Hindu architecture in England that was actually lived in. Sir Charles Cockerell was a 'nabob', the Hindi-derived word for a European who had made their wealth in the East. On his retirement from the East India Company he had the house built by his brother, Samuel Pepys Cockerell, an architect. The eminent landscape gardener Humphry Repton helped Cockerell to choose the most picturesque elements of Hindu architecture from the Daniells' drawings.

Pavilion Inspiration

Some modern materials, like cast iron, were thought to complement the intricacies of traditional Mogul design. The garden buildings took on elements from Hindu temples, with a lotus shaped temple pool, Hindu columns supporting a bridge and the widespread presence of snakes, sacred bulls and lotus buds. The Prince of Wales was an early visitor. The experience obviously made some impression as the extremely Mogul Brighton Pavilion arose not long after. Betjeman was a regular guest at Sezincote during his undergraduate days. 'Stately and strange it stood, the nabob's house, Indian without and coolest Greek within, looking from Gloucestershire to Oxfordshire.'

Measuring Up in Bourton-on-the-Hill

This walks begins and ends in Bourton-on-the-Hill, a pretty village that would be exceptional were it not for traffic streaming through it on the A44. Nevertheless, there is quite a lot to see here. The church owes its impressive features to the fact that the village was formerly owned by Westminster Abbey, whose income was handsomely supplemented by sales of wool from their vast flocks on the surrounding hills. There is a fine 15th-century clerestory, lighting an interior notable for its substantial nave columns and a rare bell-metal Winchester Bushel and Peck (8 gallons/35.2 litres and 2 gallons/8.8 litres respectively). These particular standard English measures date from 1816, but their origins go back to the 10th century when King Edgar (reigned AD 959–975) decreed that standard weights be kept at Winchester and London. They were used to settle disputes, especially when they involved tithes. Winchester measures finally became redundant in 1824 when the Imperial system was introduced, though many Winchester equivalents remain in the United States. Further down the village, the 18th-century Bourton House has a 16th-century barn in its grounds.

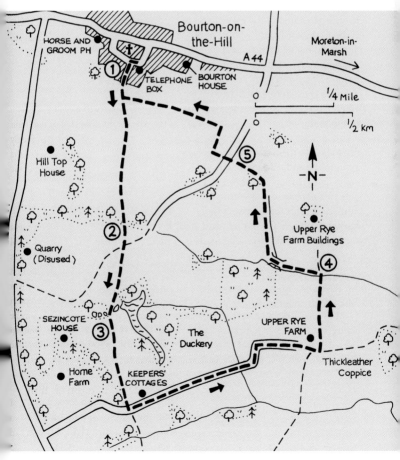

Walk 11 **Directions**

① Walk up the road from the **telephone box** with the church to your right. Turn left down a signposted track between walls. Go through a gate into a field and then continue forward to pass through two more gates.

② Cross a stile, followed by two kissing gates among the trees. This is the **Sezincote Estate** – go straight ahead, following markers and crossing a drive. Dip down to a gate among trees, with ponds on either side. Go ahead into a field, from where **Sezincote House** is visible to the right.

③ Walk into the next field and go right to the end, aiming for the top, right-hand corner. Pass through a gate to a narrow road and turn left. Walk down this road, passing the **keepers' cottages** to your left, and through a series of gates. The road

will bottom out, curve left and right and then bring you to **Upper Rye Farm**. Pass to the right of the farmhouse, go through a gate and, immediately before a barn, turn left along a track and a road.

④ After a second cattle grid, go left over a stile. Follow the edge of the field to a footbridge. Go over it and turn right. Now follow the right-hand margin of the field to a stile in the far corner. Cross this to follow a path through woodland until you come to a stile and a field and continue on the same line to another stile.

⑤ Cross a track to another stile and walk on. After a few paces, with Bourton-on-the-Hill plainly visible before you, turn right and follow the path to the next corner. Turn left and pass through three gates. After the third one, walk on for a few paces and turn right through a gate to return to the start.

The Lost Villages of the Ditchfords

A walk among the ghosts of former medieval agricultural communities, abandoned since the 15th century.

•DISTANCE•	5 miles (8km)
•MINIMUM TIME•	1hr 45min
•ASCENT / GRADIENT•	130ft (40m)
•LEVEL OF DIFFICULTY•	
•PATHS•	Track and field, quiet lanes, ford or bridge, 2 stiles
•LANDSCAPE•	Rolling fields, with good views at some points
•SUGGESTED MAP•	aqua3 OS Explorer OL45 The Cotswolds
•START / FINISH•	Grid reference: SP 240362
•DOG FRIENDLINESS•	Some livestock and some not very encouraging signs
•PARKING•	Lay-bys on Todenham's main street, south of village hall
•PUBLIC TOILETS•	None on route
•CONTRIBUTOR•	Christopher Knowles

BACKGROUND TO THE WALK

There are cases of so-called 'lost villages' all over England and almost as many theories and explanations for their demise. The principal culprit is often said to be the Black Death, sweeping through the countryside in the 14th century and emptying villages of their inhabitants. However, this is by no means the only possibility and in the case of the Ditchfords there do appear to be other reasons for their disappearance. Ditchford is a name that was widespread in this area (perhaps because of their proximity to the Fosse Way – 'fosse' meaning ditch in Old English). Remnants of this, in the form of the names of houses and farms, are still evident on detailed maps, but of the three villages – Ditchford Frary, Lower Ditchford and Upper Ditchford – there is almost no trace.

Abandonment
A 15th-century witness, a priest from Warwickshire called John Rouse, wrote in 1491 that the Ditchfords had been abandoned during his lifetime. Changes in agricultural practices are thought to be the principal reason for this abandonment. As farming gradually became more efficient there was a disinclination to cultivate the stony soils of the more exposed and windswept upland areas.

At the same time, in the Cotswolds, the wool trade was rapidly supplanting arable farming, as the wolds were given over to sheep. Much of the land was owned by the great abbeys who, deriving a third of their income from wool, turned vast tracts of land over to summer pasture in the uplands and winter pastures on the more sheltered lower slopes. The result was that the villagers, mostly farm labourers who had for centuries depended on access to arable land for their livelihood, lost that access. They simply had to move elsewhere in search of work. Today there are no solid remains of any of the three villages. What you can see, however, is a series of regular rolls and shapes in the land that indicate settlement. Upper Ditchford, which stood on the slope near Neighbrook Farm, is the least obvious but

Walk 12

you can see banked enclosures and terraces that probably supported buildings. The site is somewhat clearer in the case of Lower Ditchford, where there are terraces and the site of a manor house and moat. Ditchford Frary has left its name to a nearby farmhouse.

Surviving Village
Todenham survived the rigours of depopluation, and today is a quiet and unspoilt village on the edge of the Cotswolds. It's really a long, single road flanked by an assortment of houses and their leafy gardens. The manor house dates from the end of the Georgian period whilst the church is worth a visit for its decorated and Perpendicular interior. Its features include a 13th-century font with the names of 18th-century churchwardens inscribed upon it.

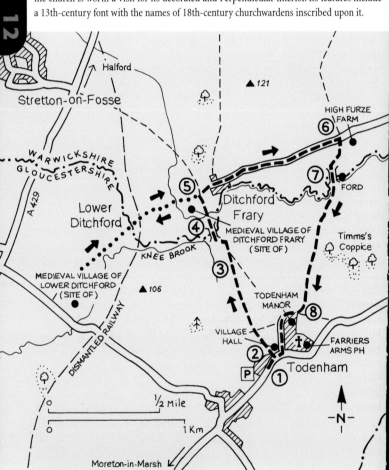

Walk 12 Directions

① From a lay-by below **Todenham village hall** walk up towards the hall and turn left just before it, along a track that runs to the right of a house.

② After a few paces go right up a bank to a gate. Pass into a field and head straight across. Go through another gate on the far side, into a field of undulations indicating medieval ploughing. Continue on the same line to a stile – cross into the neighbouring field and, staying

WHILE YOU'RE THERE ⓘ

Tuesday is **market day** in Moreton-in-Marsh; it's the largest, indeed practically the only, weekly market left in the Cotswolds. Full of bustling bargain hunters, it gives a hint, at least, of how village life must have once been.

on its upper part, go straight ahead, in the general direction of a large house.

③ Cross another stile and soon join a farm track. Where the track goes into a field on the right, go straight ahead. At the bottom of the field the path may become indistinct – look for a small bridge, with gates at either end, amid the undergrowth 50yds (46m) to your left.
④ Cross this bridge and then go straight ahead, crossing a field (the site of **Ditchford Frary**) with a farmhouse before you to the right. On the other side go through a gate, cross another field and pass through a gate to a farm track.

⑤ If you wish to see the site of **Lower Ditchford**, turn left here and keep going over the former railway line until you approach a road – the remains are to your left. Then return along the track. Otherwise turn right on the track and pass behind the farmhouse. The track becomes a metalled lane.

⑥ Just before **High Furze Farm** turn right through a gate into a field. Follow its left margin until it dips down to a ford across Knee Brook. Turn right here and after a few paces find a bridge on your left.

⑦ Cross this and then return to the faint, grassy track that rises from the ford. By staying on this line, with the brook now to your right, you will come to a gate in the top corner. Go through on to a track that rises between two high hedges. Parts of this may be boggy but soon the track will become firmer and will eventually carry you to a junction opposite an entrance to **Todenham Manor**.

WHERE TO EAT AND DRINK ⓘ

The highly attractive **Farriers Arms** is in Todenham, a short way up from the church. The market town of Moreton-in-Marsh, 3 miles (4.8km) south west, has plenty of pubs, cafés, and restaurants, including the well-known **Marsh Goose**.

⑧ Turn right here and follow this track as it curves left, around the manor, and finally brings you back to the village with the **village hall** on your right. Turn left for the **church** and the **Farriers Arms** pub, right to return to your car.

WHAT TO LOOK FOR ⓘ

As you're crossing the fields at the start of the walk, look for the pleats in the fields that indicate **medieval ridge and furrow** ploughing techniques. These are common all over central England, though many have been ploughed out by modern machinery. The furrows were created by ox-drawn ploughs, the ridges separated different farmers' workings in the same open field. Each furrow would originally have been about a furlong (201m) in length, the distance being about as far as the ploughing beast could pull before it needed a rest.

Winchcombe and Sudeley Castle

A rewarding walk above a thriving Cotswold village and the burial place of Henry's sixth queen – Catherine Parr.

•DISTANCE•	4 miles (6.4km)
•MINIMUM TIME•	2hrs
•ASCENT / GRADIENT•	490ft (150m) ▲▲▲
•LEVEL OF DIFFICULTY•	🚶🚶 🚶🚶 🚶🚶
•PATHS•	Fields and lanes, 10 stiles
•LANDSCAPE•	Woodland, hills and villages
•SUGGESTED MAP•	aqua3 OS Explorer OL45 The Cotswolds
•START / FINISH•	Grid reference: SP 024282
•DOG FRIENDLINESS•	On leads (or close control) throughout – much livestock
•PARKING•	Free on Abbey Terrace; also car park on Back Lane
•PUBLIC TOILETS•	On corner of Vine Street
•CONTRIBUTOR•	Christopher Knowles

BACKGROUND TO THE WALK

At the end of a long drive just outside Winchcombe is a largely 16th-century mansion called Sudeley Castle. The first castle was built here in 1140 and fragments dating from its earlier, more martial days are still much in evidence. Originally little more than a fortified manor house, by the mid-15th century it had acquired a keep and several courtyards. It became a royal castle after the Wars of the Roses before being given to Thomas Seymour, Edward VI's Lord High Admiral. Seymour lived at Sudeley with his wife, Catherine Parr – he was her fourth husband. Seymour was executed for treason. Consequently the castle passed to Catherine's brother, William, but he was executed too. Queen Mary gave the property to Sir John Brydges, the first Lord Chandos. Sudeley Castle was a Royalist stronghold during the Civil War. It was disarmed by the Parliamentarians and left to decay until its purchase by the wealthy Dent brothers in 1863.

Married at Nine Years Old

Catherine Parr, sixth wife of Henry VIII and the only one to outlive him, is buried in Sudeley's chapel. She was born in 1512 into an influential northern family and educated in Henry's court. She was first married at the tender age of nine, but widowed six years later. Back at court, she was at the centre of a group of educated, capable women, using her influence with the King to protect her second husband, Lord Latimer, from the machinations of courtly politics. When Latimer died in 1543, Catherine was left one of the wealthiest and best-connected women in England, and an obvious choice of wife for Henry. She looked after him and his affairs during the years until his death in 1547. She quickly married Seymour and moved to Sudeley, where the future Queen Elizabeth was often her companion until Catherine's death in childbirth in 1548.

The village of Winchcombe has a considerable history. In Anglo-Saxon times it was a seat of the Mercian kings and the capital of Winchcombshire until the shire's incorporation into Gloucestershire in the 11th century. It became a significant place of pilgrimage due to the presence of an abbey established in AD 798 and dedicated to St Kenelm, the son of its founder, King Kenulf.

Grinning Gargoyles

The abbey was razed in the Dissolution, but the village's parish church survived and is a fine example of a 'wool church', financed through income from the medieval wool trade. Of particular interest are the amusing gargoyles that decorate its exterior. They are said to be modelled on real local people. Winchcombe also boasts two stimulating small museums: the Folk Museum on the corner of North Street and the Railway Museum on Gloucester Street. Unlike many villages in the area, it has has managed to retain many of its shops and other vital local services.

Walk 13 **Directions**

① From the parking area on **Abbey Terrace** in Winchcombe, walk towards the village centre and turn right, down **Castle Street**. Where it levels out cross a bridge and after a few paces turn left on a path between cottages. Pass into a field and go half right to a gate on the other side.

WHAT TO LOOK FOR ⓘ
If you go into the church at Winchcombe, note the **embroidery** behind a screen, said to be the work of Catherine of Aragon, a wife of Henry VIII. As you descend the hill on the approach to Sudeley Hill Farm, look out for **St Kenelm's Well**. This is a 19th-century version of a holy well connected with the martyred prince, patron saint of the vanished Winchcombe Abbey.

② Turn right along a lane. At the end of a high stone wall to your right, turn left into a field. Go half right across this field to find a well-concealed gap in the hedge, about 50yds (46m) left of a gateway, with a plank across a ditch. Cross this and then turn left to a gate. Go through and continue half right to another gap in the hedge. Pass through and maintain your direction to a protruding corner. Once you are round it, keep close to the fence on your left and continue into the next corner to find a (possibly overgrown) path leading to a stile.

③ Cross the next field to another stile. Continue up the following field to a gate. Go through and then go half right to the far corner to another stile, again possibly

WHILE YOU'RE THERE ⓘ
There is enough to detain you for a day in Winchcombe itself. Not only can you visit Sudeley Castle (► Background to the Walk) which has gardens, a plant centre and special exhibitions, but you will also find the fascinating Folk and Police Museum in the Victorian Town Hall building in the centre of the village. The Police Collection includes uniforms and equipment from a variety of police forces around the world, while the Folk Collection concentrates on the history of Winchcombe and its people.

concealed. Cross this and then another stile almost immediately. Continue until you come to a stile beside a gate with a stone barn above you to the right.

④ Don't go over the stile but turn right to head downhill to a gate (at first hidden) in the hedge about 250yds (229m) below the barn. Go through this on to a track and follow it as it curves towards a house. Cross a stile.

⑤ Just before the house turn right, cross the field and go over a stile. In the next field go to the bottom left-hand corner to emerge on a road. Turn left and, after a few paces, turn right along a lane, towards **Sudeley Lodge Parks Farm**.

WHERE TO EAT AND DRINK ⓘ
For a small town, **Winchcombe** has a disproportionately large number of possibilities, ranging from pubs to tea rooms and restaurants. It also has a bakery (and a supermarket). If you visit **Sudeley Castle**, there's a good café.

⑥ Opposite a cottage turn right on to a footpath across a field. At the bottom nip over a stile and turn right. At the next corner turn left, remaining in the same field. Cross another stile, continue for a few paces and then turn right over a stile. Walk half left, following the obvious waymarkers to a fence, with **Sudeley Castle** now on your right-hand side.

⑦ Go through two kissing gates to enter the park area. Cross a drive and then cross a field to another gate. Go through this and bear half right to the farthest corner. You will emerge on **Castle Street** in Winchcombe where you can turn left to return to the village centre.

The Sacred Tombs of Belas Knap

A walk from Winchcombe to discover the secrets of one of the best preserved neolithic barrows in the country.

•DISTANCE•	5 miles (8km)
•MINIMUM TIME•	2hrs 30min
•ASCENT / GRADIENT•	710ft (216m) ▲▲▲
•LEVEL OF DIFFICULTY•	👫 👫 👫
•PATHS•	Fields and lanes, 6 stiles
•LANDSCAPE•	Wooded escarpment and village
•SUGGESTED MAP•	aqua3 OS Explorer OL45 The Cotswolds
•START / FINISH•	Grid reference: SP 024282
•DOG FRIENDLINESS•	Pretty good, but livestock in parts
•PARKING•	Abbey Terrace or car park on Back Lane, Winchcombe
•PUBLIC TOILETS•	On corner of Vine Street
•CONTRIBUTOR•	Christopher Knowles

BACKGROUND TO THE WALK

The Cotswolds are riddled with settlement remains from all eras, including early tombs. Belas Knap (it means beacon hill), a huge green mound in a field overlooking Winchcombe, is one of the most evocative.

Burial Sites

Barrows (often known in Scotland and Wales as cairns) are widespread throughout the country, especially in the south and west of England. The earliest types, neolithic long barrows, were built over a vast time span, between 4000 and 1800 BC. Usually constructed of earth or chalk, they are normally between 98ft and 295ft (30m/90m) long and between 30ft and 98ft (9m/30m) wide. They were used, it is thought, as the burial places of tribal chiefs and their families. Utensils – food vessels for example – were often buried with them in mortuary chambers of wood or of stone, which then, over a period of time, were covered with earth. The burial chamber, containing between six and eight bodies, tended to be at one end rather than at the centre.

Round Barrows

Round barrows were a feature of the Bronze Age (1800–550 BC). They are much more variable in size and form, but in general they are shaped like bowls, bells or discs and are up to about 20ft (6m) in height and between 12ft and 99ft (4m/30m) in diameter.

Barrows were not a purely prehistoric phenomenon and they continued to be built – albeit only irregularly – by both the Romans and the Saxons (until about AD 750). Once the parish system took hold, however, and as the rites of the Christian Church became established, so the idea of communal earthen burial chambers fell away, to be replaced by permanent buildings dedicated to public worship. The desire for grandiose memorials did not entirely go away, of course, as the mausoleums of the great and the good testify.

Long Barrows

The long barrow at Belas Knap, dating to approximately 2500 BC, has a false portal (apparently to warn off intruders) of breathtakingly exact dry-stone work. The real entrances to the burial chambers are at the sides. Just who precisely was entombed here is unknown but it is surmised that ancestor worship was widely practised and that the mound was opened many times over the centuries to admit further generations of worthy souls.

Community Project

No doubt the whole community worked at its construction over many months, and maintained it devotedly. It is possible that the barrow became the centrepiece of the settlement, seen as a tangible link with the past – certainly it would have been a significant presence on the treeless wolds. Thirty-eight skeletons have been found inside the tomb, which is constructed of slabs of limestone, covered in turf.

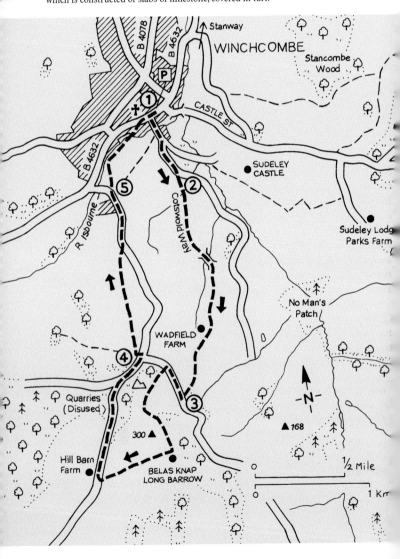

Walk 14

Walk 14 Directions

① From **Abbey Terrace**, walk along the main street in the direction of Cheltenham. Shortly turn left down **Vineyard Street**, towards Sudeley Castle. Walk down the street flanked by pretty cottages, cross a bridge and come to the entrance to the castle, near a lodge. Stay on the road as it bears right and, after 300yds (274m), go through a kissing gate on the right.

> **WHAT TO LOOK FOR** ⓘ
> Visit the church at Winchcombe and look for the embroidery behind a screen, said to be the work of Catherine of Aragon, wife of Henry VIII. Of particular interest are the amusing gargoyles that decorate the exterior, believed to be modelled on local people.

② Go half left to a stile and cross two further fields on the same line. In the far corner of the third field, cross a footbridge to a field and follow its right-hand margin to a stile on the right. Go over, turn left and follow the field margin as it rises. Cross a stile, pass **Wadfield Farm** and walk on a track to a road.

③ Turn right. After 400yds (366m) turn left on to a steep path among trees. At a field turn left and follow its margin to the top. Go through a

> **WHERE TO EAT AND DRINK** ⓘ
> Winchcombe has a good choice of eateries, ranging from pubs to tea rooms and restaurants. If you are planning a picnic then pay a visit to the bakery and small supermarket. **Sudeley Castle** has a good café.

gate and turn left. Eventually go through another gate to arrive at **Belas Knap**. Leave the site on the opposite side and walk ahead until you come to a track. Turn right and descend for ½ mile (800m) to a road at a sharp corner.

④ Go left over a stile into a field and descend half right to a stile at the bottom. Turn right along a track. At the road turn left. After 500yds (457m) go right through a kissing gate into a field.

⑤ Turn left and follow the margin until you come to a kissing gate and footbridge. Beyond, go up a path to the road. Turn right and make your way back to **Abbey Terrace**.

> **WHILE YOU'RE THERE** ⓘ
> This is a good place to come if you are interested in old railways. The **Railway Museum** on Gloucester Street has lots of hands-on exhibits as well as a Victorian garden. Just outside the town, on the road to Stanway, is Toddington Station, and the **Gloucestershire and Warwickshire Railway**. Run by dedicated volunteers, this currently operates on a restored stretch of line between Toddington and Gotherington, 6½ miles (10.5km) away and hopes to extend its passenger services to Cheltenham racecourse in 2003.

Walk 15

Thomas Cromwell and the Destruction of Hailes Abbey

How an important abbey was destroyed by a King's Commissioner.

•DISTANCE•	5 miles (8km)
•MINIMUM TIME•	2hrs
•ASCENT / GRADIENT•	605ft (185m)
•LEVEL OF DIFFICULTY•	
•PATHS•	Fields, tracks, farmyard and lanes, 7 stiles
•LANDSCAPE•	Wide views, rolling wolds and villages
•SUGGESTED MAP•	aqua3 OS Explorer OL45 The Cotswolds
•START / FINISH•	Grid reference: SP 050301
•DOG FRIENDLINESS•	Mostly on leads – a lot of livestock in fields
•PARKING•	Beside Hailes church
•PUBLIC TOILETS•	None on route
•CONTRIBUTOR•	Christopher Knowles

BACKGROUND TO THE WALK

In the decade from 1536 to 1547 just about every English religious institution that was not a parish church was either closed or destroyed – this was the Dissolution, Henry VIII's draconian policy to force the old Church to give up its wealth. The smaller monasteries went first, then the larger ones and finally the colleges and chantries. All their lands and tithes became Crown property. Much of them were sold off to laypeople, usually local landowners. The Church as a parish institution was considerably strengthened as a result of the Dissolution, but at the expense of the wider religious life. The suppression of the chantries and guilds, for example, meant many people were deprived of a local place of worship.

Hailes Abbey

Hailes Abbey was one of the most powerful Cistercian monasteries in the country, owning 13,000 acres (5,265ha) and 8,000 sheep. It was a particular target for reformers. In 1270 Edmund, Earl of Cornwall, the son of its founder, had given the monastery a phial supposed to contain the blood of Christ. Thomas Cromwell was the King's Commissioner responsible for seeing to the closure of the monasteries. He is reputed to have surveyed the destruction of the monastery from a vantage point near Beckbury Camp. There is still a fine view of the abbey from here, as you should find as you pass Point ⑤ on this walk. According to Hugh Latimer of Worcester, who had been working with him, Cromwell also spent an afternoon in 1539 examining the so-called 'blood'. Cromwell concluded that it was nothing more than an 'unctuous gum and compound of many things'. Once the valuables had been removed, local people took what was left.

  The monastery lands were disposed of in a typical manner. First they were confiscated by the Crown and then sold to a speculator who sold the land on in lots. In about 1600 the site of the abbey was bought by Sir John Tracy, the builder of Stanway House. The monks were dispersed: a few managed to secure positions as part of the parish clergy, whilst others took up posts with the cathedrals at Bristol and Gloucester. Others returned to the laity.

Charming Remains

Hailes church is all that remains of the village of Hailes. It predates the abbey and survived the Dissolution, perhaps because it had been a parish church and was not directly linked to the neighbouring monastery. It is a church of real charm, sadly ignored by the many visitors to the monastery's ruins. Although very small, it has several special features, including a panelled chancel – floored with tiles from the monastery – and a nave with 14th-century wall paintings. Didbrook church also survived the upheavals. Built in Perpendicular style, it was rebuilt in 1475 by the Abbot of Hailes, following damage caused by Lancastrian soldiers after the Battle of Tewkesbury.

Walk 15

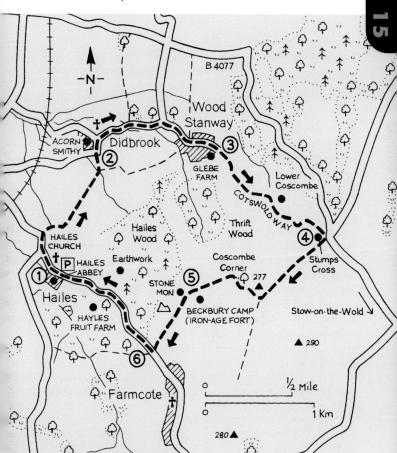

Walk 15 **Directions**

① From **Hailes church** turn right and follow the lane to a T-junction. Turn right and after 200yds (183m) turn right on to a footpath. Cross an area of concrete and follow a track as it goes right and left, becoming a grassy path beside a field. Go through a gate, followed by a stile. After about 75yds (69m) turn left, through a gate, and cross a field to a gate at a road.

② Turn right and follow the road as it meanders through the pretty village of **Didbrook** then a stretch

Walk 15

of countryside. At a junction turn right for **Wood Stanway**. Walk through this village into the yard of **Glebe Farm**.

③ At a gate and a stile cross into a field and walk ahead, looking for a stile on the left. You are now on the **Cotswold Way**, well marked by arrows with a white dot or acorn. Cross into a field and go half right, keeping to the left of some telegraph poles, to a gap in a hedge. Bear half left across the next field, heading towards a house. Cross a stile and turn sharp right, up the slope, to a stile on your right. Cross this and turn immediately left up the field. Go left over a ladder stile by a gate. Follow the footpath as it wends its way gently up the slope. At the top go straight ahead to a gate at a road.

④ Turn right and right again through a gate to a track. Follow this, passing through a gate, until at the top (just before some trees), you turn right to follow another track for 50yds (46m). Turn left through a gate into a field and turn sharp

right to follow the perimeter of the field as it goes left and passes through a gate beside the ramparts of an Iron-Age fort, **Beckbury Camp**. Continue ahead to pass through another gate which leads to a stone monument with a niche. According to local lore, this is the point from where Thomas Cromwell watched the destruction of Hailes Abbey in 1539.

⑤ Turn right to follow a steep path down through the trees. At the bottom go straight across down the field to a gate. Pass through, continue down to another gate and, in the field beyond, head down to a stile beside a signpost.

⑥ Cross this and turn right down a lane, all the way to a road. To the left is **Hayles Fruit Farm** with its café. Continue ahead along the road to return to **Hailes Abbey** and the starting point by the church.

In Search of King Cod Around Cutsdean and Ford

The origins of the Cotswolds, once the focus of England's most valued export.

•DISTANCE•	5½ miles (8.8km)
•MINIMUM TIME•	2hrs 30min
•ASCENT / GRADIENT•	265ft (80m)
•LEVEL OF DIFFICULTY•	
•PATHS•	Tracks, fields and lane, 3 stiles
•LANDSCAPE•	Open wold, farmland, village
•SUGGESTED MAP•	aqua3 OS Explorer OL45 The Cotswolds
•START / FINISH•	Grid reference: SP 088302
•DOG FRIENDLINESS•	Best on leads – plenty of livestock, including horses
•PARKING•	Cutsdean village
•PUBLIC TOILETS•	None on route
•CONTRIBUTOR•	Christopher Knowles

BACKGROUND TO THE WALK

Cutsdean can claim to be the centre of the Cotswolds, according to one theory about the origin of the name 'cotswold'. Today it is nothing more than a small, pretty village on the high, voluptuous wolds above the beginnings of the River Windrush. However, it may once have been the seat of an Anglo-Saxon chief by the name of 'Cod'. His domain would have been his 'dene' and the hilly region in which his domain lay, his 'wolds. This is plausible, even if there is no verifiable record of a King Cod. Another, possibly more persuasive, explanation concerns the sheep that still graze many hillsides in the Cotswolds, a 'cot' referring to a sheep fold and 'wolds' being the hills that support them. (In Old English a 'cot' is a small dwelling or cottage.)

Lamb's Wool to Lion's Wool

Whatever the truth of the matter, the sheep remain, even if the species that in the Middle Ages produced the finest wool in Europe dwindled to the point of extinction. The ancestors of the 'Cotswold Lion' probably arrived with the Romans, who valued the sheep's milk and their long, dense wool. After the Romans' withdrawal the Saxons continued to farm them; indeed by the 8th century Cotswold fleeces were being exported. The nature of the Cotswolds was perfect for these sheep: the limestone soil produces a calcium-rich diet, good for strong bone growth; and the open, wind-blasted wolds suited this heavy-fleeced breed, able to graze all year long on abundant herbs and grasses. The hills teemed with Cotswold sheep; at one point the Cotswold wool trade accounted for half of England's income.

Distinctive Forelock

It is believed that the medieval Cotswold sheep differed a little from its modern counterpart. Its coat was undoubtedly long and lustrous, but it may have been slightly shorter than that of its descendants. It was the distinctive forelock and the whiteness of its fleece that inspired the nickname, Cotswold Lion, characteristics that persist in the modern sheep.

Under Threat

Why, then, did the fortunes of this miraculous animal plummet? To some extent this is a misconception, since serious decline occurred only with the move to arable farming in the Cotswolds in the mid-20th century. Demand for the wool was strong in the 18th and 19th centuries and the Cotswold was also prized for its meat and its cross-breeding potential. However, the market for long-stapled wool began to decline in favour of finer wool, and crop growing became more attractive to local farmers. Incredibly, by the 1960s, there remained only some 200 animals. Suddenly, it was clear that a living piece of English history was on the verge of extinction. The Cotswold Breed Society was reconvened and steps were taken to ensure the sheep's survival. Farmers have since rediscovered the animal's many qualities, and it is no longer quite such a rare sight on the wolds.

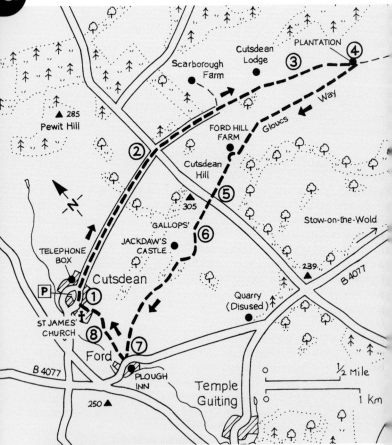

Walk 16 Directions

① With the **Church of St James** to your right-hand side and, after a few paces, a telephone box away to your left, walk out of the village of **Cutsdean**. Continue uphill on this straight country road for just over a mile (1.6km), until you come to a T-junction with another road.

② Cross this to enter another lane, at the margin of **woodland**. Emerge from the woods, and, where the track veers left towards a house, keep straight on.

③ Eventually you will come to a field. Walk straight on for 200yds (183m) and then go quarter right over the brow of a slope to head for a **plantation**.

④ Pass through the plantation. At a junction turn right and right again, the plantation now on your right. Follow this track – passing through the precincts of **Ford Hill Farm** – all the way to a road.

⑤ Cross over, to enter a track which runs to the left of a 'gallops', used for training racehorses. Keep straight on where the track veers left into a neighbouring field. Shortly after this the track becomes a metalled lane, still running alongside the gallops.

⑥ Soon after passing the stables of **Jackdaw's Castle** across to your right, you need to turn sharp right across the gallops area (watch out for horses) to join a track, where you turn left. The track descends gently for just under a mile (1.6km), the gallops and greensward to your left. Keep descending until you are near the bottom, at the beginning of a

> ### WHERE TO EAT AND DRINK
> The route passes close to the old and very attractive **Plough Inn** in Ford. It serves Donnington's, the local beer brewed in a charming lakeside brewery near Stow-on-the-Wold. The nearest towns with a greater choice are Winchcombe and Stow.

village. This is **Ford**: if you walk into the village you will see the welcoming **Plough Inn** directly in front of you.

⑦ Otherwise turn right, right again and then left, to walk along a grassy path between railings. On the far side turn right, with the railings to your right, and soon arrive at a bank. Follow the path down among trees as it bears left to a stile.

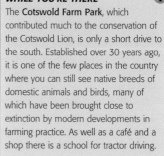

> ### WHILE YOU'RE THERE
> The **Cotswold Farm Park**, which contributed much to the conservation of the Cotswold Lion, is only a short drive to the south. Established over 30 years ago, it is one of the few places in the country where you can still see native breeds of domestic animals and birds, many of which have been brought close to extinction by modern developments in farming practice. As well as a café and a shop there is a school for tractor driving.

⑧ Cross into a field and then go half right across it. Go down a bank, across a rivulet (possibly dried up in summertime) and up the bank on the other side to a stile. Cross into a field and turn left along the side of the field towards **Cutsdean**. Pass to the right of the church, which sits back across a wall to your left. At the edge of the village come to a stile: cross this to join a track. After a few paces emerge on to the **main street** through the village and your starting point.

> ### WHAT TO LOOK FOR
> **Horses** are very important to the local economy. The countryside is covered in 'gallops', earthy tracks where racehorses can be exercised in safety. You'll also notice a large number of jumps, like the hurdles at a proper racecourse. Many racehorses are bred here, and some may get to race at nearby Cheltenham, home to the pre-eminent steeplechase course in the country and host to the huge Cheltenham Festival racing event.

Walk 17

Empires and Poets at Adlestrop and Daylesford

Embracing the legacies of Warren Hastings and the poet Edward Thomas.

•DISTANCE•	5 miles (8km)
•MINIMUM TIME•	2hrs
•ASCENT / GRADIENT•	230ft (70m)
•LEVEL OF DIFFICULTY•	
•PATHS•	Track, field and road, 6 stiles
•LANDSCAPE•	Rolling fields, woodland and villages
•SUGGESTED MAP•	aqua3 OS Explorer OL45 The Cotswolds
•START / FINISH•	Grid reference: SP 241272
•DOG FRIENDLINESS•	Some livestock but some open areas and quiet lanes
•PARKING•	Car park (donations requested) outside village hall
•PUBLIC TOILETS•	None on route
•CONTRIBUTOR•	Christopher Knowles

BACKGROUND TO THE WALK

Warren Hastings is a name that is simultaneously familiar and elusive; his role, however, in the making of the British Empire, was paramount. Born in the nearby village of Churchill, in 1732, he spent much of his childhood in Daylesford, where his grandfather was rector. When debt forced the sale of the manor, Hastings was sent to London to train for a career in commerce. He joined the East India Company, which was de facto ruler of India, and by 1773 he had attained the rank of Governor-General of Bengal, with the specific remit of cleaning up the corruption that was rife among the British and Indian ruling classes. His draconian methods were often resented but his determination and guile were effective. That India became the fulcrum of the British Empire was largely due to his work. Upon his return to England, he used his savings to repurchase Daylesford, where he died in 1818. The years before his death were bitter. A change in attitude to colonialist methods meant that Hastings was impeached for corruption. The seven year trial bankrupted him and ruined his health, although he was eventually vindicated and made Privy Councillor to George III.

Spacious Parkland

Daylesford House was rebuilt by Warren Hastings to the design of the architect Samuel Cockerell, who had been a colleague of Hastings at the East India Company. The building is in a classical style with Moorish features. The parkland around Daylesford House was laid out in 1787 by the landscape gardener Humphrey Repton in the spacious style of the day, made popular by Lancelot 'Capability' Brown. The village grew largely out of a need for cottages to house the workers who helped to make the estate profitable. Similarly, Daylesford church was rebuilt by Hastings in 1816 as a place of worship for the estate workers. By 1860 the congregation had outgrown the church, so it was redesigned to accommodate it. Inside there are monuments to the Hastings family, whilst the tomb of Warren Hastings himself lies outside the east window.

If Hastings represents the British Empire at its strongest then, in Adlestrop, you will find echoes of the changing world which signalled its decline. This small village, so characteristic of rural southern England, has come to be associated with one of the best-known poems in English, written by the war poet, Edward Thomas (1878–1917). Called simply *Adlestrop*, the poem captures a single moment as a train halts briefly at the village's station. Its haunting evocation of the drowsy silence of a hot summer day is all the more poignant when it is borne in mind that Thomas was killed by an exploding shell at Ronville near Arras in April 1917. Though trains still run on the line, the station was closed in 1964. You'll find the old station sign now decorates a bus shelter and the old station bench has the poem inscribed upon it.

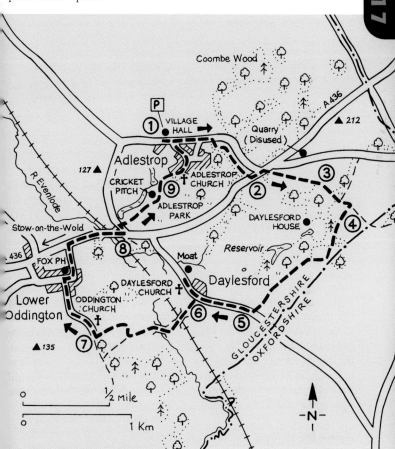

Walk 17 Directions

① From the car park turn left along the road. Pass a road on the right, the **bus shelter** bearing the Adlestrop sign, and some houses. Some 200yds (183m) after another road, turn right over a stile. Follow a woodland path to the left. Continue on this path until it meets a stile at a road.

② Cross the road with care and turn left along the verge. Before a road on the right, turn right through a gate on to a path in the **Daylesford Estate**. The path curves left towards a fence. Stay to the left of the fence until you reach a stile. Go over and cross the paddock. Pass through a gate, turn right and then left between fences.

③ Cross a bridge and follow a tree-lined avenue towards buildings. Traverse the farmyard and then turn right, passing the **estate office**.

> **WHERE TO EAT AND DRINK** ⓘ
> The **Fox** in Lower Oddington is very homely. There is also the **Horse and Groom** in the sibling village of Upper Oddington. Stow-on-the-Wold, a short drive to the west, has many and varied pubs, restaurants and tea rooms.

④ Walk along the drive between paddocks, soon following the estate wall. Pass the gateway to the garden offices and then, as it goes sharp right, stay on this drive, eventually coming to a road. Turn right.

⑤ Walk along the road, with the estate on your right, until you come to **Daylesford estate village**. Opposite the drive to Daylesford House is a shaded footpath leading to **Daylesford church**. After visiting the church, return to the road, turn right and retrace your steps. Before the pavement ends, turn right over a stile.

> **WHILE YOU'RE THERE** ⓘ
> **Bledington church**, about 3 miles (4.8km) south of the Oddingtons, contains an outstanding series of Perpendicular windows of beautiful, medieval stained glass. North of Adlestrop is the handsome Stuart manor house of **Chastleton**, Stow-on-the-Wold's **Toy Museum** will delight children and probably adults, too; Stow also has a set of stocks and several antique shops.

> **WHAT TO LOOK FOR** ⓘ
> As you walk around **Daylesford Park**, try to catch a glimpse of the house – it's almost impossible as it's very cleverly concealed behind ornamental parkland. This it seems was a deliberate ruse, fashionable in the 18th century, to preserve privacy whilst creating a harmonious landscape in keeping with the surrounding countryside. In Adlestrop, look out for the site of the old **station**, immortalised by Edward Thomas.

⑥ Cross this field to a railway footbridge. Go over it and straight ahead into a field (not the field on the left) then head, bearing slightly right, for another footbridge. Cross into a field, turn right and then left at the corner. Follow the grassy field margin as it passes into another field. At the next corner, enter the field in front of you. Turn right and then left. At the next corner, go right to a track.

⑦ Turn right and pass **Oddington church**. Continue to a junction in the village and turn right. Pass the **Fox** pub and continue to another junction. Turn right and walk along the pavement. Where this ends, cross the road carefully to the pavement opposite.

⑧ Beyond the bridge, turn left along the **Adlestrop road** and turn immediately right over two stiles. Walk towards **Adlestrop Park**. As you draw level with the cricket pitch go diagonally left to a gate about 100yds (91m) to the right of the pavilion.

⑨ Follow the track past **Adlestrop church**. At the next junction turn left through the village until you reach the **bus stop**. Turn left here to return to the car park at the start of the walk.

Adlestrop to Chastleton

From a timeless village to an age-old house.

•DISTANCE•	4 miles (6.4km)
•MINIMUM TIME•	2hrs
•ASCENT / GRADIENT•	427ft (130m) ▲▲▲
•LEVEL OF DIFFICULTY•	🚶🚶 🚶🚶 🚶
•PATHS•	Meadows, lanes, woodland, 8 stiles
•LANDSCAPE•	Low rolling hills north of Chipping Norton
•SUGGESTED MAP•	aqua3 OS Explorer OL45 The Cotswolds
•START / FINISH•	Grid reference: SP 241271
•DOG FRIENDLINESS•	Some road walking; not permitted in Chastleton House
•PARKING•	Car park (donations) beside village hall, Adlestrop
•PUBLIC TOILETS•	None on route
•CONTRIBUTOR•	Ann F Stonehouse

BACKGROUND TO THE WALK

The walk starts in the sleepy village of Adlestrop. It was not always so quiet, for trains used to stop here. The poet Edward Thomas (1878–1917) wrote a wistful little verse in which he recalled stopping here unexpectedly on the express train, apparently in the middle of nowhere, and listening to the birdsong (► Walk 17). Set in deep, lush countryside, Adlestrop still feels well off the beaten track. Its houses are a pleasing harmony of old and new, stone roofs alternating with thatch, and cottage gardens to die for.

Chastleton House

One of the finest Jacobean mansions in England, Chastleton House stands on the hillside above its village, aloof and self-contained. The house has a magical stillness about it. It was built between 1603 and 1618 by a local wool merchant, Walter Jones, on land purchased from Robert Catesby, one of the Gunpowder plotters. Unusually, the house was to be occupied for the next 400 years by the same family.

Time-worn Perfection

Its handsome grey stone frontage, with its tall windows and symmetrical gables and staircase towers, is seen clearly from the road. If you want to see inside, however, you are urged to book ahead, for opening hours and numbers are strictly limited. Chastleton is no grand showplace and, since its recent acquisition, the National Trust has been careful to conserve it in its peaceful, time-worn perfection, rather than attempt to restore it to some former glory. There is a panelled hall, an ornate great chamber and a vast long gallery with plastered ceiling on the top floor looks out over the gardens. Much of the furniture is original, and chambers are richly furnished with embroideries, quilts and tapestries.

Chastleton may have led a quiet life, but hardly a dull one. A secret room above the parlour was used to hide a fugitive in the Civil War. Arthur Jones was a Royalist, and had fought for the King – and lost – at the Battle of Worcester in 1651. He fled to his father's house at Chastleton and was forced into the hiding place when a party of soldiers arrived in hot pursuit. Arthur's wife, Sarah, was obliged to put them up for the night. This resourceful woman laced their ale with laudanum and, while his pursuers snored, Arthur made his escape. He was able to return at the Restoration and planted an oak in the grounds to celebrate his narrow escape.

Croquet on the Lawn
The formal gardens at Chastleton are contemporary with the house, its lawns studded with dark topiary. It is sometimes claimed that croquet was invented here. In fact, the game had been around for centuries, but was only introduced to England in 1852. The rules of the game were set out for the first time here at Chastleton in 1865.

Walk 18 Directions

① From the car park in Adlestrop turn left on to the road and left again up a broad track, signposted 'Macmillan Way'. Climb a stile by a gate and enter a meadow. Bear left (yellow waymarker). Walk up the field, with **Fern Farm** up to your right. Cross a stile in the top left corner and continue up the fence. Soon cross a stile to your left and continue up the same line, passing a bulging oak tree on your right. Cross another stile and continue straight ahead up the field. The hill gets steeper.

② Cross a stile by a wooden gate and walk up through the line of trees. Continue straight across the next field. Go over the crest of the hill and through an iron gate, into the **Chastleton Estate**. Continue straight ahead up an avenue of trees. Go through two gates to reach the road.

> **WHAT TO LOOK FOR**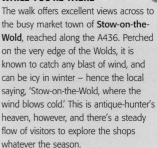
> Walking into the green ring of **Chastleton Barrow** is an eerie experience. Surrounded by a bank or rampart planted with trees, it clearly functioned once as a defensive site, most probably in the Iron Age. An ancient track linked the camp with the Rollright Stones (▶ Walk 22). This wide grassy amphitheatre on the hilltop is now used to hold cattle.

③ Turn right and walk along the road, passing **Chastleton House** on your left, then **St Mary's Church**. Pass the arcaded dovecote on the right. Stay on the road, which bends up right, and pass a car park on your right.

④ Where the road bends sharply right, turn left into a private road. Cross a cattle grid and immediately turn right. Go through a gate and take the bridleway diagonally left up the field, parallel with the road. On a level with **Barrow House** farm, go through a small gate, cross the drive and take the left of two gates opposite. Go through two more gates to enter the tree circle of **Chastleton Barrow**.

⑤ When you have seen the barrow, retrace your route to the drive and turn left. At the road turn left. After a short distance turn right across a stile. Walk ahead through the trees and follow the path, which leads diagonally left across the field, with

> **WHILE YOU'RE THERE** ⓘ
> The walk offers excellent views across to the busy market town of **Stow-on-the-Wold**, reached along the A436. Perched on the very edge of the Wolds, it is known to catch any blast of wind, and can be icy in winter – hence the local saying, 'Stow-on-the-Wold, where the wind blows cold.' This is antique-hunter's heaven, however, and there's a steady flow of visitors to explore the shops whatever the season.

views to Stow-on-the-Wold. Keep straight on down, passing some barns to your left. Cross a track and walk ahead down the edge of woodland. At the bottom corner bear right into the woods. Follow the winding path, cross a stile and emerge at a field.

⑥ Turn left along the track. Turn right before you reach the gateway, and walk down the edge of the field. Go through a gate into the **Long Drive**. Follow this path through the trees and emerge on to the road. Cross over, go through a gateway on the other side and soon turn right along a narrow footpath. Follow this through the trees; cross a stile and turn left along the road. Take the first turning left and walk through **Adlestrop** village, keeping right to return to the car park and the start of the walk.

> **WHERE TO EAT AND DRINK** ⓘ
> The venerable villages of Lower Oddington and Upper Oddington offer an appealing diversion on your way to Stow-on-the-Wold and are served by two good pubs. The **Fox** at Lower Oddington is set opposite a beautiful little manor house. Continue through the villages to reach the **Horse and Groom** at Upper Oddington, which describes itself as village inn and has the bonus of a big car park behind.

A Ghostly Trail Around Prestbury

A gentle ramble around this unassuming old village which claims to be one of Britain's most haunted.

•DISTANCE•	3½ miles (5.7km)
•MINIMUM TIME•	1hr 30min
•ASCENT / GRADIENT•	100ft (30m)
•LEVEL OF DIFFICULTY•	
•PATHS•	Fields (could be muddy in places) and pavement, 10 stiles
•LANDSCAPE•	Woodland, hills and villages
•SUGGESTED MAP•	aqua3 OS Explorer 179 Gloucester, Cheltenham & Stroud
•START / FINISH•	Grid reference: SO 972238
•DOG FRIENDLINESS•	Lead necessary as some fields stocked with farm animals; some stiles have dog slots
•PARKING•	Free car park near war memorial
•PUBLIC TOILETS•	None on route
•CONTRIBUTOR•	Christopher Knowles

BACKGROUND TO THE WALK

The village of Prestbury, on the north east fringe of Cheltenham, is reputedly the second most haunted village in England, with The Burgage its oldest and most haunted street. The largest building along it is Prestbury House, now a hotel. During the Civil War it was occupied by Parliamentary troops. Expecting Royalists camped on Cleeve Hill to send a messenger to Gloucester, they laid a trap. A rope was stretched across The Burgage. When the Cavalier rode through the village, he snagged on the rope and was catapulted from his mount. No doubt relieved of his despatches and interrogated, the unfortunate rider was then executed. A skeleton discovered near by in the 19th century is thought to be his. It is said that the sound of hooves can often be heard here, as well as a horse's snorting and stamping.

Exercise and Exorcism
More paranormal activity has been experienced in the hotel grounds, where they meet Mill Street. Here there have been sightings of rowdy parties of people in Regency dress. On this site, it turns out, there was once a fashionable meeting place, called the Grotto. It was where the local gentry would take their ease. By the time of its closure, in 1859, it had become known as a place of ill-repute.

Spectral abbots are regularly seen in Prestbury. The Black Abbot used to walk the aisle of St Mary's Church but, since his exorcism, he prefers the churchyard – a vicar came across him here, seated on a tombstone. The Abbot has also been spotted in the early morning near the Plough Inn on Mill Street. In fact, there have been sightings of the Black Abbot almost everywhere in the village. Perhaps this may be explained by the fact that the Bishops of Hereford owned a palace here from the 12th century, whilst the Prior of Llanthony lived in the priory close to the church. There are several other haunted places you will come across in the village. At Sundial Cottage, in The Burgage, a lovelorn girl plays the spinet; the Three

Queens house in Deep Street had to be exorcised; there are three stone cottages next to Three Queens, the middle one of which is haunted by soldiers from the Civil War, and the third of which is haunted by the Black Abbot. And another abbot (or perhaps the same one) with 'an unpleasant leer', is said to haunt Morningside House, next to the car park.

There is more to the village than ghosts, however. The manor of Prestbury, belonging to the Bishop of Hereford, was established by AD 899. Remains of the moated hall can still be found on Spring Lane, close to Cheltenham racecourse. By the 13th century Prestbury had gained a charter to hold a weekly market in The Burgage. This was also the site of the annual fair. The village is closely associated with the jockey Fred Archer, as a plaque on the King's Arms testifies, whilst the cricketer Charlie Parker, who played for England, was also born here. Another great English cricketer, Tom Graveney, was once landlord of the Royal Oak on The Burgage.

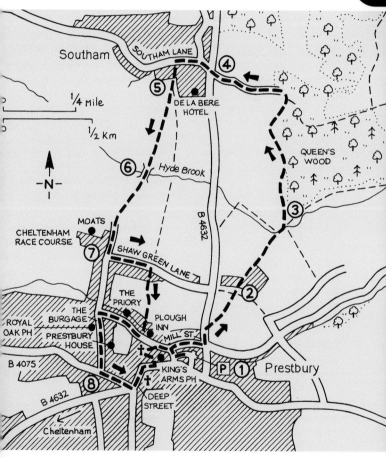

Walk 19 Directions

① Leave the car park, turn right into **The Bank** and right again into **Mill Street**. At the main road turn left. After 100yds (91m) cross the road to a stile. Go into a field and go diagonally left to another stile.

② Cross this and follow the track that is ahead of you and slightly to

Walk 19

your left. Where it goes right, cross a stile in front of you. Cross a field heading slightly to the right, to another stile. Go over this into a field and head for **Queen's Wood** in front of you.

③ Stay to the left of the woods. Eventually cross a track and enter another field. Where the woods sweep uphill, continue straight on through bushes to a bridle gate. Go through on to a woodland path and turn left, downhill, to reach the main road.

④ Ahead of you are the medieval buildings of the **De La Bere Hotel**. Cross the road and turn right. Follow the pavement as it bears left into **Southam Lane**. After 200yds (183m) turn left along a track to a gate. Go through this and a kissing gate to a field.

WHERE TO EAT AND DRINK ℹ

There are several pubs to choose from. The **King's Arms** welcomes children, the **Royal Oak** also serves lunches and the **Plough Inn**, on Mill Street, is a very fine old pub with a flagstone floor and a gorgeous garden. **Prestbury House** offers an excellent light lunch or dinner in a more formal setting.

---

⑤ Head across, bearing slightly right, with the De La Bere on your left. Follow an obvious path across a series of paddocks and fields via stiles and gates. Finally, at a stile amid bushes in a corner, cross on to a track and follow this as it leads to a bridge stile.

⑥ Cross and continue straight ahead into a field with a hedge on your right. Go over the brow of the slope and down to a gate in the hedge to your right. Go through to a track and follow this to a road.

WHILE YOU'RE THERE ℹ

Cheltenham, of which Prestbury is really a suburb, is a very handsome town and definitely worth a visit. It has many streets of fine Regency and Georgian architecture, as well as two excellent small museums, one in the birthplace of the composer Gustav Holst (1874–1934), the other with features devoted to the arctic explorer Edward Wilson, a native of the town, and to the Arts and Crafts Movement, which was very strong in this area.

---

⑦ Turn left along **Shaw Green Lane**. After about 400yds (366m) turn right along a footpath passing between houses. Eventually this will bring you out on to **Mill Street**, opposite the church. Turn right, to walk past the **Priory** and the brick wall that marks the site of the haunted Grotto, until you come to **The Burgage**. Turn left here, passing the **Royal Oak**, **Prestbury House** and **Sundial Cottage**.

⑧ At the junction with **Tatchley Lane** turn left and then left again into **Deep Street**, passing the **Three Queens** and the trio of stone cottages. Just before the **King's Arms** turn left on a footpath leading to the **church**. Turn right just before the church and pass through the churchyard to return to **Mill Street**, opposite the **Plough Inn**. Turn right and return to the car park at the start.

WHAT TO LOOK FOR ℹ

Don't forget that you are very close to one of Europe's greatest **racecourses**. As you walk across the fields towards Queen's Wood, you will have some wonderful views across the racecourse to Cheltenham. The **De la Bere Hotel** is a striking Elizabethan mansion that was once the home of Lord Ellenborough, a former Governor-General of India.

Guiting Power to the People

A gentle ramble in quintessential Gloucestershire, from a typical village with an atypical place name and atypical ownership.

•DISTANCE•	5 miles (8km)
•MINIMUM TIME•	2hrs
•ASCENT / GRADIENT•	295ft (90m) ▲ ▲ ▲
•LEVEL OF DIFFICULTY•	ŤŤ ŤŤ ŤŤ
•PATHS•	Fields, tracks and country lanes, 10 stiles
•LANDSCAPE•	Woodland, hills and village
•SUGGESTED MAP•	aqua3 OS Explorer OL45 The Cotswolds
•START / FINISH•	Grid reference: SP 094245
•DOG FRIENDLINESS•	Fairly clear of livestock but many horses on roads
•PARKING•	Car park outside village hall (small fee)
•PUBLIC TOILETS•	None on route
•CONTRIBUTOR•	Christopher Knowles

BACKGROUND TO THE WALK

It is remarkable how much detailed history is available about English villages, even ones, like Guiting Power, that are distinguished only by their comeliness. Looking from the village green, surrounded by stone cottages, with its church and secluded manor house, it is easy to imagine that very little has changed here in 1,000 years.

What's in a Name?

The eccentric name comes from the Saxon word 'gyte-ing', or torrent, and indeed the name was given not only to Guiting Power but also to neighbouring Temple Guiting, which in the 12th century was owned by the Knights Templars. Guiting Power though, was named after the pre-eminent local family of the 13th century, the Le Poers.

Over the years the village was variously known as Gything, Getinge, Gettinges Poer, Guyting Poher, Nether Guiting and Lower Guiting. Its current name and spelling date only from 1937. In 1086, the Domesday Book noted that there were 'four villagers, three Frenchmen, two riding men, and a priest with two small-holders'. Just under 100 years later the first recorded English fulling mill was in operation at the nearby hamlet of Barton. In 1330 permission was given for a weekly market to be held at Guiting Power, which may explain the current arrangement of the houses about the green. Guiting had its share of the prosperity derived from the 15th-century wool trade, as the addition of the little tower to the church testifies.

Slow to Catch Up

And yet, in other ways, history was slow to catch up with small villages like Guiting. Its farmland, for example, was enclosed only in 1798, allowing small landowners such as a tailor called John Williams, who owned 12 acres (4.86ha) in the form of medieval strips scattered throughout the parish, to finally consolidate their possessions. Local rights of way were enshrined in law at this time. By the end of the 19th century the rural depression had reduced the population to 431, and it continued to decline throughout the 20th century.

Nonetheless, it is recorded that apart from public houses (there were at least four), there were two grocers, two bakers, two tailors, two carpenters, two policemen and a blacksmith.

Local Village for Local People
There are still two pubs in Guiting Power but everything else, apart from the post office and a single grocery store, has disappeared. The village is unusual in that it hasn't succumbed to the inflationary effects of second homeowners from the cities pushing local housing beyond the reach of existing locals. Much of this is down to the far-sightedness of Moya Davidson, a resident in the 1930s, who purchased cottages to be rented out locally. Today these are managed by the Guiting Manor Amenity Trust. It has meant that younger people are able to stay in the village to live and work and there still a few families here who can trace their roots back in Guiting Power for several generations.

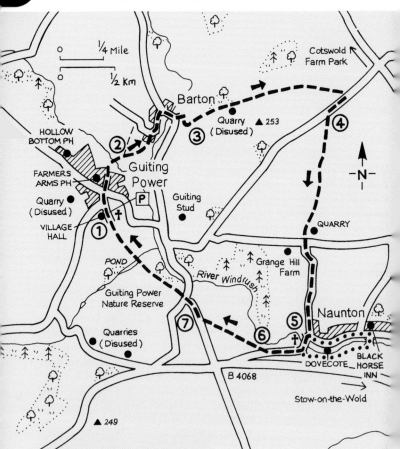

Walk 20 **Directions**

① From the **village hall** car park walk down the road to the **village green**. Cross the road to walk down a lane. At the bottom go over a stile into a field and turn right. Walk up the bank, up to another stile. Don't cross the one in front of you but clamber over the one to your right into a field.

② Turn left and walk straight across this field to another stile. Cross this and two more to pass a farmhouse in **Barton** village. Follow the lane down to a larger road and turn right. Cross a bridge and turn left up a track and, after 100yds (91m), turn right up another track.

> **WHERE TO EAT AND DRINK**
> Guiting Power's two pubs are the **Farmers Arms**, just off the village green, and the **Hollow Bottom** on the other, Winchcombe, side of the village. Naunton has the very pleasant **Black Horse Inn**.

③ After a few paces bear left and walk along this track for about a mile (1.6km), until you reach another road. Turn right, walk along here for about 250yds (229m) and turn left on to a track.

④ Follow this all the way to a road, passing a **quarry** as you go. Cross the road and enter a lane descending past a house. This quiet lane will bring you all the way into the village of **Naunton**.

> **WHILE YOU'RE THERE** ⓘ
> Located between Guiting Power and Stow-on-the-Wold is the **Cotswold Farm Park**, a sort of zoo specialising in rare breeds of British farm livestock. Animals include the Cotswold 'lion'. This breed of sheep was the foundation of the medieval wool trade and has fortunately been saved from extinction.

⑤ At the junction turn right. Walk through the village and cross the pretty stone bridge by the old mill, passing the old **rectory** to the left and the church concealed to the right. (To get to the Black Horse Inn, turn left and walk along the street for 400yds (366m). Return by entering a drive opposite the pub, turning sharp right over a stile, and

walking back along the side of the river to emerge at a road near the church, where you turn left.) Continue up, out of the village.

⑥ After ¼ mile (400m) turn right over a stile into a field. Turn left, walk to a stile and go into the next field. Cross this field, enter the next one and follow the path to the right of some trees to a gate at the road.

⑦ Turn right along the road and continue to a junction at the bottom. Cross the road to enter a field and walk straight across. At the end go down some steps and pass to the right of a pond. Walk across the next field and then cross a stile to walk to the left of the **church** and return to the start.

> **WHAT TO LOOK FOR** ⓘ
> The Norman doorway in **Guiting church** is an exceptionally rich golden hue. In Naunton, if you stroll back from the Black Horse Inn towards the church on the opposite side of the river then you will be rewarded with a view of a large but charming 17th-century **dovecote**. Many villages had dovecotes for eggs and winter meat.

Walk 21

Churchill and Cornwell

A walk linking two intriguing villages on the D'Arcy Dalton Way.

•DISTANCE•	5½ miles (8.8km)
•MINIMUM TIME•	2hrs 30min
•ASCENT / GRADIENT•	459ft (140m) ▲ ▲ ▲
•LEVEL OF DIFFICULTY•	🚶 🚶 🚶
•PATHS•	Open farmland, village lanes, quiet roads, 12 stiles
•LANDSCAPE•	Broad, open valley once used by a railway line
•SUGGESTED MAP•	aqua3 OS Explorer OL45 The Cotswolds
•START / FINISH•	Grid reference: SP 270270
•DOG FRIENDLINESS•	Some road walking, otherwise good
•PARKING•	Lay-by beside phone box at Cornwell
•PUBLIC TOILETS•	None on route
•CONTRIBUTOR•	Ann F Stonehouse

BACKGROUND TO THE WALK

There's a slightly theatrical air about Cornwell, as if this neat and charming village were poised and waiting for the next act, or a film camera to roll. It huddles on one side of a small valley, smugly holding on to its secrets, for, as part of the Cornwell Manor Estate, it is private and inaccessible. You may look, but not touch. The manor itself, where owner Peter Ward and his family live today, is carefully screened from prying eyes, except for the lovely stone front, which boldly faces up to the road from behind its high wrought iron gate.

Cornwell

Cornwell's best known secret is that it was thoroughly remodelled just before World War II by the architect-cum-salvage king, Clough Williams-Ellis (1883–1978). Born in Northamptonshire, Williams-Ellis developed an eclectic design style that mixed architectural details in a particularly flamboyant way. By the time he was working on Cornwell, his own pet project at Portmeirion in North Wales – what he called his home for fallen buildings – was already well established. The then owner of Cornwell, Mrs Anthony Gillson, employed Williams-Ellis to modernise the village, but also to create the magnificent terraced gardens at the manor, along with other alterations including the addition of a ballroom. His influence may be clearly seen on the village hall (originally the school), with its bowed end and eccentric chimney stack-cum-bellcote.

The little Church of St Peter remained untouched at this time, though the handsome wooden candelabras are attributed to the style of Clough Williams-Ellis. It dates back to Norman times, and its position away from the village, in fact on the opposite side of the manor, is curious. It is believed that a village once surrounded the church, but disappeared during the ravages of the plague years.

Churchill

In direct contrast to Cornwell, Churchill's attractions are up-front and open to view. The tower of All Saints' Church dominates the skyline for miles around, and if it looks familiar that's because it's a scaled-down model of the tower of Magdalene College, Oxford. As the choristers of that famous establishment sing from their tower to greet the dawn on May Day, so local choristers gather at the top of All Saints' to do the same. The church was built in 1826 by James Langston, a mover and shaker in the village, and it is he who is affectionately remembered with the large and elaborate fountain next door.

Churchill boasts two famous sons. The first is Warren Hastings (1732–1818), a colourful figure who rose to become Governor-General of India, and lost his fortune in successfully defending himself against a charge of cruelty and corruption. The second is William Smith (1769–1839), who produced the first geological map of England.

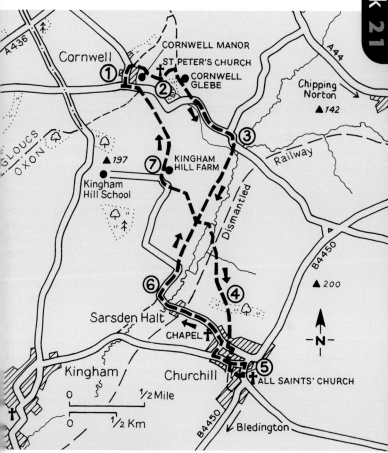

Walk 21 Directions

① Turn left and walk down and up through **Cornwell**. Pass a farm, right, and turn right, signposted 'D'Arcy Dalton Way'. Where the track veers left, keep ahead, by a fingerpost. Walk down an orchard and bear left. Go right at the corner through the hedge. Soon go through a gate on your left. Turn right and walk downhill. Cross a stile, right; follow the path down towards **St Peter's Church**.

② Go through a gate into the churchyard. Pass the church, and leave via a squeeze gate. Walk straight ahead down the hill, cross

Walk 21

the bridge at the bottom and go up to the gate. Turn right along the drive, passing **Cornwell Glebe**. Bear left along the road. Pass a turning to Salford.

③ Turn right along a bridleway, signed 'Kingham'. Follow this for ½ mile (800m), then cross a stile on the left and walk ahead down the field edge. Cross a footbridge and follow the path diagonally right. Cross another footbridge and bear right along the stream. Soon bear left and cross a stile. Cross the track. Cross a footbridge opposite, and bear diagonally right up the field. Cross a footbridge in a hedge and continue on this line through another hedge.

WHAT TO LOOK FOR ⓘ

The hamlet of **Sarsden Halt** was once a stop on the railway line – hence the appearance and railway theme of some of its buildings. The line ran along the valley floor, linking Chipping Norton in the east with the main line at Kingham Station to the west. Its route is crossed twice in the course of the walk.

④ Cross a stile into the woods. Follow the path down, over a footbridge and right up the other side. Go through a gate and ahead towards **Churchill**. Cross a stile, then bear right beside a house. Cross a stile and turn left up the road. Pass a post-box and turn right along a path. At the next road turn left. At the top turn right.

⑤ Turn right again before you reach the church and follow the path round the back of the old pub. Cross a stile, pass a barn and maintain your direction into a field. Soon turn right over a stile and walk down a lane. When you get to the road turn left; turn right at the

WHERE TO EAT AND DRINK ⓘ

The pub in Churchill was closed at the time of writing. It's therefore worth making your way westwards to Bledington, where the venerable **King's Head Inn** looks out on the huge village green, with its streams and tiny bridges. In a beautiful setting, the pub is a free house, offering restaurant food and accommodation, with plenty of tables to sit at outside. A children's play area is near by.

next junction, then left at the end. Follow this road out of the village, passing the old chapel. Continue through **Sarsden Halt**.

⑥ Follow the road right, then keep straight ahead along the green lane. After ½ mile (800m) climb the stile on your left and bear diagonally up the field. Walk up the hedge and turn right along the road.

⑦ Continue walking straight ahead through **Kingham Hill Farm**. Pass through a gate at the other side and carry on straight across two fields. Cross a stile, then a footbridge and stile and keep straight on. Pass an old gate and continue up the field. Cross another stile and continue, bearing slightly left over the hill crest. Take the gate to the left of the main gate and turn left up the road to return to your car and the start of the walk.

WHILE YOU'RE THERE ⓘ

Chipping Norton is the highest town in Oxfordshire, its wealth built on the wool trade. It centres on a large market square, with a little town hall dating from 1835 and some handsome Georgian frontages. There are lots of opportunities for shopping and eating out. The distinctive **Bliss Valley Tweed Mill** with its tall Tuscan-style chimney, on the north side of town, has been converted to flats.

Myths of the Rollright Stones

From Chipping Norton to an ancient site associated with a charming legend.

•DISTANCE•	8 miles (12.9km)
•MINIMUM TIME•	4hrs
•ASCENT / GRADIENT•	295ft (90m) ▲▲▲
•LEVEL OF DIFFICULTY•	🚶 🚶 🚶
•PATHS•	Field paths and tracks, country roads, 9 stiles
•LANDSCAPE•	Rolling hills on the Oxfordshire/Warwickshire border
•SUGGESTED MAP•	aqua3 OS Explorer 191 Banbury, Bicester & Chipping Norton
•START / FINISH•	Grid reference: SP 312270
•DOG FRIENDLINESS•	Under control or on lead across farmland, one lengthy stretch of country road and busy streets in Chipping Norton
•PARKING•	Free car park off A44, in centre of Chipping Norton
•PUBLIC TOILETS•	At car park
•CONTRIBUTOR•	Nick Channer

BACKGROUND TO THE WALK

Commanding a splendid position overlooking the rolling hills and valleys of the north east Cotswolds, the Rollright Stones comprise the Whispering Knights, the King's Men and the King Stone. These intriguing stones are steeped in myth and legend.

Mystical Theories

It seems a king was leading his army in this quiet corner of Oxfordshire while five of his knights stood together conspiring against him. The king met a witch near by who told him he would be King of England if he could see the settlement of Long Compton in seven long strides. As he approached the top of the ridge a mound of earth suddenly rose up before him, preventing him from seeing the village and so the king, his soldiers and his knights were all turned to stone.

In reality the Rollright Stones form a group of prehistoric megalithic monuments created from large natural boulders found within about 600yds (549m) of the site. The stones are naturally pitted, giving them astonishing and highly unusual shapes. The Whispering Knights, of which there are five, are the remains of a Portal Dolmen burial chamber, probably constructed around 3800–3000 BC, long before the stone circle. It would have been very imposing in its day and it is the easternmost burial chamber of this kind in Britain. The King Stone stands alone and apart from the others, just across the county boundary in Warwickshire. The 8ft (2.4m) tall single standing stone was almost certainly erected to mark the site of a Bronze Age cemetery which was in use around 1800–1500 BC.

Finally, you come to the King's Men Stone Circle – a ceremonial monument thought to have been built around 2500–2000 BC. There are over 70 stones here, but it has been said they are impossible to count! Originally there were about 105 stones forming a continuous wall except for one narrow entrance. The King's Men Stones are arranged in an unditched circle about 100ft (30m) across and ranging in size from just a few inches to 7ft (2m). Here and there the stones are so close they almost touch.

It is not clear what the stone circle was used for but it may well have had some significance in religious and secular ceremonies. Between 200 and 300 people can fit within the circle, though it is not known how many people would attend these ceremonies or what form they took. Most mysterious of all is why this particular site was chosen. Many visitors to the Rollright Stones have questioned their origin over the years but they remain a mystery. Appropriate for such a legend as this, the remote hilltop setting of these timeless stones has more than a hint of the supernatural about it.

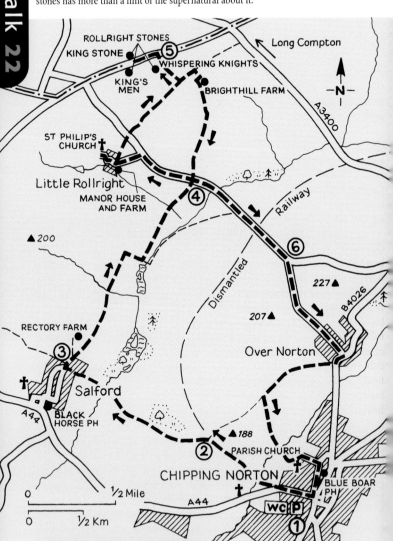

Walk 22 Directions

① Follow the **A44** downhill. Pass **Penhurst School**, then veer right, through a kissing gate. Skirt the left-hand edge of the recreation ground and aim for a gate. Descend to a bridge and, when the path forks, keep right. Go up the slope to

Walk 22

three stiles and keep ahead along the right edge of the field. Make for gate and drop down to some double gates in the corner.

② Cross a track just beyond the gates and walk towards Salford, keeping the hedge on the left. Continue into the village and soon turn right by a patch of grass and a sign, 'Trout Lakes – Rectory Farm'.

③ Follow the track to a right-hand bend. Go straight ahead here, following the field edge. Make for a gate ahead and turn right in the next field. About 100yds (91m) before the field corner, turn left and follow the path across to an opening in the boundary. Veer left, then immediately right to skirt the field. Cross a little stream and maintain your direction in the next field to reach the road.

④ Turn left, then left again for **Little Rollright**. After visiting the church, retrace your steps to the **D'Arcy Dalton Way** on the left. Follow the path up the field slope to the road. Cross over and continue

on the way between fields. Head for some trees and approach a stile. Don't cross it; instead, turn left and skirt the field, passing close to the **Whispering Knights**.

⑤ On reaching the road, turn left and visit the site of the **Rollright Stones**. Return to the Whispering Knights, head down the field to the stile and cross it to an immediate second stile. Walk ahead along a grassy path and turn right at the next stile towards **Brighthill Farm**. Pass alongside the buildings to a stile, head diagonally right down the field to a further stile, keep the boundary on your right and head for a stile in the bottom right corner of the field. Make for the bottom right corner of the next field, go through a gate and skirt the field, turning left at the road.

⑥ Keep right at the next fork and head towards the village of **Over Norton**. Walk through the village to the T-junction. Turn right and when the road swings to the left by **Cleeves Corner**, join a track signposted 'Salford'. When the hedges give way, look for a waymark on the left. Follow the path down the slope, make for two kissing gates and then follow the path alongside a stone wall to reach the parish church. Join Church Lane and follow it as far as the T-junction. Turn right and return to the town centre.

Regenerating Bourton-on-the-Water

On the wilder side of Bourton-on-the-Water to see its natural regeneration.

•DISTANCE•	4¾ miles (7.7km)
•MINIMUM TIME•	2hrs
•ASCENT / GRADIENT•	230ft (70m) ▲ ▲ ▲
•LEVEL OF DIFFICULTY•	🚶 🚶 🚶
•PATHS•	Track and field, can be muddy and wet in places, 26 stiles
•LANDSCAPE•	Sweeping valley views, lakes, streams, hills and village
•SUGGESTED MAP•	aqua3 OS Explorer OL45 The Cotswolds
•START / FINISH•	Grid reference: SP 169208
•DOG FRIENDLINESS•	Some stiles may be awkward for dogs; occasional livestock
•PARKING•	Pay-and-display car park on Station Road
•PUBLIC TOILETS•	At car park
•CONTRIBUTOR•	Christopher Knowles

BACKGROUND TO THE WALK

Despite Bourton-on-the-Water's popularity the throng is easily left behind by walking briefly eastwards to a chain of redundant gravel pits. In the 1970s these were landscaped and filled with water and fish. As is the way of these things, for some time the resulting lakes looked every inch the artificial creations they were, but now they have bedded into their surroundings and seem to be an integral part of the landscape.

Migrating Birds

The fish and water have acted as magnets for a range of wetland birds, whose populations rise and fall with the seasons. During the spring and summer months you should look out for the little grebe and the splendidly adorned great crested grebe, as well as the more familiar moorhens and coots, and mallard and tufted ducks. Wagtails will strut about the water's edge, swans and geese prowl across the water and kingfishers, if you are lucky, streak from bush to reed. Come the autumn, the number of birds will have increased significantly. Above all there will be vast numbers of ducks – pintail, shoveler, widgeon and pochard among them – as well as occasional visitors like cormorants. Either around the lakes or by the rivers you may also spy dippers and, in the hedgerows, members of the finch family.

Immigrant Birds

Should you get drawn into the village – as you surely will – keep listening for birdsong and you will hear some improbable 'visitors'. Bourton-on-the-Water has a large bird sanctuary which houses, among many other birds, one of the largest collections of penguins in the world, some of which featured in the film *Batman* (1989). A penguin seems an odd choice for an adversary, given its endearing reputation, and at first glance one might think that a penguin was a mammal and a bat was a bird, not vice versa. The reason for the presence of so many penguins in the Cotswolds is that the sanctuary's founder was also the owner of two small islands in the Falklands.

Long History

Penguins aside, Bourton-on-the-Water has a long history. The edge of the village is bounded by the Roman Fosse Way and many of its buildings are a pleasing mix of medieval, Georgian and Victorian. Although the village can become very crowded during the summer months, with the riverbanks at its centre like green beaches, strewn with people picnicking and paddling, it can still be charming. Arrive early enough in the morning, or hang around in the evening until the daytrippers have gone and you will find the series of bridges spanning the Windrush (one of which dates back to 1756) and the narrow streets beyond them highly picturesque. They retain the warm honeyed light that attracts people to the Cotswolds. You'll see far fewer visitors in little Clapton-on-the-Hill, which overlooks Bourton. Make the brief detour just before Point ⑤ to see its handsome green and tiny church.

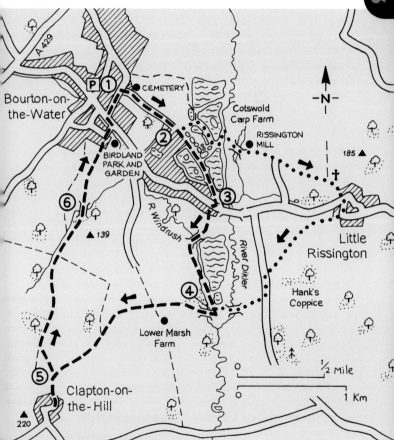

Walk 23 **Directions**

① Opposite the entrance to the main pay-and-display car park in **Bourton-on-the-Water** locate a public footpath and continue to a junction opposite the village **cemetery**. Bear right to follow a lane all the way to its end. There are two gates in front of you. Take the one on the right-hand side, with a stile beside it, to join a grassy track.

Walk 23

② Follow the track between lakes to where it curves right. Leave the track to go forward over a bridge and stile into a field. Go across the field, curving right, to come to a stile at a road.

③ Cross the road, turn right and immediately left on to a track. After 100yds (91m) go left over a stile into a field and turn right. Cross a stile and return to the track, with a lake to your left. Just before a gate turn right over a bridge and left over a stile on to a path alongside the **River Windrush**. Continue until the path comes to a stile at a field. Turn left, cross another stile and go left over a bridge before turning right beside another lake.

④ Where this second, smaller lake ends bear right to a stile, followed by a bridge and stile at a field. Keep to the right side of fields until you come to a track. At a house leave the track and continue to a stile. In the next field, after 25yds (23m), turn left over a stile and then sharp right. Continue to a stile and then go half left across a field. Continue

on the same line across the next field to a stile. Cross this and follow the right margin of a field, to climb slowly to a junction of tracks. Turn left to visit the village of **Clapton-on-the-Hill**, or turn right to continue.

⑤ Follow a track to a field. Go forward then half right to pass right of **woodland**. Continue to a stile, followed by two stiles together at a field. Go half left to a stile and then follow a succession of stiles, a stream appearing to the left.

⑥ Cross a bridge and then go half right across a field to a bridge. Continue to more stiles and then walk along a grassy track towards houses. Cross one more stile and follow a path to a road in **Bourton**. Walk ahead to cross the river and turn left, then right, to return to the start.

Extending the Walk
You can extend this walk to include the pretty village of **Little Rissington.** As you leave Bourton on the lane after the **cemetery**, at Point ②, follow a path to the left, past lakes and meadows to **Rissington Mill**. Field paths take you into the village and you can meet up with the main route again across the bridge near Point ④.

Painswick's Traditions

From the Queen of the Cotswolds through the Washpool Valley.

•DISTANCE•	7½ miles (12.1km)
•MINIMUM TIME•	3hrs 30min
•ASCENT / GRADIENT•	705ft (215m) ▲▲▲
•LEVEL OF DIFFICULTY•	👫 👫 👫
•PATHS•	Fields, tracks, golf course and a green lane, 16 stiles
•LANDSCAPE•	Hills, valleys, villages, isolated farmhouses, extensive views
•SUGGESTED MAP•	aqua3 OS Explorer 179 Gloucester, Cheltenham & Stroud
•START / FINISH•	Grid reference: SO 865094
•DOG FRIENDLINESS•	Off leads along lengthy stretches, many stiles
•PARKING•	Car park (small fee) near library, just off main road
•PUBLIC TOILETS•	At car park
•CONTRIBUTOR•	Christopher Knowles

BACKGROUND TO THE WALK

Local traditions continue to thrive in Painswick, the 'Queen of the Cotswolds'. These are centred around its well-known churchyard, where the Victorian poet Sydney Dobell is buried. The churchyard is famously filled, not only with the 'table' tombs of 18th-century clothiers, but also with 99 beautifully manicured yew trees, planted in 1792. The legend goes that only 99 will ever grow at any one time, as Old Nick will always kill off the hundredth. Should you be minded to do so, try to count them. You will almost certainly be thwarted, as many of them have grown together, creating arches and hedges.

This old tale has become confused with an ancient ceremony that still takes place here on the Sunday nearest to the Feast of the Nativity of St Mary, in mid-September. This is the 'clipping' ceremony, which has nothing to do with cutting bushes or flowers. It derives from the old Saxon word, 'clyping', which means 'embrace' and is used in conjunction with the church. Traditionally, the children of the village gather together on the Sunday afternoon and join hands to form a circle around the church or churchyard, and advance and retreat to and from the church, singing the *Clipping Hymn*. Perhaps this ceremony is the distant descendant of an a pagan ceremony involving a ritual dance around an altar bearing a sacrificed animal. The children wear flowers in their hair and are rewarded with a coin and a bun for their efforts. There was, and maybe still is, a special cake baked for the day, known as 'puppy dog pie', in which a small china dog was inserted. Was this a reminder of the ancient ritual sacrifice? There are yew trees in other gardens in the village, many older than those in the churchyard, and one of which is said to have been planted by Elizabeth I.

The other famous tradition that continues to be observed in the area takes place further along the escarpment, at Cooper's Hill. Here, on Spring Bank Holiday Monday, the cheese-rolling races take place. From a spot marked by a maypole, competitors hurtle down an absurdly steep slope in pursuit of wooden discs representing Gloucester cheeses. The winner, or survivor, is presented with a real cheese; but the injury rate is high and there has been a lot of controversy about whether the event should be allowed to continue. Fortunately, tradition has won the day so far and people are still able to break their necks in the pursuit of cheese if they want to.

Walk 24

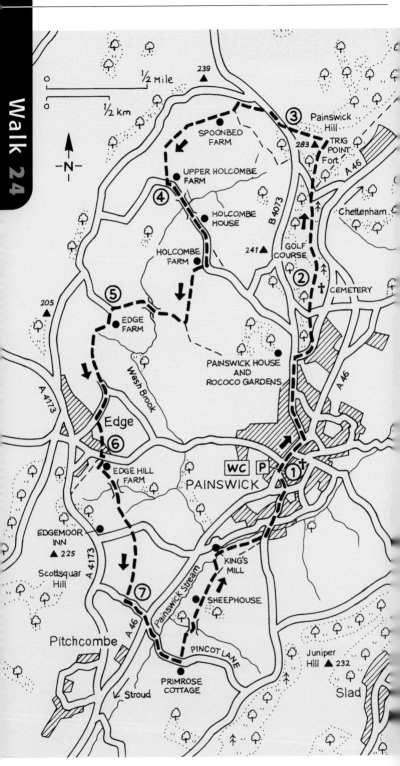

½ Mile

½ km

–N–

239

③ Painswick Hill

SPOONBED FARM

283 TRIG POINT Fort

A 46

UPPER HOLCOMBE FARM

④

HOLCOMBE HOUSE

B 4073

Cheltenham

HOLCOMBE FARM

241

GOLF COURSE

205

⑤

EDGE FARM

② CEMETERY

Wash Brook

PAINSWICK HOUSE AND ROCOCO GARDENS

A 46

A 4173

Edge

⑥

EDGE HILL FARM

WC P

PAINSWICK

①

EDGEMOOR INN

▲ 225

Scottsquar Hill

A 4173

KING'S MILL

Painswick Stream

⑦

SHEEPHOUSE

A 46

Pitchcombe

PINCOT LANE

Juniper Hill ▲ 232

PRIMROSE COTTAGE

Slad

← Stroud

Walk 24 Directions

① Turn right out of the car park and along the main street. Turn left along the **Gloucester road**, join another road and turn right towards the golf club. Bear left through the car park, turn left along a track and immediately right across a fairway (look out for flying golf balls).

> **WHAT TO LOOK FOR** ⓘ
> Just before you leave the golf course, at the highest point of the walk, you should be able to identify the ramparts and ditches of the **hill fort** beneath your feet. Like many such features on the Cotswold escarpment, this one is believed to date back to the Iron Age.

② Keep to the left of a **cemetery**, then cross another fairway to a woodland path. Continue to a road. After a few paces turn right. Walk along the edge of the golf course to the top of a promontory, passing to the left of a **trig point**. Descend the other side and turn left down a path. At a track go left to a road.

③ Turn right to a bus stop. Cross to a path going right. Turn left down to **Spoonbed Farm**. Walk through to a gate, then take a path to a field. In a second field keep left of a tree to reach a stile. After another stile cross a field to the right of a telegraph pole. Keep to the right of **Upper Holcombe Farm** to a stile.

④ Turn left, eventually ascending to **Holcombe Farm**. Continue along a track, passing some gates on the left, and go left into the next field. Cross a stile and bear right to another stile. Turn right down to a bridge, then take the rightmost path. Ascend the field to a stile.

⑤ Turn left towards **Edge Farm**, then fork right to a gate. Cross two fields to another gate. Pass a house, soon arriving at a road. Keep right. Opposite a house turn left over a stile, bear half right to another stile and enter **Edge**.

⑥ Turn left, then sharp right. Before the farm turn left over a stile, then another, to a bridge. Ascend a field to a stile, then head for a gate at a track, to the right of a farm. Go through another gate opposite and turn left up to a gate. Turn left and, after a few paces, turn right on to a track. Cross fields on the same line, passing right of a house to a road.

> **WHERE TO EAT AND DRINK**
> There are several possibilities in Painswick – a pub, a tea room, a couple of restaurants and several shops. There is also a pub in Edge, the **Edgemoor Inn**, (a few minutes walk off the route).

⑦ Turn left, cross the **A46** and walk along **Pincot Lane**. At **Primrose Cottage** turn left over a stile and then cross to another. Cross a bridge, a stile and a gate to the left of **Sheephouse**. Walk along the drive and, where it forks, go left down to **King's Mill**. Bear right over the weir and then continue on the same line to arrive at a lane. Turn left to return to the start.

> **WHILE YOU'RE THERE**
> Just outside the village are the **Painswick Rococo Gardens**. Here an 18th-century house is set in gardens that have been restored to how they would have appeared at the time of the house's construction. The detail for this restoration came from a contemporary painting. The garden is particularly well-known for the masses of snowdrops that appear there in the winter.

The Medieval Looters of Brimpsfield

A walk through a vanished castle and secluded valleys, taking in charming Syde and tiny Caudle Green.

•DISTANCE•	4 miles (6.4km)
•MINIMUM TIME•	2hrs
•ASCENT / GRADIENT•	180ft (55m) ▲ ▲ ▲
•LEVEL OF DIFFICULTY•	🚶 🚶🚶 🚶🚶
•PATHS•	Fields, tracks and pavement, 9 stiles
•LANDSCAPE•	Woodland, steep, narrow valleys and villages
•SUGGESTED MAP•	aqua3 OS Explorer 179 Gloucester, Cheltenham & Stroud
•START / FINISH•	Grid reference: SO 938124
•DOG FRIENDLINESS•	Some good, long stretches free of livestock
•PARKING•	Brimpsfield village; lay-bys on Cranham road
•PUBLIC TOILETS•	None on route
•CONTRIBUTOR•	Christopher Knowles

BACKGROUND TO THE WALK

There is something poignant about a vanished castle. The manor of Brimpsfield was given by William the Conqueror to the Giffard family. In early Norman French a 'gifard' was a person with fat cheeks and a double chin. The Giffards built two castles, the first of wood on another site, and its successor of stone, near Brimpsfield church. In 1322 John Giffard fell foul of King Edward II, following a rebellion that was quelled at the Battle of Boroughbridge in Yorkshire – Giffard was hanged at Gloucester.

Plundering Populace
Consequently the family castle was 'slighted', that is to say, put beyond military use. In such circumstances local people were never slow to remove what was left for their own, non-military use. Now almost nothing remains of the castle apart from the empty meadow just before the church and some earthworks to its right. Some of the castle masonry found its way into the fabric of the church. On the stone shed to the left of the church there are details that appear to be medieval and which perhaps originally decorated the castle. The other possibility is that they formed part of a 12th-century priory, long since disappeared, that belonged to the abbey of Fontenay in Burgundy. Brimpsfield church, rather lonely without its castle, distinguishes itself on two counts. Several medieval tombstones, thought to commemorate members of the Giffard family, have been brought inside their protection.

Mysterious Masonry
The other, highly unusual feature, is the huge base of the tower, which separates the nave from the chancel. It is not clear how this came about, but it is surmised that the east wall would originally have contained an arch over which a bell turret was built in the 13th century, requiring the addition of more masonry. When the turret was replaced by a 15th-century tower still more masonry was needed to keep it upright.

Syde overlooks the Frome Valley and perched on the valley slope, the early Norman church has a saddleback tower and a rustic, 15th-century roof. It's worth peering inside to search out the 15th-century octagonal font and the small round window featuring St James, dating from the same period. The box pews are from the 17th century. Don't miss the tithe barn just to the south of the church. Caudle Green is a typical example of a hamlet that has grown up around a single farm and expanded only very slightly over the centuries. It is dominated by an elegant 18th-century farmhouse overlooking the village green.

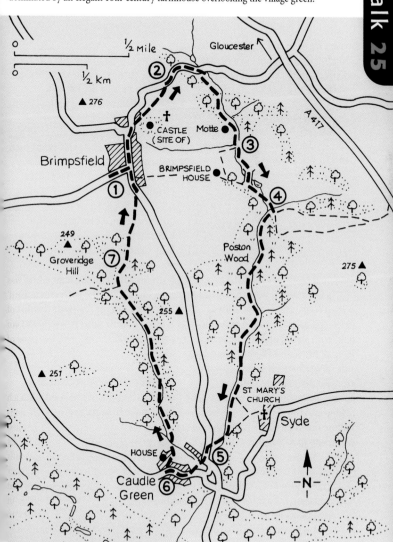

Walk 25 **Directions**

① Go to the end of the road towards the centre and turn left.

Walk through the village and turn right through a gate towards the **church**. Before the church bear left to a stile. In the next field go half right to a corner and a road.

② Turn right and follow the road down to just before a cottage near the bottom. Turn right here on to a drive. After a few paces drop down to the left on to a parallel path which will bring you back on to the drive. Next, just before a cottage, turn left and go down into woodland to follow a path with the stream on your left. Follow this for 550yds (503m), ignoring a bridge on your left, to cross two stiles and emerge on to a track.

WHILE YOU'RE THERE ℹ

In nearby Miserden the Elizabethan mansion, **Misarden Park**, is set in pretty gardens; they are open on certain days throughout the summer months. Sir Edward Lutyens designed the war memorial here. Further west is **Whiteway**, where a group of libertarians from Essex established a proto-anarchist community, based on the ideas of Leo Tolstoy, in 1898.

---

③ Turn left and follow the track as it rises to the right. After 100yds (91m) go forward over a stile into a field with **Brimpsfield House** to your right. Go half right to another stile, pass a gate on your right and cross another stile at the next corner. Follow the path to cross a bridge and bear left up to a track. Follow this for 250yds (229m), until you come to a crossways.

④ Turn right to follow a footpath along the bottom of a valley. After ¾ mile (1.2km) the track will become grassy. Where houses appear above you to the left you can go left up the slope to visit the church at Syde. Otherwise remain on the valley floor and continue

---

WHERE TO EAT AND DRINK ℹ

There is nowhere on the route where refreshment is available, unless you make a diversion to the **Golden Hart** at Nettleton Bottom, (on the road to Cirencester). Otherwise you can seek out the **Carpenter's Arms** in Miserden to the south, or the **Black Horse** in Cranham to the west.

---

until you come to some gates. Take the one furthest to the right and go ahead to pass to the left of a cottage. Follow a drive up to a road.

⑤ Turn left and follow the road as it turns sharp left. At this point turn right over a stile into a field and walk up a steep bank to arrive in **Caudle Green**.

⑥ Turn right. At the green, just before a large house ahead of you, bear right to a stile and follow a winding path down to the valley bottom. Turn left, through a bridle gate, and follow the path along the valley bottom on the same line for ¾ mile (1.2km) until you come to a stile at a field.

⑦ Once you are in the field, continue up the slope until you come to a gate at a road. Turn left to re-enter **Brimpsfield**.

WHAT TO LOOK FOR ℹ

The little stream encountered at certain points during the walk is the infant **River Frome**, which, in its later, stronger stages to the south, runs through the Stroud Valley. The Frome powered the dozens of weaving mills that existed until the latter part of the 19th century. As you ascend the valley slope into Syde look out for the old **sheep dip** just below the village.

Musing on the Past at Northleach

A modest Cotswold village is home to a pair of diverse museums.

•DISTANCE•	4 miles (6.4km)
•MINIMUM TIME•	1hr 45min
•ASCENT / GRADIENT•	165ft (50m) ▲▲ ▲
•LEVEL OF DIFFICULTY•	🚶🚶 🚶 🚶🚶
•PATHS•	Fields, tracks and pavement, muddy after rain, 3 stiles
•LANDSCAPE•	Valley track, wolds and villages
•SUGGESTED MAP•	aqua3 OS Explorer OL45 The Cotswolds
•START / FINISH•	Grid reference: SP 113145
•DOG FRIENDLINESS•	Some clear stretches without livestock, few stiles
•PARKING•	Northleach village square
•PUBLIC TOILETS•	In village square
•CONTRIBUTOR•	Christopher Knowles

BACKGROUND TO THE WALK

For a small country village to have one museum is unusual – to have two, as Northleach does, is remarkable. One, the Cotswold Countryside Collection, is closely associated with its surroundings; the other, Keith Harding's World of Mechanical Music, is one of those eccentricities that has, by happenstance, ended up here in Northleach.

Mechanical Music Museum

The World of Mechanical Music is in the High Street at Oak House, a former wool house, pub and school. There are daily demonstrations of all manner of mechanical musical instruments, as well as musical boxes, clocks and automata. Some of the instruments, early examples of 'canned' music, date back more than 200 years. The presentation is simultaneously erudite and light-hearted. (You may also listen to early, live recordings of concerts given by some of the great composers including Gershwin and Grieg.) This is something more than a museum – both serious historical research and highly accomplished repairs are carried out here.

House of Correction

To the west of the village centre, at a corner of a Fosse Way crossroads, lies the Cotswold Countryside Collection. It is housed in an 18th-century prison, or 'house of correction', built by a prison reformer and wealthy philanthropist, Sir Onesipherous Paul. He was a descendant of a family of successful clothiers from Woodchester, near Stroud, who were also responsible for the construction of, what is now, the Prince of Wales's house at Highgrove. Paul's intentions were surely good, but conditions in the prison were still harsh and the treadmill was still considered effective as the unrelenting instrument of slow punishment. As well as a restored 18th-century cell block, you'll find the museum houses an interesting collection of agricultural implements and machinery, and displays plenty of fascinating photographs showing what rural life in the Cotswolds was once like.

Then and Now

Northleach itself, like Cirencester and Chipping Campden, was one of the key medieval wool trading centres of the Cotswolds and therefore also one of the most important towns in Europe. Though once on a crossroads of the A40 and the Fosse Way, neither now passes through the town, the completion of the A40 bypass in the mid-1980s leaving the town centre a quiet and very attractive place to visit.

The main street is lined with houses, some half-timbered, dating from between the 16th and 19th centuries. Many of these retain their ancient 'burgage' plots at the rear that would originally have served as market gardens. Above the market square is a tiny maze of narrow lanes, overlooked by the Church of St Peter and St Paul, the town's impressive 15th-century Perpendicular 'wool church'. Its features include an array of brasses commemorating the wool merchants on whose wealth the church and town were founded.

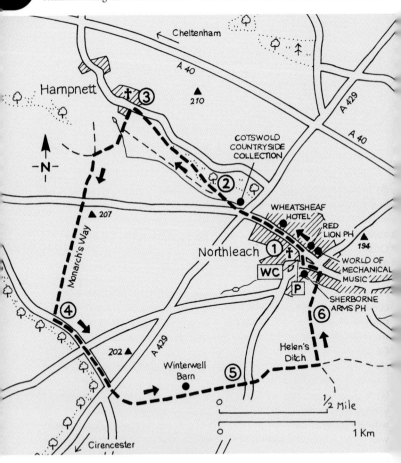

Walk 26 Directions

① From **Northleach square**, with the church behind you, turn left and walk along the main street to

the traffic lights at the **A429**. Cross with care, keep left of the **Cotswold Countryside Collection** and, immediately after passing the museum, turn right through a gate into a field. Go ahead, turn left with

Walk 26

the river to your right and then turn right to cross the river into the next field.

② Turn left and go half right up the field to a stile. Go over this into the next field and, keeping fairly close to the field's right-hand margin, head for another stile on the far side. Pass into the next field and follow a path across it in the general direction of **Hampnett church**. This will bring you to a gate at a road.

> ### WHAT TO LOOK FOR ⓘ
> Leaving Northleach, look out for some interesting old houses. **Walton House**, for example, was formerly the King's Head, an important inn on the old London to Gloucester route. Further on, set back from the road, are the buildings of the old brewery.

③ Turn left and almost immediately come to a track on your left. To visit the church walk ahead and then return to this track. Otherwise, turn left down the track and follow it as it descends to pass farm buildings. Where the track begins to bear right, turn left to climb a track towards a gate. Go through it and continue to follow the track, eventually striking a road. Cross this to walk along another track all the way to another road.

④ At this road turn left and walk until you reach the **A429**. Cross with great care to a gate and then walk along a track until you come

> ### WHERE TO EAT AND DRINK ⓘ
> Although only fairly small Northleach has two pubs, the **Red Lion** and the **Sherborne Arms**, and a hotel, the **Wheatsheaf**. Further along the Fosse Way is the **Fossebridge Inn**, located in a hollow in a rare curve in the Fosse Way, with a large garden beside a stream.

to a farmyard. Walk through the yard and out the other side along a track to another road.

⑤ Cross to a track and follow this for 500yds (457m). Turn left through a gap in a hedge to enter a field and follow the left margin with a stone wall to your left. **Northleach** will soon come into view. Where the field comes to an end, cross a stile and continue ahead, bearing slightly right, to a gate at the bottom of the next field, beside a playground.

⑥ Go through and walk towards some tennis courts. Just before these, turn right to cross a stream. Walk the length of an alley and, at the top, turn left to return to the starting point.

> ### WHILE YOU'RE THERE ⓘ
> As well as the two fine **museums** in Northleach (► Background to the Walk), you are close to the National Trust's 4,000 acre (1,620ha) **Sherborne Park Estate** (► Walk 27). This was bequeathed by Lord Sherborne in 1982 and includes the estate village and richly planted parkland. The highlight is Lodge Park, a 17th-century deer course with an ornate grandstand boasting spectacular views. The grandstand has been extensively restored and can be visited by prior arrangement. Call 01451 844794 for information.

Sherborne and the Sherborne Estate

A walk from a picturesque village through the woods and parkland of an 18th-century estate once owned by wealthy Winchcombe Abbey.

•DISTANCE•	2½ miles (4km)
•MINIMUM TIME•	1hr 15min
•ASCENT / GRADIENT•	188ft (57m) ▲ ▲ ▲
•LEVEL OF DIFFICULTY•	🚶 🚶 🚶
•PATHS•	Fields, track and pavement, 4 stiles
•LANDSCAPE•	Village and landscaped estate
•SUGGESTED MAP•	aqua3 OS Explorer OL45 The Cotswolds
•START / FINISH•	Grid reference: SP 174145
•DOG FRIENDLINESS•	Not many stiles and some clear stretches without livestock
•PARKING•	Village street
•PUBLIC TOILETS•	None on route
•CONTRIBUTOR•	Christopher Knowles

BACKGROUND TO THE WALK

Sherborne was always an estate village, originally belonging to Winchcombe Abbey. Huge flocks of sheep were gathered here for shearing, with much of the wool exported to Flanders and Italy. In the 14th century the tenants of the Abbot of Winchcombe had to work for a fortnight washing and shearing the abbey's sheep.

Abbey Habits

A century later Sherborne, because of the plentiful water supply provided by the river, essential for washing the wool, and because it was the largest of the abbey's manorial possessions, had become the principal shearing station for all the abbey's flocks. In 1485 drovers brought in 2,900 sheep from the surrounding 'holdings', or villages. Quarters were provided for all the shearers whilst the Abbot of Winchcombe rode up to supervise and inspect the weighing of the fleeces in a room set aside for the purpose.

He bought as much of the tenants' wool as he required and then sold it on. The abbot of course wanted to make sure that he made as much money as possible; and indeed in 1341 local tenants were fined by their abbot for attempting to set up a fulling mill in competition with his own.

Sherborne Estate

After the Dissolution, the estate was purchased by the Dutton family, who built themselves a fine house with the help of the eminent local quarryman, Valentine Strong. In the 19th century the house, said to be haunted by the hunchback and gambler known as 'Crump' Dutton, was rebuilt using estate stone but eventually it became a boarding school and has now been converted into luxury flats. Today the estate, and much of the village, belongs to the National Trust. The village of Sherborne has some very pretty cottages, one of which, in the eastern part, has somehow acquired a Norman arch, which originally graced a

12th-century chapel that apparently stood in the grounds of one of the nearby farms. From the road near the church are sweeping rustic views across Sherborne Brook and its water-meadows, where once the medieval flocks of sheep would have grazed.

Lodge Park
South of Sherborne, near the village of Aldsworth, is Lodge Park, originally part of the Sherborne Estate. This was created in 1634 by Crump Dutton and is a unique survival of a deer course, park and grandstand, which has been painstakingly reconstructed using archaeological evidence.

Sherborne was also the birthplace of an eminent scientist. James Bradley, born here in 1693, was appointed the third Astronomer Royal in 1742, and is remembered as the first person to calculate the speed of light in 1729. He also established the time line at Greenwich.

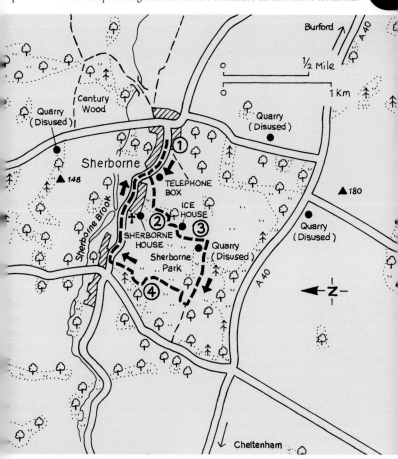

Walk 27 **Directions**

① From the main part of the village, east of the church, walk back towards **Sherborne House**.

Continue to a road on the left beside the war memorial. Enter the **Sherborne Estate** through a doorway beside the telephone box and follow the main path. The house will appear to the right. The path bears sharp left and after 150yds (137m) turns right. After a further 150yds (137m) turn left on to another gently ascending path.

② Stay left of a tree surrounded by a metal seat on a mound and take a path on the far side to head for a gate. Go through the smaller of two gates, pass the old **Ice House** and head for another gate.

WHERE TO EAT AND DRINK ℹ️

There is nowhere to eat or drink on the route itself, although you'll find the small post office and store in Sherborne is a useful place to stock up on snacks. The nearest pub is the **Fox**, just outside Little Barrington, about 2½ miles (4km) away to the east in the Windrush Valley. It has a lovely riverside location, a good range of locally-brewed real ales and an extensive menu.

WHAT TO LOOK FOR ℹ️

Sherborne Park is a typical example of 18th-century estate design, where the intention has been to bring order to unruly nature without undermining its exuberance. The estate is now owned and managed by the National Trust. In the church, look out for the sculpture to the Dutton family by Flemish-born John Michael Rysbrack (1694–1770), a leading sculptor of his day and best known for his monument to Sir Isaac Newton in Westminster Abbey. There is also a memorial in the village church to the locally born Astronomer Royal, James Bradley.

---

④ Stay left and keep to the path as it skirts the woods, bearing right to flatten out at the bottom. Stay on it all the way to a doorway in a wall. Emerge at a road and turn right. Follow the pavement through the village, passing the **church** on the right, and return to your starting point.

③ Follow the main path through the trees. Join another path and, at a gate, go through on to a farm track and turn right. Follow this to a gate at a farmyard. Go through this and turn immediately right to pass through another gateway. Pass a gate on the right and turn right into a field to follow the right hand margin. Follow this as it bears left at the corner and descend to the bottom corner where the path will take you into conifer woodland. Follow this wide path down until you come to a fork.

WHILE YOU'RE THERE ℹ️

The walk can easily and briefly be extended by walking a little way east of Sherborne to a point east of Century Wood, where the old **water-meadows** have been restored to become a haven for wildlife once again.

The Stone Secrets of the Windrush Valley

An insight into the character of Cotswold stone, which makes up the building blocks of the region's beauty.

•DISTANCE•	6 miles (9.7km)
•MINIMUM TIME•	2hrs 30min
•ASCENT / GRADIENT•	120ft (37m)
•LEVEL OF DIFFICULTY•	
•PATHS•	Fields, tracks and pavement, 11 stiles
•LANDSCAPE•	Streams, fields, open country and villages
•SUGGESTED MAP•	aqua3 OS Explorer OL45 The Cotswolds
•START / FINISH•	Grid reference: SP 192130
•DOG FRIENDLINESS•	Some care required but can probably be off lead for long stretches without livestock
•PARKING•	Windrush village
•PUBLIC TOILETS•	None on route
•CONTRIBUTOR•	Christopher Knowles

BACKGROUND TO THE WALK

The Cotswolds, characterised by villages of gilded stone, lie mainly in Gloucestershire. Stone is everywhere here – walk across any field and shards of oolitic limestone lie about the surface like bits of fossilised litter. This limestone, for long an obstacle to arable farming, is a perfect building material. In the past almost every village was served by its own quarry, a few of which are still worked today.

Golden Hue

Limestone is a sedimentary rock, made largely of material derived from living organisms that thrived in the sea that once covered this part of Britain. The rock is therefore easily extracted and easily worked; some of it will actually yield to a handsaw. Of course this is something of a generalisation as, even in a small area, the quality of limestone varies considerably in colour and in texture, suiting certain uses more than others. But it is for its golden hue, due to the presence of iron oxide, that it is most famous.

Slated

The composition of the stone dictates the use to which it will be put. Some limestone, with a high proportion of grit, is best suited to wall building or to hut building. Some outcrops are in very thin layers and are known as 'presents' because they provide almost ready-made material for roof-slates. Sometimes the stone needs a little help and in this case it is left out in the winter so that frost freezes the moisture trapped between layers, forcing them apart. The stone can then be shaped into slates and hung on a wooden roof trellis by means of a simple nail. The smallest slates are placed at the top of the roof, the largest at the bottom. Because of their porous nature, they have to overlap and the roof is built at a steep pitch, so that the rain runs off quickly.

Construction Types

There are four basic types of traditional stone construction to be seen in the Cotswolds – dr[y]
mortared rubble, dressed stone and ashlar. Dry-stone, without any mortar, is used in th[e]
boundary walls you'll see as you walk around the region. Mortared rubble, on the other hand, [relies]
on the use of lime pointing in order to stay upright. You'll see it's use in many of the simpler b[uildings]
or as a cheaper backing to buildings faced with better stone. Dressed stone refers to the
chopping and axing stone to give it a more polished and tighter finish. This is used in high[er]
buildings and houses.

Ashlar is the finest technique, where the best stone is sawn and shaped into perfectly
blocks that act either as a facing on rubble, or which, more rarely, make up the entire wall. As [it is]
used in the finer houses and, occasionally, in barns. The quality of Cotswold stone has lo[ng been]
recognised and the quarries here, west of Burford, provided building material for St Paul's C[athedral]
and several Oxford colleges.

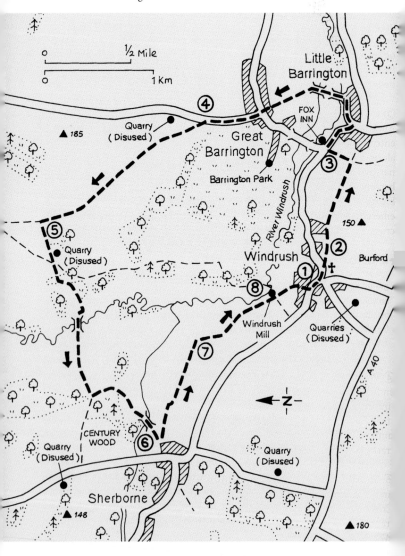

Walk 28 Directions

① Walk out of the village, keeping to the left of the church and, after about 100yds (91m), go right, through a gate into a field. Go across this field to the other side, keeping to the left.

② Go through the right-hand gate and continue across a series of stiles until you emerge in a large field at a wide grass strip (careful here, as it is used for 'galloping' horses) with the houses of **Little Barrington** opposite. Cross two thirds of the field, then turn left and head for the hedge at the bottom.

③ Go through a gap to a road. Ahead is the **Fox Inn**. Turn right, enter Little Barrington and turn left along a 'No Through Road' which narrows to a path. Where the path becomes a lane, go left across a bridge and continue, eventually emerging in **Great Barrington** at a cross. Take the road in front of you.

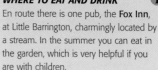

WHAT TO LOOK FOR

Towards Little Barrington you should see **Barrington Park**, in the middle distance on your left. This Palladian house was built by William Kent for Earl Talbot (George II's Lord Chancellor) in the 18th century.

④ Where the wall on your left ends, go left on to a track and immediately right. Stay on this track for a little over 1 mile (1.6km) until you come to a junction of tracks with large hedges before you.

⑤ Turn left and follow this track until you enter scrubby woodland. Cross the river and follow a grassy track until, just before **Century Woods**, you turn left into a field.

Follow the margin of the woods. Cross another bridge into a field and turn half right to the far corner. Go over the bridge, cross a stile and go half left to another stile.

⑥ Take the track before you and then turn left over another stile. Cross this field to go through a gate and walk along the right-hand margin on the same line through several fields.

WHERE TO EAT AND DRINK

En route there is one pub, the **Fox Inn**, at Little Barrington, charmingly located by a stream. In the summer you can eat in the garden, which is very helpful if you are with children.

⑦ Come to a stile at a corner. Go over into the next field and cross it on a right diagonal, in the general direction of a distant village. On the far side go through a gap into another field, with a stone wall on your right. Continue for several fields and pass a **stone barn** to the right, at which point the **River Windrush** will appear to your left. Finally, pass a tin barn to your left-hand side, just as you arrive at a gate by a lane.

⑧ Opposite, go up to a stile. In the next field follow its perimeter as it goes right and brings you to a stile. Cross to a path and follow it into **Windrush** village.

WHILE YOU'RE THERE

To the east is the small but magnificent town of **Burford** in Oxfordshire. Its main street, flanked by a cascade of beautiful houses, leads down to the River Windrush, spanned by a bridge dating from 1322. Wool drove Burford's early prosperity; then, in the 18th century, it was an important stop on the coaching route to Oxford and London.

Walk 29

Wanderings at Wychwood

A gentle walk through rolling Oxfordshire farmland and a corner of an ancient forest.

•DISTANCE•	5¾ miles (9.2km)
•MINIMUM TIME•	2hrs 30min
•ASCENT / GRADIENT•	574ft (175m) ▲▲▲
•LEVEL OF DIFFICULTY•	🚶🚶 🚶🚶 🚶
•PATHS•	Field paths, quiet roads, woodland tracks, no stiles
•LANDSCAPE•	Gently rolling hills of arable farmland, ancient woods
•SUGGESTED MAP•	aqua3 OS Explorer 180 Oxford, Witney & Woodstock
•START / FINISH•	Grid reference: SP 318194
•DOG FRIENDLINESS•	Lead essential for road stretches, otherwise excellent
•PARKING•	On village street near phone box, Chilson
•PUBLIC TOILETS•	None on route
•CONTRIBUTOR•	Ann F Stonehouse

BACKGROUND TO THE WALK

The Wychwood takes its name from a local Saxon tribe, the Hwicce. At the time of the Norman conquest, Wychwood Forest was one of four royal hunting grounds in England, and covered most of western Oxfordshire. The leafy remains of this once magnificent demesne are now mostly confined to the hilltops that lie between Ascott-under-Wychwood, Charlbury, Ramsden and Leafield, and private land ownership means that access for walkers is sometimes frustratingly limited.

A National Nature Reserve
At its heart is a National Nature Reserve, which preserves some 360 species of wild flowers and ferns, including the elusive yellow star of Bethlehem and the bizarre toothwort, a parasitic plant that is found on the roots of some trees. This walk takes you through the edge of the old woodland, on a path that in spring is carpeted with vivid drifts of bluebells that stretch away under the trees as far as the eye can see. The rich variety of wild flowers means a corresponding abundance of butterflies, including peacock, tortoiseshell and orange tip.

The Shrinking Forest
By 1300 the once-flourishing 'forest' had been split into three sections: Woodstock, based around the royal hunting lodge first built there during the reign of Ethelred II; the area around Cornbury Park; and a section around Witney, where the Bishop of Winchester had built his palace. The forest continued to decline and, by 1857, only some 10 square miles (26sq km) were left to be removed from Forest Law by an act of parliament. As the enclosure of land became commonplace in the 1860s, Kingstanding Farm, passed on this walk, was one of seven new farms built at this time to take advantage of the newly available land.

The Ascott Martyrs
The village of Ascott-under-Wychwood is tucked in the valley below the remnants of the Wychwood, along with its near-neighbours Shipton-under-Wychwood and Milton-under

Wychwood. Ascott may not be the prettiest of these Cotswold villages, but it has another claim to fame: the Ascott Martyrs. These 16 young women played their part in the Agricultural Revolution of the 19th century when, in 1873, they attempted to dissuade Ramsden men from taking over the jobs of local men, who had been sacked for membership of the Agricultural Workers' Union. Indeed, the women were accused of encouraging the imported labourers to join the same union. Their punishment – imprisonment with hard labour – caused a riot outside the court in Chipping Norton and the women had to be secretly transferred to Oxford gaol. Their sentences were later remitted by Queen Victoria and some accounts say she sent each woman a red flannel petticoat and five shillings. The union presented them with blue silk for dresses and £5 each. These bold women are remembered with a bench on the village green.

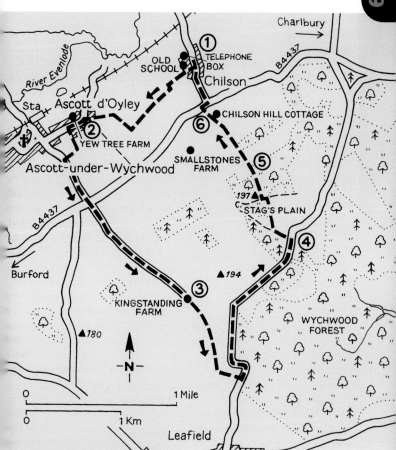

Walk 29 **Directions**

① From the phone box, turn south along the village street, and right up **School Lane**, passing various houses and the **Old School** at the end, on the right. Follow the path straight on into the field ahead, with the hedge to your right. Stay on the path round the edge of the field as it kinks left then right. Keep straight on, descend steadily, and follow as the track bends right.

Walk 29

At the hedge turn right then immediately left through a gateway; take the track diagonally left across the field towards Ascott-under-Wychwood, to meet a lane.

② Turn left along the lane through **Ascott d'Oyley**, passing **Yew Tree Farmhouse** on the right. Beyond d'Oyley House and just before a recreation ground turn left up a track, **Priory Lane**, which becomes a grassy path. This bends sharp right, and emerges at a road by a house. Turn left up the road, and cross the main road at the top with care. Continue straight ahead up the lane, signed 'Leafield'. Follow this straight uphill for a mile (1.6km), to pass through the buildings of **Kingstanding Farm**.

③ Continue down the stony track and keep straight on. It leads along the bottom of a winding, secret valley, with the solid spire of **Leafield church** up to your right. Emerge at a main road; turn left and follow the road as it snakes uphill, with **Wychwood Forest** to your right. After about 1 mile (1.6km) the road descends into woodland. As it ascends again, look for a wooden gate on the left, signed 'Circular Walk Footpath'.

④ Turn left through here and follow the path up the edge of the woods. Keep right and cross the

clearing of **Stag's Plain**. Bend left and right and continue on the path through the woods, carpeted with bluebells in spring.

⑤ Start to descend and emerge from the woods. Continue straight ahead, following the track downhill, with a hedge on your right. Pass **Smallstones Farm**, over to the left. Bend left at the bottom of the field, cross a stile, and take the path that leads to the left, down the hill and past **Chilson Hill Cottage** (right).

⑥ At the bottom of the drive turn right along the main road and immediately left down the road that leads into **Chilson** village. Enter the village and keep straight on past the tiny triangular green, passing the old **Primitive Methodist chapel** on your left. Pass the end of **School Lane** and return to your car.

Walking with Rosie in the Slad Valley

A stroll through the countryside around Slad, backcloth to Laurie Lee's most popular novel.

•DISTANCE•	4 miles (6.4km)
•MINIMUM TIME•	2hrs
•ASCENT / GRADIENT•	425ft (130m) ▲▲▲
•LEVEL OF DIFFICULTY•	🚶 🚶 🚶
•PATHS•	Tracks, fields and quiet lanes, 13 stiles
•LANDSCAPE•	Hills, valleys and woodland
•SUGGESTED MAP•	aqua3 OS Explorer 179 Gloucester, Cheltenham & Stroud
•START / FINISH•	Grid reference: SO 878087
•DOG FRIENDLINESS•	Mostly off leads – livestock encountered occasionally
•PARKING•	Lay-by at Bull's Cross
•PUBLIC TOILETS•	None on route
•CONTRIBUTOR•	Christopher Knowles

BACKGROUND TO THE WALK

The Slad Valley is one of the least spoiled parts of the Cotswolds, notwithstanding its invariable association with the area's most important literary figure, the poet Laurie Lee (1914–97). And yet he is not instantly remembered for his poetry but for *Cider With Rosie* (1959). This autobiographical account of a Cotswold childhood has, for thousands of students, been part of their English Literature syllabus.

A Childhood Gone Forever

For anyone coming to the area, *Cider With Rosie* is well worth reading, but it is especially pertinent here as it is largely set in Slad, where Lee was brought up and lived for much of his life. The book charts, in poetic language, the experiences of a child living in a world that is within living memory and yet has quite disappeared. Some of the episodes recounted in the book are said to have been products of Lee's imagination but, as he said himself, it was the 'feeling' of his childhood that he was endeavouring to capture.

A Spanish Odyssey

The story of his life is, anyway, an interesting one. He spent a considerable time in Spain and became involved in the Spanish Civil War and the struggle against Franco. Afterwards he established a reputation as a poet, mixing with the literati of the day. He was never very prolific – much of his energy appears to have been poured into love affairs. He did, however, write plays for radio and was involved in film-making during the Second World War. But it was with the publication of *Cider With Rosie* that he became a household name. Readers from all over the world identified with his magical evocation of rural English life and the book has not been out of print since. To some extent Lee became a prisoner of a *Cider with Rosie* industry. The picture of an avuncular figure living a bucolic idyll was not a strictly accurate one – much of his time was spent in London. He was susceptible to illness all his life. Nonetheless, in his later years he managed to complete his autobiographical trilogy. His second volume, *As I Walked Out One Midsummer Morning* (1969) describes his journey from Gloucestershire to Spain as an itinerant fiddle player. The third, *A Moment of War* (1991), recounts his experiences there during the Civil War. Lee died in 1997 and is buried in Slad churchyard. Many of the places in and around the village mentioned in *Cider With Rosie* are readily identifiable today. Although it is no longer possible to frolic in the roads with impunity, the valley remains as beautiful as it ever was.

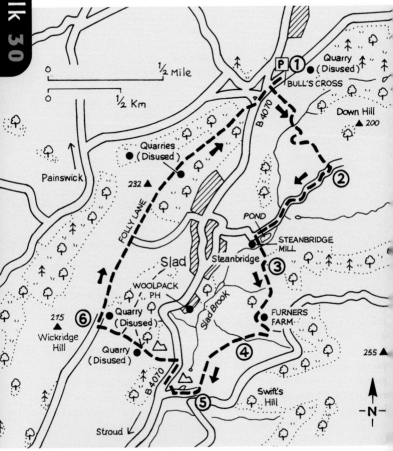

Walk 30 Directions

① From **Bull's Cross** walk to the end of the lay-by (going south) and turn left on to a tarmac-covered drive. Follow it down and, immediately before some buildings, turn left over a stile into a field. Go half right, down the field and up the other side, to a gate at the top.

Turn left along a track. Where it joins another track stay right and continue to a lane.

② Turn right and walk to the bottom. Pass between a large pond and **Steanbridge Mill**. If you want to visit Slad, follow the lane into the village. To continue the walk turn left immediately after the pond and walk to a stile. Cross into a field,

Walk 30

with a hedge on your right, and continue to a stile at the top.

③ Cross and follow a path to another stile. Cross the next field and another stile, then continue as the path curves right towards a farm. Pass through a gate on to a track, stay to the right of **Furners Farm** and curve left. About 30yds (27m) after the curve turn right over a stile on to a wooded path and then, after a few paces, go right again over a stile into a field. Walk ahead, with the farm above you to the right. Cross another stile and then keep to the right of a pond.

WHAT TO LOOK FOR ⓘ
There are a number of landmarks on or near the walk that are readily associated with *Cider With Rosie*, including **Steanbridge Mill**. From Folly Lane, a short distance south of where you join it, there are often excellent **views** across to the River Severn and its bridges.

right along the pavement. After 150yds (137m) cross to a public footpath and climb steeply. At a junction of footpaths bear left and continue to a field. Follow the margin of the field up, then follow the path as it weaves in and out of **woodland**.

⑥ At the top turn right on to **Folly Lane** and continue to a junction. If you want to go into Slad, turn right, otherwise continue ahead on to a path that will soon take you into woodland. Walk through the woods, finally emerging at your starting point at **Bull's Cross**.

WHILE YOU'RE THERE ⓘ
In its heyday **Stroud** was the centre of the 19th-century wool weaving industry. The small town centre offers a pleasant stroll featuring the Shambles, the Town Hall and the Subscription Rooms. There are a couple of museums to enjoy, including the Stroud Museum and the Industrial Museum.

④ At the top of the pond cross a stile into a field. Go half left across it to a gate and stile. In the next field head straight across its lower part. At a point where a telegraph pole almost meets a hedge, turn right over a stile on to a track. Turn left to meet a lane.

⑤ Turn right and follow the lane to the valley bottom. Start to climb the other side and at a corner go over a stile on your right. Ascend steeply to another stile at the road. Turn

WHERE TO EAT AND DRINK ⓘ
The **Woolpack** in Slad features in *Cider With Rosie*. Laurie Lee was a regular there in his later years. It has since become well-known for its food. In the neighbouring village of Sheepscombe is the **Butcher's Arms**.

Uley and its Magnificent Fort on the Hill

The vast bulk of the ancient fort of Uley Bury forms the centrepiece for this walk along the Cotswold escarpment.

•DISTANCE•	3 miles (4.8km)
•MINIMUM TIME•	1hr 30min
•ASCENT / GRADIENT•	345ft (105m) ▲▲▲
•LEVEL OF DIFFICULTY•	🚶 🚶 🚶
•PATHS•	Tracks and fields
•LANDSCAPE•	Valley, meadows, woodland and open hilltop
•SUGGESTED MAP•	aqua3 OS Explorer 168 Stroud, Tetbury and Malmesbury
•START / FINISH•	Grid reference: ST 789984
•DOG FRIENDLINESS•	Good – little or no livestock, few stiles
•PARKING•	Main street of Uley
•PUBLIC TOILETS•	None on route
•CONTRIBUTOR•	Christopher Knowles

BACKGROUND TO THE WALK

Uley is a pretty village, strung along a wide street at the foot of a high, steep hill. It is distinctive for several reasons. It has its own brewery, which produces some fine beers including Uley Bitter and Uley Old Spot. In the past the village specialised in the production of 'Uley Blue' cloth, which was used in military uniforms. And then there is Uley Bury, dating back to the Iron Age and one of the finest hill forts in the Cotswolds.

Peaceful Settlements

There are many hundreds of Iron-Age forts throughout England and Wales. They are concentrated in Cornwall, south west Wales and the Welsh Marches, with secondary concentrations throughout the Cotswolds, North Wales and Wessex. Although the term 'hill fort' is generally used in connection with these settlements, the term can be misleading. There are many that were built on level ground and there are many that were not used purely for military purposes – often they were simply settlements located on easily-defended sites. Broadly speaking, there are five types, classified according to the nature of the site on which they were built, rather than, say, the date of their construction. Contour forts were built more or less along the perimeter edge of a hilltop; promontory forts were built on a spur surrounded by natural defences on two or more sides; valley and plateau forts (two types) depended heavily on artificial defences and were located, as their names suggest, in valleys or on flat land respectively; and multiple-enclosure forts were usually built in a poor strategic position on the slope of a hill and were perhaps used as stockades.

Natural Defences

Uley Bury, covering about 38 acres (15.4ha), is classified as an inland promontory fort and was built in the 6th century BC. It falls away on three sides, the fourth side, which faces away from the escarpment, is protected by specially constructed ramparts which would have been surmounted by a wooden palisade. The natural defences – that is, the Cotswold escarpment, facing west – were also strengthened by the construction of a wide and deep ditch, as well as two additional ramparts, an inner one and an outer one, between which the footpath largely threads its course. The three main entrances were at the northern, eastern and southern corners. These, being the most vulnerable parts of the fort, would have been fortified with massive log barriers.

Although some tribespeople would have lived permanently in huts within the fort, most would have lived outside, either on other parts of the hill or in the valleys below. In an emergency, therefore, there was space for those who lived outside the fort to take shelter within. Eventually the fort was taken over by the Dobunni tribe – Celtic interlopers from mainland Europe who arrived about 100 BC – and appears to have been occupied by them throughout the Roman era.

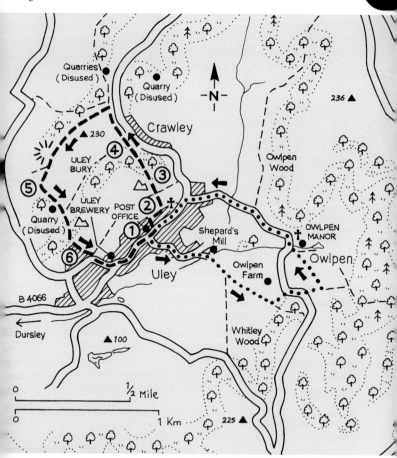

Walk 31 **Directions**

① From the main street locate the **post office** (on your left as you walk up the street). Walk along the

narrow lane (to the right, as you look at it). Pass between houses as the lane dwindles to a track. Immediately before a stile turn right along an enclosed path towards the **church**.

Walk 31

② When the churchyard can be seen on the right, turn left up a narrow path beside a cottage. This rises fairly sharply and brings you to a kissing gate. Pass through into a meadow. Climb steeply up the grassland towards woodland.

③ At the treeline keep left of the woods. In a corner go through a gate and follow a winding woodland path, climbing among the trees. When you come to a fence stay on the path as it bears left. Go over a stile and then continue ascending, to emerge from the woods. Stay on the path as it rises across grassland to a junction.

> **WHAT TO LOOK FOR** ℹ
> There are **magnificent views** westward from the summit of Uley Bury. You should easily be able to see the estuary of the River Severn, as well as the Tyndale Monument. Look out too for the **brewery** in Uley and the statue of a pig outside it. This is a Gloucester Old Spot, a breed of pig peculiar to the county, now making something of a comeback.

④ Turn right to follow the contour of the hill – the edge of the ancient fort. You are following the perimeter of the fort in an anti-clockwise direction, with steep drops to your right. When you meet another junction of paths go left along the edge of the hill, with views to the west.

⑤ At the next corner continue to follow the edge of the fort, disregarding a stile that invites you to descend. At the next corner, at the fort's south eastern point, bear right on a path that descends through hillocks and then quite steeply through bushes, keeping left. This will bring you to a stile into a meadow and a tarmac path.

> **WHERE TO EAT AND DRINK** ℹ
> The **Old Crown** on the main street opposite the church in Uley is a very picturesque village local, with lots of memorabilia on the walls, exposed beams and a small, sunny garden. Beers come from the local brewery and include Uley Bitter and Uley Old Spot, named after the Gloucestershire pigs.

⑥ Walk along the path, all the way to a cottage and then a kissing gate. Go through this and pass beside the cottage to arrive at a lane. Turn left here and follow the lane, soon passing the **Uley Brewery**, to reach the main road. Turn left, passing **South Street**, to return to the start.

Extending the Walk
While you're in Uley you can make an interesting additional circuit by walking up **South Street** from the main street. Cross fields to the right of **Owlpen Farm** then pick out a route into **Owlpen** village with its ancient **manor house**. You can return to Uley on the road.

> **WHILE YOU'RE THERE** ℹ
> Two sites are worth a closer look while you're in the area. Near by is the little village of North Nibley, over which towers the 111ft (34m) **Tyndale Monument**. Built in 1866 this is a tribute to William Tyndale (c1494–1536). He was born at Dursley near Gloucester, and was the first to translate the New Testament of the Bible from Latin into English. It is possible to climb to near the top of the tower for magnificent views. Just to the north of Uley Bury, and still on the escarpment, is Uley Long Barrow, better known as **Hetty Pegler's Tump**. This is a neolithic chambered tomb some 180ft (55m) in length. A narrow stone doorway leads into a passage, off which four semicircular chambers would have contained cremated remains.

Weaving Along the Stroud Valley

Discover the impact of the Industrial Revolution in the Cotswold valleys.

•DISTANCE•	6 miles (9.7km)
•MINIMUM TIME•	3hrs
•ASCENT / GRADIENT•	495ft (150m) ▲▲▲
•LEVEL OF DIFFICULTY•	👥 👥 👥
•PATHS•	Fields, lanes, canal path and tracks, 3 stiles
•LANDSCAPE•	Canal, road and railway, valley and steep slopes, villages
•SUGGESTED MAP•	aqua3 OS Explorer 168 Stroud, Tetbury and Malmesbury
•START / FINISH•	Grid reference: SO 892025
•DOG FRIENDLINESS•	Good, with few stiles and little livestock
•PARKING•	Lay-by east of Chalford church
•PUBLIC TOILETS•	None on route
•CONTRIBUTOR•	Christopher Knowles

BACKGROUND TO THE WALK

Wool has been associated with the Cotswolds for many centuries. During the Middle Ages the fleece of the 'Cotswold Lion' breed was the most prized in all of Europe. Merchants from many countries despatched their agents to purchase it from the fairs and markets of the wold towns in the northern part of the region – most famously Northleach, Cirencester and Chipping Campden. Woven cloth eventually became a more important export and so the industry moved to the southern Cotswolds, with its steeper valleys and faster-flowing streams, which were well suited to powering woollen mills.

Mechanisation

The concentration of mills in the Stroud area was evident by the early 15th century. Indeed, its importance was such that in a 1557 Act of Parliament that restricted cloth manufacture to towns, the villages of the Stroud area were exempted. By 1700 the lower Stroud Valley was producing 30,000 bolts (about 4.59 million sq m) of cloth every year. At this time the spinning and weaving was done in domestic dwellings or workhouses, the woven cloth then being returned to the mill for fulling, roughening and shearing. The mills were driven by the natural flow of the streams but the Industrial Revolution was to bring rapid change. There was great opposition to the introduction of mechanical spinning and shearing machines. This was heightened in 1795 by the development of the improved broadloom with its flying shuttle. The expectation was that, as well as compelling weavers to work in the mills rather that at home, it would bring mass unemployment. Progress marched on, however, and by the mid-19th century there were over 1,000 looms at work in the Stroud Valley. They came with their share of political unrest too, and in 1825 and 1828 strikes and riots had to be quelled by troops. The industry went into decline through the course of the 19th century, as steam replaced water power and it migrated northwards to the Pennines. By 1901 only 3,000 people were employed in the cloth industry, compared with 24,000 in the mid-17th century. Today, only one mill remains.

Graceful Elevations

This walk begins in Chalford, an attractive village built on the steep sides of the Stroud Valley. Its streets are lined with terraces of 18th- and 19th-century clothiers' houses and weavers' cottages. On the canalside the shells of woollen mills are still plentiful.

The 18th-century church contains fine examples of craftsmanship from the Arts and Crafts period of the late 19th century. Nether Lypiatt Manor is a handsome manor house now owned by Prince and Princess Michael of Kent. Known locally as 'the haunted house', it was built in 1702 for Judge Charles Cox. Its classical features and estate railings, all unusual in the Cotswolds, inspired wealthy clothiers to spend their money on the addition of graceful elevations to their own houses.

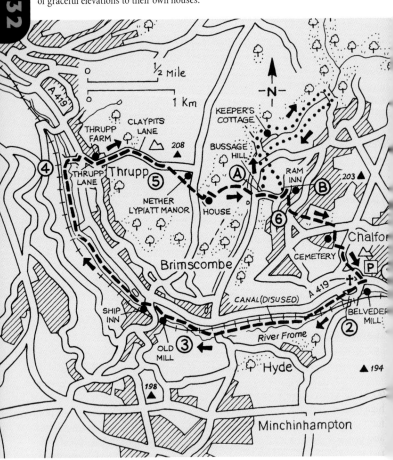

Walk 32 **Directions**

① Walk towards **Chalford church**. Immediately before it, cross the road and locate a path going right, towards a canal roundhouse. Note the **Belvedere Mill** across to your left and follow the tow path alongside the **Thames and Severn Canal** on your right.

② Cross a road and continue along the tow path as it descends steps. Now follow this path for about 2 miles (3.2km). It will soon

Walk 32

disappear under the railway line via a gloomy culvert, so that the **railway** will now be on your right, beyond the old canal. Old mills and small factories line the route.

③ Shortly before arriving in **Brimscombe** the path passes beneath the railway again. Soon after, it becomes a road leading into an industrial estate. At a road opposite a large, old mill turn left, to come to a junction. Cross and turn right. Immediately after the **Ship Inn** turn left along a road among offices and workshops. Continue straight on along a path, with factory walls to your right. The canal reappears on your left. As you walk on into the country you will pass beneath three brick bridges and a metal footbridge.

> **WHILE YOU'RE THERE** ℹ
> High up on the far side of the Stroud Valley, there are a number of places to go. **Woodchester** has a well-preserved, Roman mosaic and an unfinished, 19th-century Gothic mansion. **Rodborough Common** is the site of an 18th- and 19th-century fort that was originally built as a luxurious palace by a wealthy wool dyer. At **Selsley** is a little church filled with stained glass designed by members of the Arts and Crafts Movement.

④ At the next bridge, with a hamlet high on your left, turn right to follow a path to a road. Cross this and turn left. After a few paces turn right up a short path to meet **Thrupp Lane**. Turn right. At the top, turn left into **Claypits Lane**, turn right just before **Thrupp Farm** and climb up steeply.

⑤ After a long climb, as the road levels out, you will see **Nether Lypiatt Manor** in front of you. Turn right, beside a tree, over a stile

> **WHAT TO LOOK FOR** ℹ
> As you walk along the Stroudwater Canal look out for the **birds** that like to creep among the reeds: moorhens and coots, of course, but occasionally a heron will suddenly launch itself up from out of the undergrowth. Voles and stoats can be seen, and even the occasional adder.

into a field. Go half left to the far corner. Cross a stone stile and follow a narrow path beside trees to a road. Descend a lane opposite. Where it appears to fork, go straight on, to descend past a house. Enter **woodland** and fork right near the bottom. Keep a pond on your left and cross a road to climb **Bussage Hill**. After 100yds (91m) pass a lane on the left. At the top fork left. Opposite the **Ram Inn** turn right.

⑥ After a telephone box and bus shelter turn left to follow a path among houses into woodland. Go ahead until you meet a road. Turn left and immediately right down a path beside a **cemetery**. Descend to another road. Turn right for 50yds (46m), then turn left down a steep lane among trees, leading back to **Chalford**. At the bottom turn left to return to the start of the walk.

> **WHERE TO EAT AND DRINK** ℹ
> There are two easy possibilities en route: the **Ship Inn** at Brimscombe and the **Ram Inn** at Bussage. Only a short distance from Brimscombe is Stroud, which has several restaurants and cafés.

Extending the Walk

Between points ⑤ and ⑥ you descend into the **Toadsmoor Valley**, one of the less accessible Cotswold valleys. You can make an interesting detour up the valley, which has fine woodland and a pond, from Point Ⓐ, returning to the main route at Point Ⓑ near the **Ram Inn**.

Spring Fashions – Dressing the Wells of Bisley

From beautiful Bisley, this ramble follows undulating field paths taking in small villages and hamlets along the way.

•DISTANCE•	5½ miles (8.8km)
•MINIMUM TIME•	3hrs
•ASCENT / GRADIENT•	150ft (46m) ▲▲▲
•LEVEL OF DIFFICULTY•	🚶 🚶 🚶
•PATHS•	Tracks, fields, lanes, 9 stiles
•LANDSCAPE•	Secluded valleys, villages, open wold
•SUGGESTED MAP•	aqua3 OS Explorer 168 Stroud, Tetbury & Malmesbury
•START / FINISH•	Grid reference: SO 903060
•DOG FRIENDLINESS•	Quite good – little livestock.
•PARKING•	In Bisley village near Bear Inn
•PUBLIC TOILETS•	None on route
•CONTRIBUTOR•	Christopher Knowles

BACKGROUND TO THE WALK

There are many beautiful villages in the Cotswolds and this walk takes you to one of the loveliest. Bisley is well known in the area for its well-dressing ceremony which takes place on Ascension Day – a Thursday 40 days after Easter. This tradition, usually associated with the Peak District where wells have been dressed for centuries, was originally a pagan ceremony. But in the 14th century it became a thanksgiving for wells that remained uncontaminated during the Black Death. In Bisley the tradition dates from the restoration of the wells in Wells Street in 1863 by the Revd Thomas Keble – the vicar of Bisley at the time and the younger brother of John Keble (1792–1866) the poet, theologian and founder of Keble College in Oxford.

Keeping Traditions Alive

The problem of keeping such traditions alive are twofold – fostering local enthusiasm and in this case, obtaining the necessary funds for the children's refreshments and for paying the brass band. Moss and flowers are collected to cover the frames and hoops carried by 22 children from the local Bluecoat school in the procession to the wells. In the past all of this was done in secret, in the spirit of competition, whilst these days most of the decorative work is done in school. Another problem is finding enough flowers at this time of year and keeping them fresh enough to use in the ceremony.

On Ascension Day itself, a service is held in the parish church, then the children's procession forms; the oldest children have the privilege of carrying the largest floral stars at the front. The procession, preceded by the band and the vicar, marches through the village down to the wells where the vicar performs a short blessing. The flowers are arranged by the children to spell 'Ascension' and 'AD' and the current year, whilst garlands, floral hoops, and Stars of David are laid about the wells. A hymn is sung and the children sit down to a tea. Finally, in the late afternoon, there are village sports, such as egg and spoon and sack races.

Remarkable Village

Bisley is remarkable in a number of ways. In the churchyard is a 13th-century Poor Soul's Light, the only outdoor example in the country. It was used to light Mass candles on behalf of those who were too poor to buy their own. And then there is the Bisley Boy. Legend says that the real Queen Elizabeth I is buried in Bisley churchyard. During a visit here as a girl, apparently, she fell ill and died. A local boy who closely resembled her took her place and went on to become Queen…

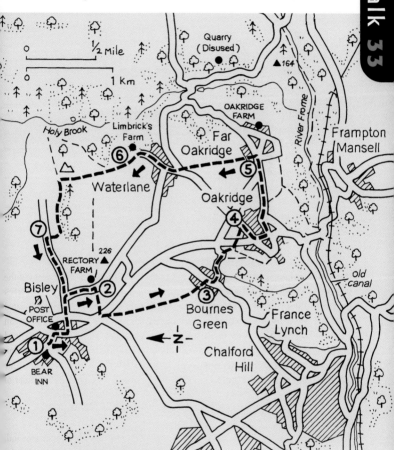

Walk 33 **Directions**

① From your parking spot in Bisley village walk down to the main street, opposite the **post office**. Turn right and take the first turn left up a street to a junction. Walk across to the road opposite, and then follow this it as it goes sharply to the right.

② After 400yds (370m), opposite **Rectory Farm**, turn right through a gate and walk through fields to a road. Cross to a stile and then a paddock to another stile. Go half right across two fields and then half right to a gap and then another. Turn left to a stile in the corner and head for a stile at the edge of trees. Go down a path to a small field. Go half right to cross a track and a

Walk 33

stile. Cross to a path alongside houses and descend left into **Bournes Green**.

③ Turn right to reach a junction and turn left. At the next junction descend a grassy bank and turn left. Follow the road down and then up again and, at a corner, turn right over a stile and go half left up a bank of trees to another stile. Continue across fields to a road. Cross this and enter another field. Walk across the field to a road.

④ Turn right. Take the next lane on the left and then turn left again when you get to the old **water pump**. Follow this lane as it bears right, up and out of the village.

⑤ After about ¾ mile (1.2km), at a crossroads at **Far Oakridge**, turn left on to a track. At the end

WHERE TO EAT AND DRINK ℹ
In Oakridge the **Butcher's Arms** is on the walk whilst there are two pubs in Bisley, both of which are good, comfortable locals. The **Bear Inn** on George Street has its origins as a building in the 16th century and has been a pub since 1766. It serves traditional British food and dogs and children are welcome. The **Stirrup Cup** also serves food along with Hook Norton and Wadworth's ales.

continue down to a junction at **Waterlane**. Take the leftmost of two lanes before you and, at a junction at a farm, turn left following this track to a gate at a spinney.

⑥ Proceed into and across a field to a stile at woodland. Follow a steep footpath down to a stile. Descend a field, turning left before you reach the bottom. Walk through fields, crossing stiles, and then bear right up to a track.

WHAT TO LOOK FOR ℹ
In Bisley look for the impressive building which houses the famous **well**. The structure, restored by Thomas Keble, is a semi-circular stone building and the water pours out of five gothic-arched recesses into a shallow stone trough. Water also emanates from channels at either side, into deeper troughs before flowing away underground.

⑦ Turn left and walk all the way to a junction. Turn right along a track and enter a field. Go half left to the other side and then left along a footpath to a road. Cross the road (watch out for traffic here as it can be busy) and descend some steps to central **Bisley**.

Sapperton, Daneway and the Thames & Severn Canal

Sapperton, both the focus of a major engineering project and a cradle for cultural change.

•DISTANCE•	6 miles (9.7km)
•MINIMUM TIME•	3hrs
•ASCENT / GRADIENT•	345ft (105m) ▲▲▲
•LEVEL OF DIFFICULTY•	🚶🚶 🚶🚶 🚶🚶
•PATHS•	Woodland paths and tracks, fields, lanes and canalside paths, 12 stiles
•LANDSCAPE•	Secluded valleys and villages
•SUGGESTED MAP•	aqua3 OS Explorer 168 Stroud, Tetbury and Malmesbury
•START / FINISH•	Grid reference: SO 948033
•DOG FRIENDLINESS•	Good – very few livestock
•PARKING•	In Sapperton village near church
•PUBLIC TOILETS•	None on route
•CONTRIBUTOR•	Christopher Knowles

BACKGROUND TO THE WALK

Sapperton was at the centre of two conflicting tendencies during the late 18th and early 20th centuries – the Industrial Revolution and the Romantic Revival. In the first case, it was canal technology that came to Sapperton. Canal construction was widespread throughout England from the mid-18th century onwards. Just as 'dot com' companies attracted vast sums of money in the late 1990s, so investors poured their money into 18th-century joint stock companies, regardless of their profitability. Confidence was high and investors expected to reap the rewards of commercial success based on the need to ship goods swiftly across the country.

Tunnel Vision

One key project was thought to be the canal that would link the River Severn and the River Thames. The main obstacle was the need for a tunnel through the Cotswolds, the cost of which could be unpredictable. But these were heady days and investors' money was forthcoming to press ahead with the scheme in 1783. During the tunnel's construction, the diarist and traveller John Byng visited the workings. With obvious distaste he wrote, 'I was enveloped in thick smoke arising from the gunpowder of the miners, at whom, after passing by many labourers who work by small candles, I did at last arrive; they come from the Derbyshire and Cornish mines, are in eternal danger and frequently perish by falls of earth.'

Legwork

The Thames and Severn Canal opened in 1789, linking the Thames at Lechlade with the Stroudwater Navigation at Stroud. The Sapperton Tunnel, at 3,400yds (3,109m) long, is still one of the longest transport tunnels in the country. Barges were propelled through the tunnel by means of 'leggers', who 'walked' against the tunnel walls and who patronised the inns that are at both tunnel entrances. Yet the canal was not a success: either there was too much or too little water; rock falls and leakages required constant attention. The cost of maintaining the tunnel led to the closure of the canal in 1911.

The Arts and Crafts Movement

It isn't just the great canal tunnel that is of interest in Sapperton. Some of the cottages here were built by disciples of William Morris (1834–96). He was the doyen of the Arts and Crafts Movement in design. It aspired to reintroduce to English life a simple yet decorative functionality, in part as a reaction to the growing mass-production methods engendered by the Industrial Revolution. Furniture makers and architects like Ernest Gimson (from Leicestershire), Sidney and Ernest Barnsley (from Birmingham), and Norman Jewson, all worked in Daneway, at Daneway House. Gimson and the Barnsley brothers are buried at Sapperton church.

You'll find the finest example of the Arts and Crafts vernacular-style architecture in Sapperton is Upper Dorval House. The entrance to the western end of the Sapperton Tunnel is in fact in the hamlet of Daneway, a short walk along the path from the Daneway Inn, which was formerly called the Bricklayer's Arms. Daneway House, the 14th-century house that was let to followers of William Morris by Earl Bathurst, is a short distance up the road from the pub.

Walk 34 Directions

① With the church to your left, walk along a 'No Through Road'. This descends rapidly and, at the entrance to a house at the bottom, turn left on to a footpath.

② Continue uphill into **woodland**. Take the main path, ignoring a footpath on the left, but where it then forks, go left uphill. Climb to a junction of tracks. Turn left and stay on the track for ½ mile (800m) to a gate at a lane.

③ Turn left and then immediately right over a stile (opposite **Daneway House**). Take the first left and walk along a wide grassy area, with a fence to the right, to a stile at a lane. Turn right for 250yds (229m) then turn left over a stile.

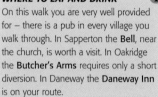

WHILE YOU'RE THERE
Cirencester is not far away. As well as the **Corinium Museum** and the largest **parish church** in England, you can explore **Cirencester Park**. This fine estate was partly designed by the poet Alexander Pope for Lord Bathurst and can be entered from Sapperton.

④ Walk down a drive. Just before the house go left through a hedge and turn immediately right, following a path to a stile. Cross this, then a bridge and a field, and a stile into woodland. Follow a path to a gate at a field, which you cross half right. Pass through a gate and head left of **Oakridge Farm** to another gate on to a lane.

⑤ Turn left and pass a junction. At a sharp right corner go ahead into a field. Walk to a stile on the far side. Cross the next field and find a stile in the top right corner. Follow the left margin of the next field to a road. Turn left along the road through **Oakridge**.

⑥ At a crossroads turn right, climbing to a road. Turn left. At the **green** go to the end and bear right to a stile. Enter a field, keep close to a hedgerow on the left-hand side and cross two further stiles. Bear right across a field to a stile into woodland. Descend steeply and turn left on to a footpath, which you follow to a junction. Turn left down to a road.

WHERE TO EAT AND DRINK
On this walk you are very well provided for – there is a pub in every village you walk through. In Sapperton the **Bell**, near the church, is worth a visit. In Oakridge the **Butcher's Arms** requires only a short diversion. In Daneway the **Daneway Inn** is on your route.

⑦ Turn left then, at a junction, turn right to cross a bridge. Bear left and, a few paces after, turn left again over a footbridge then right on to a footpath. Follow the canal for 600yds (549m). Cross a bridge and turn left on a path to a road by the **Daneway Inn**. Turn right and then left to continue by the canal to the **Sapperton Tunnel**. Walk above the tunnel's portico to a field. Bear half right up to a stile. Cross to a path and walk up to a lane which leads back into **Sapperton**.

WHAT TO LOOK FOR
Emerging on the road after Oakridge Farm you are at the edge of the hamlet of **Far Oakridge**. Painter William Rothenstein lived at Iles Farm between 1913 and 1920, hosting the poets W H Davies and Rabindranath Tagore. Writer and caricaturist Max Beerbohm resided at nearby Winstons Cottage, as did, later, the poet John Drinkwater.

Woven Charm of Bibury

The outer charm of a weavers' village conceals miserable workings conditions.

Walk 35

•DISTANCE•	6¼ miles (10.1km)
•MINIMUM TIME•	2hrs 30min
•ASCENT / GRADIENT•	165ft (50m) ▲ ▲ ▲
•LEVEL OF DIFFICULTY•	🚶🚶 🚶🚶 🚶🚶
•PATHS•	Fields, tracks and lane, may be muddy in places, 6 stiles
•LANDSCAPE•	Exposed wolds, valley, villages and streams
•SUGGESTED MAP•	aqua3 OS Explorer OL45 The Cotswolds
•START / FINISH•	Grid reference: SP 113068
•DOG FRIENDLINESS•	On leads throughout – a lot of sheep and horses
•PARKING•	Bibury village
•PUBLIC TOILETS•	Opposite river on main street, close to Arlington Row
•CONTRIBUTOR•	Christopher Knowles

BACKGROUND TO THE WALK

Arlington Row is the picturesque terrace of cottages that led William Morris to refer to Bibury as the most beautiful village in England. It was originally built, it is thought, in the late 14th century, to house sheep belonging to Osney Abbey in Oxford. The wool was washed in the river and then hung out to dry on Rack Isle, the marshy area in front of the cottages. Following the dissolution of the monasteries the land was sold off and the sheep houses converted to weavers' cottages. Before mechanisation transformed the wool weaving industry, most weaving took place in the houses of the poor. Firstly, women and children spun the wool either at home or at the workhouse. Then it was transferred to the houses of the weavers, who worked on handlooms at home at piece rates.

A typical weaver's cottage might have had four rooms, with a kitchen and workshop downstairs and a bedroom and storeroom upstairs. There were very few items of furniture in the living rooms, whilst the workroom would have contained little more than a broadloom and the appropriate tools. The woven cloth was then returned to the clothier's mill for fulling and cutting. Work on cloth was often a condition of tenure imposed by landlords. The merchant landlord fixed a piecework rate and, provided that the work was satisfactory, the cottage could stay in the weaver's family from generation to generation. Weaving went on this way for some 200 years, until the introduction of steam power in the 18th century. Consequently it tended to take place in the mills of the Stroud Valley. Despite their unfavourable working conditions, the cottage weavers greatly resisted this change but to no avail – the cottage weaving industry went into inexorable decline.

Strictly speaking, much of what is considered picturesque in Bibury is in the neighbouring village of Arlington, but they are now indistinguishable. Apart from Arlington Row, there is plenty to enjoy in the village, especially the church, which has Saxon origins and is set in pretty gardens. Across the bridge is the old mill, open to the public. Nearby Ablington has an enchanting group of cottages, threaded by the River Coln. A minor classic, *A Cotswold Village* (1898), which describes local life in the late 19th century, was written by J Arthur Gibbs, the squire who lived at Ablington Manor. You pass the walls of the manor on the walk. Close by, further into the village, are a couple of beautiful 18th-century barns.

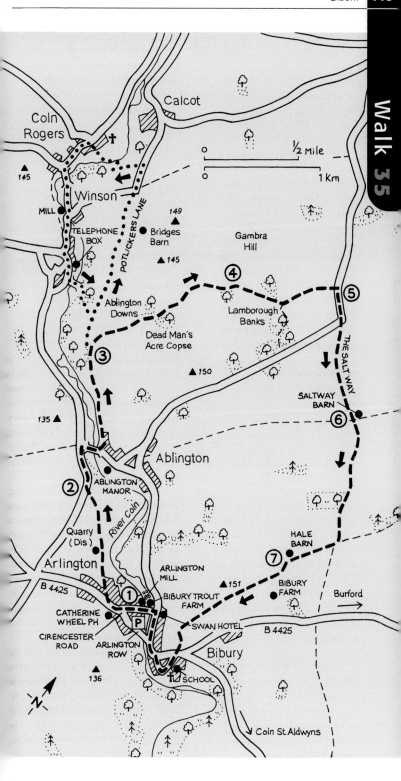

Calcot

Coln Rogers

✝

▲ 145

Winson

MILL

TELEPHONE BOX

POTLICKERS LANE

▲ 149

Bridges Barn

▲ 145

Gambra Hill

Ablington Downs

④

⑤

Dead Man's Acre Copse

Lamborough Banks

③

▲ 150

THE SALT WAY

▲ 135

SALTWAY BARN

⑥

Ablington

②

ABLINGTON MANOR

River Coln

Quarry (Dis)

HALE BARN

Arlington

⑦

BIBURY FARM

B 4425

ARLINGTON MILL

①

BIBURY TROUT FARM

▲ 151

Burford →

CATHERINE WHEEL PH

P

SWAN HOTEL

B 4425

CIRENCESTER ROAD

ARLINGTON ROW

Bibury

▲ 136

✝ SCHOOL

N

↓ Coln St. Aldwyns

½ Mile

1 km

Walk 35 Walk 35 Directions

① From the parking area opposite the mill, walk along the **Cirencester road**. Immediately after the **Catherine Wheel** pub turn right along a lane and then keep left at a fork. Pass some cottages and go through gates and stiles into a field. Walk on the same line across several stiles and fields until you pass to the right of a house to a road.

② Turn right and walk down to a junction. Turn right into **Ablington** and cross the bridge. After a few paces, turn left along a track with houses on your right and a stream to your left. Continue to a gate and then follow the track, arriving at another gate after ½ mile (800m).

WHAT TO LOOK FOR ℹ

Ablington Manor is to your right (behind high stone walls) as you cross the bridge in the village. Look out, too, not just for the 18th-century barns (mentioned above) but also for **Ablington House**, guarded by a pair of lions that once stood at the Houses of Parliament.

---

③ Go into a field and turn sharp right along the valley bottom. Follow a twisting route along the bottom of the valley. When you reach the next gate continue into a field, still following the contours of the valley. The route will eventually take you through a gate just before a barn and another immediately after.

④ Keep to the track as it bears right and gently ascends a long slope, with woodland to your left. When the track goes sharp right, with a gate before you, turn left through a gate on to a track. Follow it all the way to a road.

⑤ Turn right. After 250yds (229m), where the road goes right, continue straight on, to enter a track (the **Salt Way**). Continue along this for over ½ mile (800m), until you reach the remains of **Saltway Barn**.

WHERE TO EAT AND DRINK ℹ

The **Catherine Wheel** is a pleasant pub on the Cirencester road, just beyond the mill. The **Swan Hotel** has a good restaurant and also serves teas. A variety of snacks are available at **Bibury Trout Farm** and at the mill.

---

⑥ Do not walk ahead but, immediately after the barns, turn left into a field and then right along its right-hand margin. Walk on for just under ¾ mile (1.2km), passing hedge and woodland and, where the track breaks to the right, turn right through a gate into a field with a wall on your right.

⑦ Walk on to pass to the left of **Hale Barn**. Enter a track, with the large buildings of **Bibury Farm** away to your left, and keep on the same line through gates where they arise. Eventually you will descend to a drive which will, in turn, bring you to a road in **Bibury**. Cross the road to walk down between a row of cottages. At the end, near the church and school, turn right. Walk along the pavement into the village, passing **Arlington Row** and the river on your left.

Extending the Walk
You can extend the walk up the **Coln Valley** to **Winson** and **Coln Rogers** by leaving the main route at Point ③ to continue on **Potlickers Lane**. Cross the river and return along the road through the villages until a path brings you back to Point ③ where you can continue the main walk.

Burford – a Classic Cotswold Town

Discover the delights of an ancient settlement with a long history on this attractive walk through the Windrush Valley.

•DISTANCE•	5 miles (8km)
•MINIMUM TIME•	2hrs 30min
•ASCENT / GRADIENT•	250ft (76m)
•LEVEL OF DIFFICULTY•	
•PATHS•	Field and riverside paths, tracks, country roads, 7 stiles
•LANDSCAPE•	Undulating Windrush Valley to the east of Burford
•SUGGESTED MAP•	aqua3 OS Explorer OL45 The Cotswolds
•START / FINISH•	Grid reference: SP 252123
•DOG FRIENDLINESS•	Under control across farmland; on lead where requested
•PARKING•	Large car park to east of Windrush, near parish church
•PUBLIC TOILETS•	Burford High Street
•CONTRIBUTOR•	Nick Channer

BACKGROUND TO THE WALK

Often described as the gateway to the Cotswolds, the picturesque town of Burford has changed little over the years. The High Street runs down between lime trees and mellow stone houses to a narrow three-arched bridge over the River Windrush. Charles II and his mistress Nell Gwynn, whose child was named the Earl of Burford, attended Burford races and stayed at the George Hotel. When she retired to Windsor, Gwynn called her home there Burford House.

An Important Trading Centre

Situated at several major east–west and north–south crossing routes, Burford has always been regarded as an important trading centre. People would pay their tolls at the twin-gabled 15th-century Tolsey, now a museum, for the right to trade in the town and it was here that the prosperous Guild of Merchants conducted their meetings. Such was their power and influence that by the Middle Ages the merchants were running Burford as if it boasted a Mayor and Corporation.

Take a leisurely stroll through the streets of the town and you'll stumble across a host of treasures – especially in the little side roads leading off the High Street. For example, the Great House in Witney Street was the largest residence in Burford when it was built about 1690. With its Georgian façade, it certainly dwarfs the other buildings in the street. The Dolls' House, dating back to 1939 and on view in the Tolsey Museum, is modelled on the Great House.

A Gem of a Church

Burford's parish church, with its slender spire, is one of the largest in Oxfordshire. Begun about 1170, it was enlarged over subsequent centuries and one of its last additions was the south porch, noted for its elaborate stonework. The west doorway is pure Norman, as is the central part of the tower, to which another stage was added in the 15th century to provide a base for the spire. Inside, the ceiling is fan vaulted and there are five medieval screens dividing various chapels.

Levellers Revolt

This sizeable wool church is also associated with the Civil War Levellers – 800 Parliamentarian troopers who mutinied at Salisbury over pay and then marched north to join forces with other groups. On 14 May 1649 they reached Burford where they believed they would negotiate a settlement with Fairfax, the Commander-in-Chief. However, Fairfax had different plans and at midnight he and Cromwell entered the town with 2,000 horsemen. Following a skirmish, they captured 340 men. The prisoners were held in the church where one of them carved his name on the font. Two days later, on 17 May, three ringleaders were shot in the churchyard and a fourth was forced to preach a sermon.

Speaker's House

The Priory in Priory Lane is another of Burford's historic buildings. This Elizabethan house, rebuilt in the early 1800s, still has its Tudor gables and the heraldic arms over the doorway recall William Lenthall (1591–1662) who lived here and was elected Speaker to the Long Parliament in 1640.

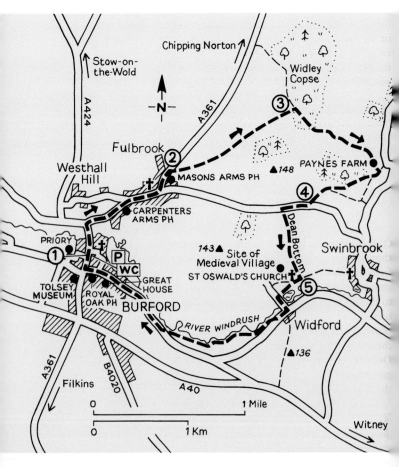

Walk **36**

Walk 36 Directions

① Head north along the **High Street** to the **Windrush**. Cross the river and turn right at the mini-roundabout towards Fulbrook. Pass the **Carpenters Arms** and continue along the road. Avoid a turning for Swinbrook and pass the **Masons Arms**. Keep ahead, passing **Upper End** on the left, and look for a footpath on the right by the **Masons Arms** sign.

② Follow the steps cut into the side of the slope up to the field edge and then swing right. Follow the boundary to a waymark just before a slope and curve left to cross the field. Go through a gap in the hedge on the far side and cross the field to an opening in the hedgerow. Cross the next field towards a curtain of woodland and make for a track.

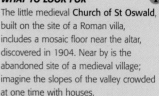

WHERE TO EAT AND DRINK
Burford has plenty of places to eat and drink – from hotel restaurants to pub food and tea shops. Just at the end of the walk is the **Royal Oak** which serves coffee and tea, as well as toasted teacakes. Various specials, snacks and ploughman's lunches are also available.

③ Keep right and follow the track through the woodland. Break cover from the trees and pass a row of cottages. Continue down the track to **Paynes Farm** and, just beyond it, turn right to join a signposted right of way. Head for a gate and follow the unfenced track towards trees. Descend the slope to a gate and continue ahead between hedges up the hill to the road.

④ Turn right and follow the road down into a dip. Swing left at the stone stile and sign for Widford and follow the grassy ride through verdant **Dean Bottom**. Make for a stile, turn right when you reach the T-junction and visit Widford's **St Oswald's Church**.

WHAT TO LOOK FOR
The little medieval **Church of St Oswald**, built on the site of a Roman villa, includes a mosaic floor near the altar, discovered in 1904. Near by is the abandoned site of a medieval village; imagine the slopes of the valley crowded at one time with houses.

⑤ On leaving the church, veer right and follow the grassy track, passing a lake on the left. Turn left at the road, recross the **Windrush** and turn right at the junction. Keep to the road until you reach a footpath sign and stile on the right. Follow the riverside path across a series of stiles, to eventually reach the road. Turn right towards Burford, pass the **Great House** and the **Royal Oak** and return to the **High Street**.

WHILE YOU'RE THERE
Visit the nearby village of **Filkins**, home to the Swinford Museum which illustrates west Oxfordshire's rural heritage. The village boasts a Victorian church built in the French Gothic style and was once the home of Sir Stafford Cripps, Chancellor of the Exchequer (1947–50) in the post-war Labour cabinet.

Mysteries at Minster Lovell

A gentle stroll through meadows and woods beside the Windrush.

•DISTANCE•	4 miles (6.4km)
•MINIMUM TIME•	1hr 30min
•ASCENT / GRADIENT•	180ft (55m) ▲ ▲ ▲
•LEVEL OF DIFFICULTY•	🚶🚶 🚶🚶 🚶🚶
•PATHS•	Meadows, tracks, pavement and lane, woodland, 17 stiles
•LANDSCAPE•	Shallow, fertile valley of River Windrush
•SUGGESTED MAP•	aqua3 OS Explorer 180 Oxford, Witney & Woodstock
•START / FINISH•	Grid reference: SP 321114
•DOG FRIENDLINESS•	Lead essential on road through Crawley and Minster Lovell
•PARKING•	Car park (free) at eastern end of Minster Lovell, above church and hall
•PUBLIC TOILETS•	None on route
•CONTRIBUTOR•	Ann F Stonehouse

BACKGROUND TO THE WALK

Crawley's industrial heart is announced by its tall mill chimney, which dominates the shallow, verdant valley to the north of Witney. By comparison, just a mile or two to the west, old Minster Lovell is the very essence of an idealised Cotswold village. Its little houses of grey-brown stone straggle up a narrow village street, adorned with impossibly pretty cottage gardens. At the top is a golden stone church, looking down over a silvery meander of the River Windrush. At the bottom is a charming old pub, the Swan, with the former mill opposite tastefully restored and now part of a discreet conference centre.

Two villages appeared on the site in the Domesday Book – Minster Lovell and Little Minster, separated by the river. There's now a newer Minster Lovell to the south west, an experimental housing and allotment development dating back to the 1840s. However, it's the picturesque older settlement which engages visitors.

No perfect Cotswold village would be complete without its manor house, of course. And Minster Lovell's is a beauty, although in ruins. The site, in a curve of the river below the church, was picked out by Lord William Lovell, 7th Baron of Tichmarsh, in the 1440s. William's son John extended the new manor house, and signboards among the broken walls show how splendid it must have been, complete with a massive gatehouse.

A Gruesome Tale

William's grandson, Francis, was politically the most successful member of the family, but came to a nasty end. Raised as a Yorkist, he served as Lord Chamberlain to Richard III and fought with him at Bosworth Field in 1485. The King died in the battle and Francis took refuge in Flanders. Two years later he returned to take part in the Lambert Simnel rebellion which backed an Oxford baker's boy for the throne. On the losing side in a battle at Stoke in 1487, Lovell fled home and was never heard of again. However in 1708, while a new chimney was being built at Minster Lovell Hall, it is said that a locked vault was discovered. In it was the skeleton of the missing Viscount Lovell, sitting with his papers at a table. Exposed to the air, the corpse dissolved into a cloud of dust in an instant. It was assumed that he had hidden here with the help of a servant, who subsequently fell ill and died, leaving unknown the secret of his master's whereabouts. John Buchan made memorable and chilling use of the legend in his novel *The Blanket of the Dark* (1931).

A pioneer of modernised agricultural techniques, Thomas Coke was the last resident at the Hall. He left in 1747 for his new Norfolk home, Holkham Hall. The old house was dismantled and the ruins are now cared for by English Heritage.

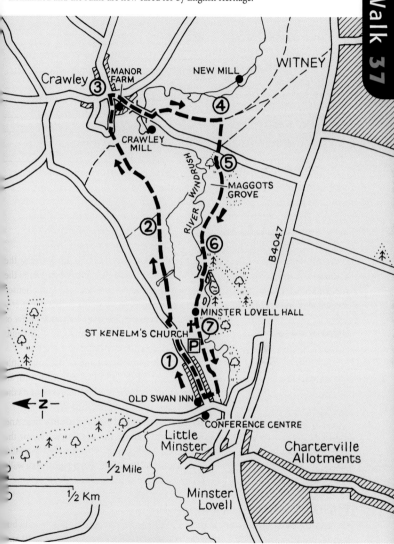

Walk 37 **Directions**

① Walk up the lane, signposted 'Crawley'. At the end of the village cross a stile, right, and take the

footpath diagonally left across the field, also signposted 'Crawley'. Look right for a view of the ruins of **Minster Lovell Hall** and the circular dovecote. Cross a stile and continue straight on along the path, with a

Walk 37

stone wall to your left. The mill chimney ahead on the horizon belongs to Crawley Mill.

② Cross a stile and go ahead up a slight incline. Cross another stile, go through a gate and continue on the path, walking up a green tunnel of a lane. Pass above **Crawley Mill**. At the road turn right and follow this down into **Crawley**. At the bottom look left to admire the diminutive village green with its stone cross. The **Lamb Inn** is on the left.

③ Turn right and follow the pavement past **Manor Farm**, with its huge pond. Cross the humpback bridge over the **Windrush** – look right for a good view of the old mill house. At the other side of the bridge cross the road and turn left through a gate, signed 'Witney'. Follow the bridleway beside the stream, marked by a line of willows.

④ At the junction of paths by a gate look ahead and left to see **New Mill**. Turn right through the gate and walk up the field edge. Pass a gate and cross the road. Climb the stile, go straight on to a second stile, and follow the path down through the woods.

⑤ At the bottom cross a stile and follow the path along the fence. The wildflower meadows of **Maggots Grove** lie to your right. Continue over three more stiles and bear left beside the trees. Cross a stile by a meander of the river.

⑥ Cross a further stile and enter the woods. At a gate bear right, following the arrows, and cross two footbridges. After a short distance cross a bridge over the river. Go through a squeeze gate towards **Minster Lovell Hall**. Climb the stile and go through a gate to explore the ruins.

⑦ Leave by the top entrance and walk through the churchyard. Cross a slab stile, continue along a grassy path with the village up to your right. Cross a footbridge and stile and veer to the right. Cross one stile and then another into **Wash Meadow** recreation ground. Keep right and go through a gate on to the high street, with the **Old Swan** pub to your left. Turn right and walk up through the village to the car park.

Side by Side with the Eastleaches

Two churches, just a stone's throw apart across a narrow stream.

•DISTANCE•	4½ miles (7.2km)
•MINIMUM TIME•	1hr 45min
•ASCENT / GRADIENT•	100ft (30m) ▲ ▲ ▲
•LEVEL OF DIFFICULTY•	🚶🚶 🚶🚶 🚶🚶
•PATHS•	Tracks and lanes, valley paths and woodland, 6 stiles
•LANDSCAPE•	Villages, open wold, narrow valley and streams
•SUGGESTED MAP•	aqua3 OS Explorer OL45 The Cotswolds
•START / FINISH•	Grid reference: SP 200052
•DOG FRIENDLINESS•	Sheep country – dogs under control at all times
•PARKING•	Village of Eastleach Turville
•PUBLIC TOILETS•	None on route
•CONTRIBUTOR•	Christopher Knowles

BACKGROUND TO THE WALK

These two Cotswold villages, sitting cheek by jowl in a secluded valley, carry an air of quiet perfection. And yet Eastleach Turville and Eastleach Martin are quite distinctive, and each has a parish church (though one is now redundant). St Andrews in Eastleach Turville faces St Michael and St Martin's across the narrow River Leach. Their origins lie in the development of the parish system from the early days of the Anglo-Saxon Church.

The Anglo-Saxon Kingdoms

The English parish has its origins in the shifting rivalries of Saxon England; for the one thing that united the various Saxon kingdoms was the Church. The first 'parishes' were really the Anglo-Saxon kingdoms. Christianity, the new power in the land, not only saved souls but also secured alliances. The Pope's aim was to invest more bishops to act as pastors and proselytisers, but at the same time their appointments were useful politically, helping to smooth the way as larger kingdoms absorbed their smaller neighbours. The number of appointments would also depend on local factors. Wessex, for example, was divided into shires and so a bishop was appointed for each one. Later the Normans appointed Archdeacons, whose job was to ensure that church buildings were maintained for worship. Over the centuries the assorted conventions and appointments that had accumulated through usage coalesced into a hierarchical English Church. For a long time, however, control was not tight. Missionaries, for example, would occasionally land from Ireland and found their own churches, quite independently of local potentates. Rulers and local landholders were certainly influential in the development of the parish system, but many parishes also derived from the gradual disintegration of the local 'minster', a central church on consecrated ground which controlled a group of client chapels. As population and congregations grew, the chapels themselves became new parish churches, with rights equal to those of the minster. This included the right to bury the dead in their own graveyard and administration of births and marriages.

Tithe Payments

With the passage of time and the establishment of a single English kingdom, the idea of a parish had diminished geographically to something akin to its modern size. By the 10th century the parish had become the accepted framework for the enforcement of the payment of tithes, the medieval equivalent of an income tax. By the 12th century much of the modern diocesan map of England was established. So in the Eastleaches, all these developments come together and you find two parish churches virtually side by side. With politics, power and bureaucracy all playing a part, it's likely that the pastoral needs of the community were quite a long way down the list of factors which led to their creation.

Walk 38 Directions

① From the **memorial cross** in **Eastleach Turville** walk along the road with the river on your right. After a few paces locate a path on your right to cross the **clapper bridge** and follow the path into the churchyard of Eastleach Martin. Pass to the right of the church and emerge at a road.

② Turn left and then turn right at a junction, taking the lower road in the direction of Holwell. Walk on for perhaps 600yds (549m) to where the road begins to rise

Walk 38

steeply. Turn left here, through a gate into a field, and follow an obvious grassy track at the base of a slope for ½ mile (800m).

③ This will bring you to a corner of **Sheephouse Plantation**. Turn left and walk into a field with the woods to your right. Continue to a gate at a field – do not go through this but continue forward with the field to your right. Soon you will reach a small area of scrubby trees, turn right here over a stile into a field and turn left.

WHAT TO LOOK FOR ⓘ
The little clapper bridge linking the two parishes is known locally as **Keble's Bridge**, after a family who were eminent in the area. John Keble, after whom Keble College in Oxford is named, was nominal curate for the two parishes in the 19th century. In the middle part of the walk the straight track to a road is part of **Akeman Street**, the Roman road that linked Cirencester with St Albans.

④ Continue, passing through gates, until you come to a gated bridge on your left. Do not cross this but continue forward towards a gate at the edge of woodland. Go through and follow a woodland path until you emerge at a clearing. Walk to the other side to re-enter woodland and continue to a track.

WHILE YOU'RE THERE ⓘ
There are two places near by worth visiting while you are in the area. To the south is **Lechlade**, Gloucestershire's only settlement on the River Thames. There is a handsome Market Square, an idyllic riverside and several fascinating old streets to wander through. To the west is **Fairford**, a handsome village noted for its fine church containing one of the only sets of medieval stained glass in the country.

WHERE TO EAT AND DRINK ⓘ
Eastleach Turville has a lovely little pub, the **Victoria**, in the western part of the village. Nearby Southrop, to the south, also has the **Swan**, a creeper-clad old pub with real fires in winter and a wide choice of food. In Coln St Alwyns, to the west, you'll find the **New Inn**, everybody's idea of a classic Cotswold pub and serving excellent food.

⑤ Turn left here and follow a track out of the woods and across fields until you come to a road. Turn left here, cross **Sheep Bridge** and, just before a turning to the right, go left into a field.

⑥ Bear right along the valley bottom, then left and right again. This will bring you to a gate. Go through it, on to a track, and soon pass the gated bridge again. Follow the wall on your right as it curves up to a gate and then stay on the same line through gates until you emerge at a road in **Eastleach Turville**. Turn left to make your way back to the start.

Around the Lakes of the Cotswold Water Park

Through an evolving landscape in the southern Cotswolds.

•DISTANCE•	5 miles (8km)
•MINIMUM TIME•	2hrs
•ASCENT / GRADIENT•	Negligible
•LEVEL OF DIFFICULTY•	
•PATHS•	Track, tow path and lanes, 10 stiles
•LANDSCAPE•	Dead flat – lakes, light woodland, canal and village
•SUGGESTED MAP•	aqua3 OS Explorer 169 Cirencester & Swindon
•START / FINISH•	Grid reference: SU 048974
•DOG FRIENDLINESS•	Good but be aware of a lot of waterfowl around lakes
•PARKING•	Silver Street, South Cerney
•PUBLIC TOILETS•	None on route
•CONTRIBUTOR•	Christopher Knowles

BACKGROUND TO THE WALK

By their very nature, ancient landscapes and historic architecture evolve very slowly, changing little from one century to another. Can they resist the demands of a brasher era? In the Cotswolds the answer to this question is essentially 'yes'. Here building restrictions are strict – even, sometimes, draconian. The result, however, is a significant area of largely unspoilt English countryside; sometimes, thoughtful development has even enhanced an otherwise lacklustre skyline. The Cotswold Water Park, located in and around old gravel pits, is an example of this.

Recreational Gravel

Gravel has been worked in the upper Thames Valley, where the water table is close to the surface, since the 1920s. The removal of gravel leads to the creation of lakes and in the areas around South Cerney and between Fairford and Lechlade there are now some 4,000 acres (1,620ha) of water, in about 100 lakes. They provide an important wetland habitat for a variety of wildlife. Most of these lakes have been turned over to recreational use of one sort or another, being a perfect place for game and coarse fishing, board sailing, walking, boating of various kinds, riding and sundry other leisure activities. Interestingly, this has been what is now called a private/public enterprise. The landscaping has not just been a case of letting nature take over where the gravel excavators left off. The crane-grabs that were used for excavation in the 1960s, for example, left the gravel pits with vertical sides and therefore with deep water right up to the shoreline. As it happens, some forms of aquatic life flourish under these conditions, but in other lakes the shoreline has been graded to create a gentler slope, to harmonise better with the flat landscape in this part of the Cotswolds and to suit the needs of swimmers and children. In the same way, trees have been planted and hills have been constructed to offer shelter and visual relief. Old brick railway bridges have been preserved. Finally, a style of waterside architecture has been developed to attract people to live here. It continues to evolve, just as the surrounding countryside has done for centuries

Walk 39

South Cerney and Cerney Wick

The walk begins in South Cerney, by the River Churn, only 4 miles (6.4km) from the source of the Thames. Look inside the Norman church for the exceptional carving on the 12th-century rood. Later the walk takes you through Cerney Wick, a smaller village on the other side of the gravel workings. The highlight here is an 18th-century roundhouse, used by the workers on the now disused Thames and Severn Canal.

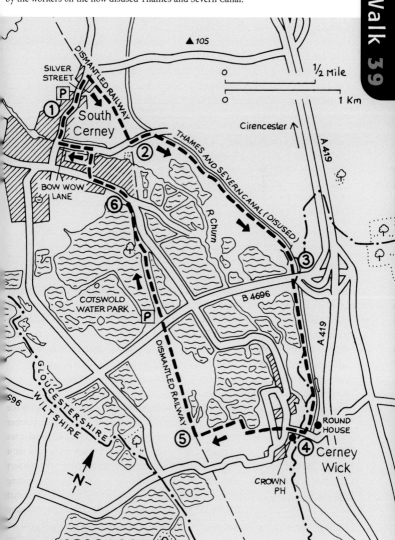

Walk 39 Directions

1) From **Silver Street** walk north out of the village. Immediately before the turning to Driffield and

Cricklade, turn right over a stile on to a bank. Stay on this obvious path for 800yds (732m), to reach a brick bridge across the path. Turn right here up a flight of steps to reach a narrow road.

② Turn left and walk along here for 200yds (183m) until you come to footpaths to the right and left. Turn right along a farm track, following a signpost for **Cerney Wick**. Almost immediately the shallow, overgrown remains of the **Thames and Severn Canal** appear to your left. When the track veers right into a farm, walk ahead over a stile to follow a path beneath the trees – the old canal tow path. At a bridge keep ahead across stiles and continue until you come to a busy road.

> **WHERE TO EAT AND DRINK** ⓘ
> The walk passes the **Crown** in Cerney Wick. There are also several pubs in South Cerney – the **Old George** and the **Eliot Arms** in Clarks Hay, and the **Royal Oak** on the High Street.

③ Cross with care. On the far side you have two choices: either continue on the tow path or take the path that skirts the lakes. If you take the lakeside path, you will eventually be able to rejoin the tow path by going left at a bridge after 600yds (549m). Continue until, after just under ½ mile (800m), you pass an old canal roundhouse across the canal to the left and, soon after, reach a lane at **Cerney Wick**.

④ Turn right here and walk to the junction at the end of the road, beside the **Crown** pub. Cross to a

> **WHILE YOU'RE THERE** ⓘ
> Visit often-overlooked **Cricklade**. The town centre is dominated by 17th- and 18th-century houses, overseen by the bulky tower of the church, visible for miles around. Unusually, it is dedicated to the Breton St Samson.

stile and enter a field. Walk straight ahead and come to another stile. Cross this aiming to the left of a cottage. Cross the lane, go over another stile and enter a field. Walk ahead and follow the path as it guides you across a stile on to the grass by a lake. Walk around the lake, going right and then left. In the corner before you, cross into a field, walk ahead towards trees and cross a stile to a track.

⑤ Turn right, rejoining the **old railway line** and following it all the way to a road. Cross this into a car park and go through a gate on to a track. Stay on this all the way to another road and follow a path that runs to its left.

⑥ Where the path ends at the beginning of **South Cerney**, continue along **Station Road**. Ignore a footpath on the right but turn right at the second one, which takes you across a bridge and bring you to a lane called '**Bow Wow**'. Turn left here between streams and return to **Silver Street**.

> **WHAT TO LOOK FOR** ⓘ
> Disused **transport systems** feature greatly in this walk. For much of it you will be beside or close to the old Thames and Severn Canal (▶ Walk 34), or following the route of the old Andoversford railway line. The line linked Cheltenham and Swindon between 1891 and 1961. The **roundhouse** seen on the far side of the old canal as you approach Cerney Wick was used by lock keepers and maintenance engineers. This design was a distinctive feature of the Thames and Severn Canal. Even the windows were rounded to afford the occupants maximum visibility of their stretch of canal. The downstairs would have been used as a stable, the middle storey as a living area and the upstairs held sleeping accommodation. The flat roof was also put to use collecting rainwater for the house's water supply.

Larks Above Down Ampney

A route based on the birthplace of one of Britain's best-known composers.

•DISTANCE•	8½ miles (13.7km)
•MINIMUM TIME•	4hrs
•ASCENT / GRADIENT•	100ft (30m) ▲ ▲ ▲
•LEVEL OF DIFFICULTY•	🚶 🚶 🚶
•PATHS•	Fields, lanes, tracks, 15 stiles
•LANDSCAPE•	Generally level fields and villages in all directions
•SUGGESTED MAP•	aqua3 OS Explorer 169 Cirencester & Swindon
•START / FINISH•	Grid reference: SU 099965
•DOG FRIENDLINESS•	On leads near livestock but plenty of stretches without
•PARKING•	Down Ampney village
•PUBLIC TOILETS•	None on route
•CONTRIBUTOR•	Christopher Knowles

BACKGROUND TO THE WALK

Ralph Vaughan Williams is considered by many to be England's greatest composer. He was born in 1872 in Down Ampney, where his father was vicar, spending the first three years of his life in the Old Vicarage. He studied music in London at the Royal College of Music with Parry, Stanford and Wood, who were the leading British musicians of the day. Then he studied in Berlin with Bruch and later in Paris with Ravel. This experience gave him the confidence to tackle large-scale works, many of which were based on English folk songs, which he had begun to collect in 1903. But Vaughan Williams was also interested in early English liturgical music, the result of which was his *Fantasia on a Theme by Thomas Tallis* (1910) for strings, which combines the English lyrical, pastoral tradition with the stricter demands of early formal composition.

Famous Works

Vaughan Williams went on to compose several symphonies, as well as a ballet based on the ideas of William Blake, and an opera based on *The Pilgrim's Progress* by John Bunyan. There were several sacred works, too, including a Mass and the Revelation oratorio. He also composed the score for the film *Scott of the Antarctic* (1948). One of his best-known hymn tunes is *Down Ampney* (1906), named in tribute to his birthplace. For many of us, however, Vaughan Williams is associated with two pieces in particular. The first is his version of *Greensleeves* (1928), the song said to have been originally composed by Henry VIII; and the second is *The Lark Ascending* (1914), the soaring work for violin and orchestra that evokes the poignancy of a bird in flight over the English countryside. Perhaps Williams was thinking of the Cotswolds. He certainly had the Cotswolds in mind when he wrote the opera, *Hugh the Drover* (1924), which is based on traditional folk songs and is set in the village of Northleach at the time of the Napoleonic wars.

There are four Ampneys altogether. Down Ampney church is the finest and definitely worth a visit. It's crowned by a 14th-century spire and contains several interesting effigies. Adjacent to the church is Down Ampney House, a 15th-century manor house that was later redesigned by Sir John Soane. The prettiest of the villages is Ampney Crucis, which takes its

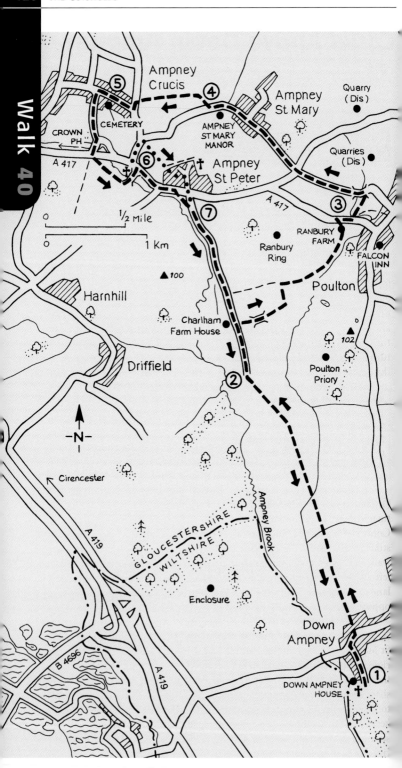

Ampney
Crucis

⑤

④

Ampney
St Mary

Quarry
(Dis)

CEMETERY

AMPNEY
ST MARY
MANOR

CROWN
PH

A 417

⑥

✝

✝ Ampney
St Peter

Quarries
(Dis)

③

RANBURY
FARM

FALCON
INN

A 417

⑦

½ Mile

1 Km

Ranbury
Ring

Poulton

▲ 100

Harnhill

Charlham
Farm House

Poulton
Priory

▲
102

Driffield

-N-

⑫

Cirencester

A 419

Ampney Brook

GLOUCESTERSHIRE

WILTSHIRE

Enclosure

Down
Ampney

B 4696

A 419

DOWN AMPNEY
HOUSE

①

✝

name from the 14th-century cross in the churchyard. The head of the cross was only rediscovered in 1854, having been secreted in the church, probably to protect it from puritan zealots in the 16th or 17th century. Ampney St Mary, the second Ampney you come to, is interesting because its original site was abandoned, leaving the little church you see today. Your route visits the fourth Ampney, Ampney St Peter, before returning to Down Ampney.

Walk 40 Directions

① From the church walk to the centre of the village. At the main road turn right and after 160yds (146m) turn left along a lane. Continue to a track and stay on this to cross a field to woodland.

② Join a track and walk along it to a house. Turn right into a field and on the far side cross a bridge into another field. Cross to a gap and turn left on to a track. At a corner turn right to join a bridleway. Pass through a farmyard to a road.

WHERE TO EAT AND DRINK ⓘ

There are two pubs near the route, the **Crown** in Ampney Crucis, and the **Falcon Inn**, just off the route when you get to Poulton. Continue along the road at Point ③ and turn right.

---

③ Turn right. After 200yds (183m) turn left over a stile beside a house. Continue to a second stile, then a stile and footbridge. In the field walk ahead to a stone stile on your left. Cross and walk ahead along a lane to a junction. Follow the lane opposite through **Ampney St Mary**.

④ After the entrance to **Ampney St Mary Manor** on your left, turn right over a stile into a field. Cross this half left to a gate and then turn sharp left to a stile. Cross and walk towards houses. On the far side keep right of a wall and arrive at a stile at a road. Turn left and first right, towards **Ampney Crucis**.

⑤ After a cemetery on the left, turn left down a lane. At the bottom turn right to a main road. Cross to a stile. Enter a field and go quarter left to the river. Find a path leading to a bridge and the churchyard of **Ampney Crucis**. Leave this on the far side and meet the road.

⑥ There are two possibilities here. The shortest is to turn right, pass a lane, then take a footpath on the right. Go half left to a lane and turn right. The other route is longer but avoids traffic. Follow a lane opposite to a junction on your right. Turn right over a stile into a field. Go quarter left to a gate and then immediately right through a gate into a paddock. Cross to another gate and a stile. Go half left to a stile and then, after a few paces, turn right through a gate. Cross a stile and then go half right to a gate. Walk along the margin of a garden and after a stile turn left to emerge in **Ampney St Peter**. Turn right to cross the road and enter a lane.

⑦ Stay on this lane as it becomes a track, from where you retrace your steps to **Down Ampney**.

WHAT TO LOOK FOR ⓘ

In **Down Ampney church** one of the effigies is of a medieval knight in black marble. The small church at Ampney St Mary boasts a complete set of Decorated windows and a Norman lintel over a doorway. In **Ampney St Peter** the churchyard, like Ampney Crucis, contains a 14th-century cross and a small, possibly Saxon, figure near the font.

Walk 41

Buscot to Kelmscott

On the Thames Path to the home of William Morris.

•DISTANCE•	4¾ miles (7.7km)
•MINIMUM TIME•	2hrs
•ASCENT / GRADIENT•	82ft (25m)
•LEVEL OF DIFFICULTY•	
•PATHS•	Riverside paths, fields, village lanes, 7 stiles
•LANDSCAPE•	Open, flat lands of the Thames floodplain
•SUGGESTED MAP•	aqua3 OS Explorer 170 Abingdon, Wantage & Vale of White Horse
•START / FINISH•	Grid reference: SU 231976
•DOG FRIENDLINESS•	Lead required around weir, not permitted in Manor gardens
•PARKING•	National Trust car park (free) in Buscot, signed 'Buscot Weir'
•PUBLIC TOILETS•	Buscot, behind phone box
•CONTRIBUTOR•	Ann F Stonehouse

BACKGROUND TO THE WALK

The village of Kelmscott is famous for its connections with the founder of the Arts and Crafts Movement, William Morris (1834–96). Today he is best remembered for his furnishing designs, rich with flowers, leaves and birds, still popular on fabric and wallpaper.

Champion of Fine Craftsmanship

Throughout his life, working with the great Pre-Raphaelite artists such as Edward Burne-Jones and Dante Gabriel Rossetti, Morris dedicated himself to a movement against what he saw as the vulgar tastes of his day, with its sentimentality, clutter and gaudy gewgaws. He put a new value on craftsmanship, studying and experimenting with the techniques of ages past, and so developing a style of apparent simplicity combined with functionality. He took it upon himself to educate as well as create, with pronouncements such as 'Have nothing in your houses that you do not know to be useful, or believe to be beautiful' emphasising the place of good design in everyday life. His philosophy of design became hugely influential.

Morris looked to the medieval artists and architects for his inspiration – a favourite outing for visitors to Kelmscott was to the magnificent Great Barn, a medieval stone-built tithe barn at nearby Great Coxwell (now cared for by the National Trust), to admire the intricacies and craftsmanship of its soaring timber roof.

Manor and Village

Kelmscott Manor itself dates from 1570 and became Morris's country home in 1871. It's a mellow old place, built of the local grey limestone, with mullioned windows and high pointed gables topped by ball finials. (The image is familiar from the woodcut designed for the Kelmscott Press, which he founded in 1890.) Morris loved the manor for its integrity and austerity, and for the harmony of the house in its setting, almost as if 'it had grown up out of the soil'. Now owned by the Society of Antiquaries of London, the house is open to the public on Wednesdays and some Saturdays through the summer, and contains many examples of Morris's work.

William Morris's influence on the area continued even after his death. As a memorial to the great man, several structures were designed to his principles and built in Kelmscott village, notably Memorial Cottages and next-door Manor Cottages. Reflecting traditional style but with a modern, practical twist, they blend effortlessly into the village and were overseen by his widow Jane and daughter May (herself an accomplished designer). On a wider scale, Morris's work did much for the emergence of a Cotswold identity in the 1920s, with his appreciation and publicising of the vernacular architecture.

Morris is buried with his wife and daughters in the churchyard at Kelmscott, under a modest tombstone, its only adornment the elegant lettering designed by Philip Webb.

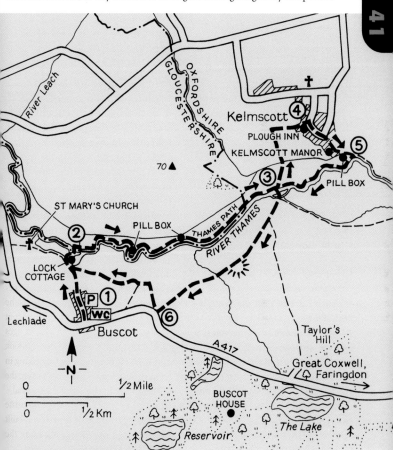

Walk 41 Directions

① Turn left and walk back into **Buscot** to admire the arcaded pump. Retrace your steps and continue ahead on the road, signed to the weir. The road becomes a track. Follow it round the edge of

the **Village Field** and cross a bridge. Keep right, to pass **Lock Cottage**. Follow the footpath over the weir. Bear left and cross the lock gate.

② Turn right, cross a stile and follow the path beside the river. Soon bear left and cross a bridge, with a view left to the main weir.

Walk 41

Turn right and follow the **Thames Path** beside the meandering river. Cross a stile, and continue past two wartime pill boxes and a gate. Go through a pair of gates. The roofs of Kelmscott appear ahead. Go through a gateway and continue towards the bridge, passing through some trees.

③ Pass the bridge, go through a gate and turn left up the field. At the far side cross a stile and two footbridges. Bear left and ahead up the hedge (yellow waymarker). At the end turn right along the path, which may be overgrown. Follow this into **Kelmscott** village.

> **WHAT TO LOOK FOR** ⓘ
> Look out for the charming relief carving of William Morris, set in the wall of the pair of **Memorial Cottages** at first floor height, between the windows. The great man is shown sitting under a tree, listening to the birds, with the old wool barn and summer house of the manor in the background.

④ Turn right to pass the **Plough Inn**. Bear left along the road, passing **Memorial Cottages** and **Manor Cottages**. Keep right to reach **Kelmscott Manor**. Maintain your direction ahead down the track, pass a World War II pill box and turn right just before you get to the river.

⑤ Cross a bridge and go through a gate to join the **Thames Path National Trail**. Cross a stile and

> **WHERE TO EAT AND DRINK** ⓘ
> The friendly **Plough Inn** at Kelmscott is a lovely old pub, with a flagstone floor and beautifully refurbished oak panelling. There's a beer garden at the front and a restaurant at the rear, with a lunch menu that changes according to the season – from mushrooms on toast to more exotic pasta dishes, as well as sandwiches. Dogs are welcome at the bar. **Buscot Village Shop** doubles as a tea room, also serving light lunches. Both are closed on Mondays.

continue, passing another old wartime pill box on your left. Go through the gate by the footbridge and turn left over the bridge. Bear left and right over another bridge. Cross a stile and walk up the track. Soon this crosses a ditch; now head diagonally right across the field. At the corner cross a stile and footbridge by the fingerpost and turn right. Keep straight on up the edge of the field, with views of **Buscot House**, left. Follow the track downhill, and bend right, then turn left over a footbridge. Continue on the path diagonally right across the next two fields.

⑥ Go through a gate by the road and turn right up a drive. Look out for a yellow waymarker and take the footpath off to the left. Soon cross a stile and veer left along the edge of the field. Cross a stile and a footbridge at the other end, walk across the **Village Field** and turn left to retrace your route back to the start of the walk in **Buscot**.

> **WHILE YOU'RE THERE** ⓘ
> **St Mary's Church** at Buscot has some good examples of stained glass from the firm of Morris and Co, founded by William Morris in 1861. The colours are rich, the foliage sumptuous in its detail and the angels elegantly Pre-Raphaelite. The window above the altar is by Burne-Jones. Look, too, for the unusual painted pulpit and two touching marble memorials to the first and second wives of Edward Loveden Loveden Esq, who died within four years of each other.

The Infant Thames at Cricklade

An easy ramble across water-meadows beside the Thames and disused canals.

•DISTANCE•	5½ miles (8.8km)
•MINIMUM TIME•	2hrs 30min
•ASCENT / GRADIENT•	Negligible
•LEVEL OF DIFFICULTY•	
•PATHS•	Field paths and bridle paths, disused railway, town streets, 15 stiles
•LANDSCAPE•	Flat river valley
•SUGGESTED MAP•	aqua3 OS Explorer 169 Cirencester & Swindon
•START / FINISH•	Grid reference: SU 100934
•DOG FRIENDLINESS•	Dogs can be off lead along old railway line
•PARKING•	Cricklade Town Hall car park (free)
•PUBLIC TOILETS•	Cricklade High Street
•CONTRIBUTOR•	David Hancock

BACKGROUND TO THE WALK

The River Thames begins life in a peaceful Gloucestershire field near Cirencester. Before long it graduates to a sizeable stream, also known as the Isis at this point, on its way to the Cotswold Water Park, a vast network of lakes and pools, before reaching Cricklade, Wiltshire's northernmost town and the only one situated on the river.

Although merely a meandering willow-fringed stream as it passes through the town, research in the 19th century revealed that the river at Cricklade had been navigable by barges weighing up to 6 tons during the 17th and 18th centuries. In 1607 the Burcot Commission was established for the purpose of improving the Thames as a navigable waterway from Clifton Hampden to Cricklade. Thomas Baskerville, writing in 1690, commented: 'So farewell Cricklade, come off ye ground, we'll sail in boats, towards London Town, for this is now the highest station by famous Tems for Navigation.' With the completion of the Thames and Severn Canal in 1789 river traffic was transferred to the canal and the upper reaches of the Thames gradually became overgrown.

Cricklade – Roman Military Post

Cricklade's advantageous position at the junction of four ancient roads may well be why it was established as the head of the navigable Thames. However, Cricklade's importance as a settlement began in Roman times when it was a significant military post on Ermine Street, the Roman road linking Cirencester and Silchester. Evidence of the Roman's occupation has been found in and around the town, with villas to the north and south east. The later fortified Saxon town was built as a defence against the Danes and had its own mint. Today, the wide High Street has worthy buildings from the 17th and 18th centuries and two contrasting parish churches. You should not miss St Sampson's, characterised by its cathedral-like turreted tower that rises high above the town and dominates the surrounding water-meadows.

Abandoned Communication Lines

This walk follows the River Thames north, away from Cricklade, via the Thames Path. Beyond North Meadow, your route passes beside a shallow ditch that was once the North Wilts Canal, which opened in 1819 and ran the 9 miles (14.5km) between Swindon and Latton, linking the Wilts and Berks Canal with the Thames and Severn Canal. Soon you will follow the old tow path beside the muddy, weed-clogged ditch that was once the Thames and Severn Canal, opened in 1789 to link the River Severn with the Thames at Lechlade. The canal closed to all traffic in 1927, and was finally abandoned in 1933. Later the walk heads south along a disused railway line, part of the Midland and South West Railway which was closed to passengers in 1961. Although a pleasing reminder of the railway era, the ever-present drone of traffic from the A419 across the water-meadows keeps the mind firmly in the 21st century.

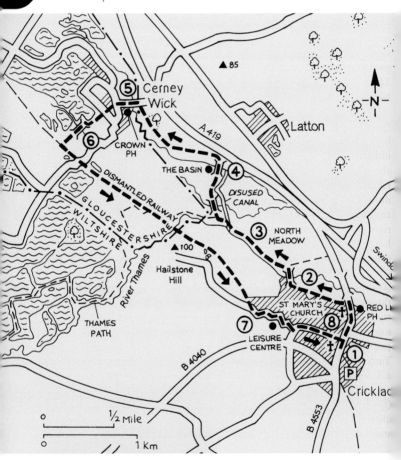

Walk 42 Directions

① Turn right out of the car park, keep ahead at the roundabout and walk along the **High Street**. Pass

St Mary's Church, then turn left along **North Wall** before the river bridge. Shortly, bear right to a stile and join the **Thames Path**. Cross a stile and continue along the field edge to houses.

Walk 42

② Go through the kissing gate on your right and bear left across the field to a gate. Follow the fenced footpath, cross a plank bridge and pass through the gate immediately on your right-hand side. Cross the river bridge and turn left through a gate. Walk beside the infant **River Thames**, crossing two stiles to enter **North Meadow**.

③ Continue to cross a stile by a bridge. Go through the gate immediately right and keep straight ahead, ignoring the Thames Path left. Follow the path beside the disused canal. Cross a footbridge and two stiles then, at a fence, bear right to cross a footbridge close to a house named **The Basin**. Cross a stile and bear right along the drive.

④ Cross a bridge and turn left through the gateway. Shortly, bear right to join the path along the left side of the old canal. Keep to the path for ½ mile (800m) to the road. Turn left into **Cerney Wick** to reach a T-junction.

⑤ Cross the stile opposite and keep ahead through the paddock to a stone stile and lane. Cross the lane and climb the stile opposite, continuing ahead to a further stile. In a few paces, cross the stile on the right and follow the path beside a lake. Bear right, then left and bear off left (yellow arrow) into trees where the path becomes a track.

⑥ Cross a footbridge and proceed ahead along the field edge to a stile. Turn left along the old railway, signed 'Cricklade'. Cross the **River Thames** in a mile (1.6km) and keep to the path along the former trackbed to a bridge.

WHILE YOU'RE THERE
Visit Cricklade's small local **museum** where collections, photographs and maps illustrate the history of the town from the Roman era to the present day. Head for the attractive village of Ashton Keynes and the heart of the **Cotswold Water Park**, Britain's largest water park, with 133 lakes providing water sports, nature trails (▶ Walk 39) and a visitor centre at **Keynes Country Park**.

⑦ Follow the gravel path to the **Leisure Centre**. Bear left on to the road, following it right, then turn left opposite the entrance to the Leisure Centre car park. Turn right, then next left and follow the road to the church.

⑧ Walk beside the barrier and turn left in front of **The Gatehouse** into the churchyard. Bear left to the main gates and follow the lane to a T-junction. Turn right to make your way back to the car park.

WHAT TO LOOK FOR
Walk across **North Meadow**, a National Nature Reserve, in spring to see many rare plants and flowers, including Britain's largest area of rare snakeshead fritillaries. At **Cerney Wick**, note the restored lock and the well-preserved roundhouse, originally the home of the lengthsman whose job was to look after the canal, ensuring that the level of water did not drop below the necessary minimum. In Cricklade, look for the Victorian **Jubilee Clock** in the High Street and the medieval carved crosses in both churchyards.

Sherston and Easton Grey's Cotswold Fringe

The infant Bristol Avon links attractive stone villages on this pastoral ramble on the south eastern fringes of the Cotswolds

•DISTANCE•	6½ miles (10.4km)
•MINIMUM TIME•	3hrs
•ASCENT / GRADIENT•	131ft (40m) ▲ ▲ ▲
•LEVEL OF DIFFICULTY•	🚶 🚶 🚶
•PATHS•	Field and parkland paths, tracks, metalled lanes, 11 stiles
•LANDSCAPE•	River valley and gently rolling farmland
•SUGGESTED MAP•	aqua3 OS Explorer 168 Stroud, Tetbury & Malmesbury
•START / FINISH•	Grid reference: ST 853858
•DOG FRIENDLINESS•	Dogs can be off lead along Fosse Way
•PARKING•	Sherston High Street; plenty of roadside parking
•PUBLIC TOILETS•	None on route
•CONTRIBUTOR•	David Hancock

BACKGROUND TO THE WALK

The Bristol Avon rises in the foothills of the Cotswolds in the north west corner of Wiltshire and is little more than a wide and shallow stream as it flows through the gently rolling pastoral countryside west of Malmesbury. Despite its size, this peaceful river enhances all the charming little stone villages in this unspoilt and somewhat forgotten area of north Wiltshire, which is typically Cotswold in appearance and character. In fact, 18 villages between Colerne and Malmesbury are officially part of the Cotswold Area of Outstanding Natural Beauty. Of these, Sherston must rank among the most attractive, with its wide High Street, doubtless once used as a market, lined with some interesting 17th- and 18th-century buildings. Sherston was a borough by the 15th century and prospered as a result of the flourishing wool trade at the time. It still has the feel of a market town, with narrow back streets and alleys, and continues to be a thriving community despite becoming a dormitory village.

Legend of a Local Hero

It has been suggested that Sherston is Sceorstan, as chronicled by Henry of Huntingdon, where in 1016 Edmund Ironside won a battle against the Danes who were led by King Canute. The early legend of John Rattlebone, a local yeoman promised land by Ironside in return for service against the Danes is deep rooted. Sadly, this brave knight was terribly wounded in battle and although he staunched his bleeding with a stone tile and continued fighting, he reputedly died as Canute's army withdrew. Other traditions say Rattlebone survived to claim his reward.

In the 17th century, the antiquary John Aubrey recorded the following local rhyme 'Fight well, Rattlebone, Thou shalt have Sherston, What shall I with Sherston do, Without I have all belongs thereto? Thou shalt have Wych and Wellesley, Easton Town and Pinkeney' Later traditions tell us that the small stone effigy on the south side of the porch outside the

Walk 43

parish church is that of Rattlebone, and that an ancient timber chest in the church, marked with the initials R B, is supposed to be where Rattlebone kept his armour. Whatever the truth is, the Rattlebone Inn opposite the church keeps his name alive.

Easton Grey – Pure Cotswold Charm

Peaceful parkland and riverside paths lead you downstream to picturesque Easton Grey. Set around a 16th-century stone bridge and climbing a short, curving street is an intimate huddle of ancient stone houses, with mullioned windows, steep, lichen-covered roofs and colourful, flower-filled gardens that touch the river bank. Set back on a rise above the river is Easton Grey House, a handsome 18th-century manor house with a classical façade and portico, surrounded by elegant gardens and lovely valley views. It was the summer retreat of Herbert Asquith, 1st Earl of Oxford, when he was Prime Minister between 1908 and 1916.

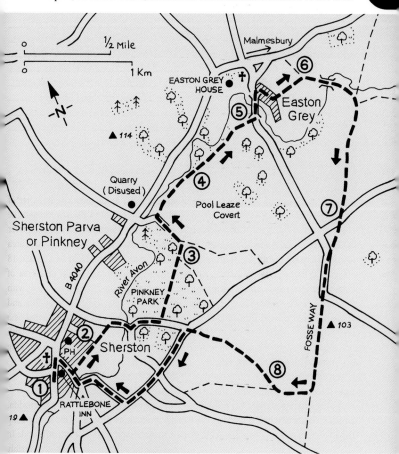

Walk 43 Directions

① On Sherton's High Street, walk towards the village stores, pass the **Rattlebone Inn** and turn right into

Noble Street. Pass Grove Road and take the footpath left up a flight of steps. Cross a cul-de-sac and follow the metalled footpath to a gate. Continue to the rear of houses to a further gate.

Walk 43

② Bear diagonally right across a field to a gate and lane. Turn right, cross the river and turn left, signed 'Foxley'. At the end of woodland on your left, take the footpath left through a gate. Follow the track across **Pinkney Park** to a gate.

③ Keep ahead, bearing left beside the wall to a gate. Follow the track ahead towards farm buildings and where the drive curves left, turn right into the farmyard. Keep right to join a concrete path to a stile. Turn left around the field edge to a stile and keep to the left-hand field edge to a stile in the corner.

WHERE TO EAT AND DRINK ⓘ

Rest weary limbs and refuel at the **Rattlebone Inn** in Sherston. A lively inn with a great atmosphere, the rambling bars are the setting for hearty lunchtime snacks and imaginative evening meals with decent wine and Youngs ales. Alternatively, try the **Carpenters Arms** which is noted for fresh fish.

---

④ Bear half-right across the field to follow the path along the field edge above the River Avon to a stile. Cross a further stile and walk beside the fence, with **Easton Grey House** left, and head downhill to a gate and lane.

⑤ Turn left into **Easton Grey**. Cross the river bridge, turn right uphill to take the footpath ahead on reaching entrance gates on your right. Cross a gravelled area, go through a gate and keep ahead to a

---

WHAT TO LOOK FOR ⓘ

The wide, hedged and dead-straight track that you follow on your return route to Sherston is the **Fosse Way**. This an the ancient Roman road that ran from Lincoln to Exeter and is so named because it was bordered on both sides by a 'fosse' or ditch.

---

stile. Maintain direction across the next field and gently descend to follow a track into the next field.

⑥ Turn right along the field edge and bear off right downhill through scrub to a footbridge. Keep ahead beside a ruin to a gate. Cross a stile and continue to a further stile and gate. Follow the track downhill to a stile and turn right along a track (**Fosse Way**). Continue for ½ mile (800m) to a road.

⑦ Cross straight over and keep to the byway to another road. Bear left and keep ahead where the lane veers sharp left. Follow this rutted track for ½ mile (800m), then cross the arrowed stile on your right. Head straight across the field to a gate and bear diagonally right across a large paddock to a stile.

⑧ Join a track, cross a racehorse gallop and go through the left-hand gate ahead. Walk through scrub to another gate and keep to the track ahead to a road. Turn left and continue to a crossroads. Proceed straight on to the next junction and keep ahead, following the lane all the way back into **Sherston**.

WHILE YOU'RE THERE ⓘ

Nearby **Luckington Court Gardens**, TV film location for Jane Austen's *Pride and Prejudice* (1995), has a 3-acre (1.2ha) formal garden and a walled flower garden. Head north just across the border into Gloucestershire to visit **Westonbirt Arboretum**, one of the finest and most important collections of trees and shrubs in the country. Visit in spring for the impressive displays of rhododendrons, azaleas, magnolias and wild flowers, and later in the year for the magnificent autumn colours.

Castle Combe and By Brook

Through the wooded By Brook Valley from a famous picture-book village.

•DISTANCE•	5¾ miles (9.2km)
•MINIMUM TIME•	2hrs 30min
•ASCENT / GRADIENT•	515ft (157m) ▲▲▲
•LEVEL OF DIFFICULTY•	👫 👫 👫
•PATHS•	Field and woodland paths and tracks, metalled lanes, 10 stiles
•LANDSCAPE•	Wooded river valley and village streets
•SUGGESTED MAP•	aqua3 OS Explorer 156 Chippenham & Bradford-on-Avon
•START / FINISH•	Grid reference: ST 845776
•DOG FRIENDLINESS•	Keep under control across pasture and golf course
•PARKING•	Free car park just off B4039 at Upper Castle Combe
•PUBLIC TOILETS•	Castle Combe
•CONTRIBUTOR•	David Hancock

BACKGROUND TO THE WALK

To many, the idyllic village of Castle Combe needs no introduction since it has featured on countless calendars, chocolate-box lids and jig-saw puzzles. Since being voted 'the prettiest village in England' in 1962, there have been more visitors to it, more photographs taken of it and more words written about it than any other village in the county. Nestling deep in a steam-threaded combe, just a mile (1.6km), and a world away, from the M4, it certainly has all the elements to make it a tourist's dream. You'll find 15th-century Cotswold stone cottages with steep gabled roofs surrounding a turreted church and stone-canopied market cross, a medieval manor house, a fast-flowing steam in the main street leading to an ancient packhorse bridge and a perfectly picturesque river.

Yet, as preservation is taken so seriously here, a palpable atmosphere of unreality surrounds this tiny 'toytown', where television aerials don't exist, gardens are immaculately kept, and the inevitable commercialism is carefully concealed. Behind this present-day façade, however, exists a fascinating history that's well worth exploring, and the timeless valleys and tumbling wooded hillsides that surround the village are favourite Wiltshire walking destinations. If you don't like crowds and really want to enjoy Castle Combe, undertake this walk on a winter weekday.

'Castlecombe' Cloth

The Castle, which gave the village its name, began life as a Roman fort and was used by the Saxons before becoming a Norman castle in 1135 and the home of the de Dunstanville family. In the 13th and 14th centuries the village established itself as an important weaving centre as Sir John Fastolf, the lord of the manor, erected fulling mills along the By Brook and 50 cottages for his workers. With the growth of the cloth trade in Wiltshire, Castle Combe prospered greatly, becoming more like a town with a weekly market and an annual fair that was regarded as 'The most celebrated faire in North Wiltshire for sheep.'

The greatest tribute to the wealth of the weaving industry is reflected in St Andrew's Church which was enlarged during the 15th century. Its impressive Perpendicular tower was built in 1436. For centuries the villages produced a red and white cloth known as Castlecombe. Cloth manufacture began to decline in the early 18th century when the diminutive By Brook was unable to power the larger machinery being introduced. People moved to the larger towns and Castle Combe became depopulated and returned to an agricultural existence. An annual fair, centred around the Market Cross, continued until 1904, and Castle Combe remained an 'estate' village until 1947 when the whole village was sold at auction.

Walk 44 **Directions**

① Leave the car park via the steps and turn right. At the T-junction, turn right and follow the lane into **Castle Combe**. Keep left at the **Market Cross**, cross the **By Brook** and continue along the road to take the path, signed '**Long Dean**', across the second bridge on your left.

② Cross a stile and follow the path uphill and then beside the right-hand fence above the valley (**Macmillan Way**). Beyond an open area, gently ascend through woodland to a stile and gate. Cross a further stile and descend into the hamlet of **Long Dean**.

③ Pass the mill and follow the track right to cross the river bridge.

> **WHERE TO EAT AND DRINK** ℹ
> The **White Hart** at Ford is the perfect halfway refuelling stop. Expect excellent real ales, interesting bar food and a riverside garden. In Castle Combe, head for the part-timbered 14th-century **White Hart** for cosy log fires, a summer patio garden and an extensive pub menu. Across the road, the more up-market **Castle Inn** offers a more contemporary menu. The impressive **Manor House Hotel** is the place to go for civilised afternoon teas.

At a mill house, keep right and follow the sunken bridleway uphill to a gate. Shortly enter sloping pasture and follow the defined path around the top edge, bearing left to reach a stile and lane.

④ Turn left and descend to the A420 at **Ford**. Turn right along the pavement and shortly turn right again into **Park Lane**. (If you want to visit the White Hart in Ford village, take the road ahead on your left, signed 'Colerne'.) Climb the gravel track and take the footpath left through a squeeze stile.

⑤ Keep right through pasture and continue through trees to a water-meadow in the valley bottom. Turn left, cross a stream and steeply ascend the grassy slope ahead of you, bearing left beyond some trees towards a waymarker post. Follow the footpath along the top of the field to a stile and gate, then walk through the woodland to a gate and the road.

⑥ Turn left, then immediately left again, signed 'North Wraxall'. Keep to the road for ¼ mile (400m) and take the arrowed bridleway right. Follow the track then, just before a gate, keep right downhill on a sunken path to a footbridge over **Broadmead Brook**.

⑦ In 20yds (18m), climb the stile on your right and follow the footpath close to the river. Cross a stile and soon pass beside **Nettleton Mill House**, bearing right to a hidden gate. Walk beside the stream, cross a stile and you will soon reach the golf course.

⑧ Turn right along the metalled track, cross the bridge and turn immediately right again. At a gate, follow the path left below the golf course fairway. Walk beside a wall to reach a stile on your right. Drop down steps to a metalled drive and keep ahead back into **Castle Combe**. Turn left at the **Market Cross** and retrace your steps.

> **WHILE YOU'RE THERE** ℹ
> Linger by the **bridge** over the By Brook and recall, if you've seen it, the 1966 film *Dr Doolittle* starring Rex Harrison. Although miles from the nearest coast, a jetty was built on the banks in front of the 17th-century cottages here to create a fishing harbour, complete with seven boats and plastic cobbles. Local people became 'extras' at £2 10s per day, with meals, alcohol and clothes all thrown in. The film put Castle Combe firmly on the tourist map!

WHAT TO LOOK FOR ℹ
St Andrew's Church, in Castle Combe, is worth closer inspection. On the parapet, note the 50 stone heads and the carving of a shuttle and scissors, the mark of the cloth industry put there by merchants who built the church. Inside, don't miss the rare faceless clock made by a local blacksmith in 1380, and the 13th-century tomb of Sir Walter de Dunstanville. Along the By Brook, note the former **fulling mills** and **weavers' cottages** at the remote and unspoilt hamlet of Long Dean.

Brunel's Great Tunnel Through Box Hill

A hilly walk around Box Hill, famous for its stone and Brunel's greatest engineering achievement.

•DISTANCE•	3¼ miles (5.3km)
•MINIMUM TIME•	1hr 45min
•ASCENT / GRADIENT•	508ft (155m) ▲▲▲
•LEVEL OF DIFFICULTY•	🚶 🚶 🚶
•PATHS•	Field and woodland paths, bridleways, lanes, 15 stiles
•LANDSCAPE•	River valley and wooded hillsides
•SUGGESTED MAP•	aqua3 OS Explorer 156 Chippenham & Bradford-on-Avon
•START / FINISH•	Grid reference: ST 823686
•DOG FRIENDLINESS•	Can be off lead on Box Hill Common and in woodland
•PARKING•	Village car park near Selwyn Hall
•PUBLIC TOILETS•	Opposite Queens Head in Box
•CONTRIBUTOR•	David Hancock

BACKGROUND TO THE WALK

Box is a large straggling village that sits astride the busy A4 in hilly country halfway between Bath and Chippenham. Although stone has been quarried here since the 9th century, Box really found fame during the 18th century when the local stone was used for Bath's magnificent buildings. The construction of Box Tunnel also uncovered immense deposits of good stone and by 1900 Box stone quarries were among the most productive in the world, employing over 700 men. Little trace can be seen above ground today, except for some fine stone-built houses in the village and a few reminders of the industry on Box Hill.

Appointed Engineer

In 1833, the newly created Great Western Railway appointed Isambard Kingdom Brunel (1806–59) as engineer. His task was to build a railway covering the 118 miles (190km) from London to Bristol. The problems and projects he encountered on the way would help to make him the most famous engineer of the Victorian age. After a relatively straightforward and level start through the Home Counties, which earned the nickname 'Brunel's Billiard Table', he came to the hilly Cotswolds. (Incidentally, the Provost of Eton thought the line would be injurious to the discipline of the school and the morals of the pupils.)

Brunel's Famous Tunnel

The solution at Box would be a tunnel, and at nearly 2 miles (3.2km) long and with a gradient of 1:100 it would be the longest and steepest in the world at the time. It would also be very wide. Already controversial, Brunel ignored the gauge of other companies preferring the 7ft (2.1m) used by tramways and roads (and, it was believed, Roman chariots). He also made the tunnel dead straight, and, never one to 'hide his light', the alignment was calculated so the dawn sun would shine through on his birthday on 9th April. Unfortunately he did not allow for atmospheric refraction and was two days out!

Box **143**

Walk 45

Passage to Narnia?

All was on a grand scale: a ton of gunpowder and candles were used every week, 3 million bricks were fired to line the soft Cotswold limestone and 100 navvies lost their lives working on the tunnel. After 2½ years the way was open, and although Brunel would ultimately lose the battle of the gauges, his magnificent line meant that Bristol was then a mere two hours from the capital. Although artificial, like many large dark holes, the tunnel has collected its fair share of mystery with tales of noises, people under the hill and trains entering the tunnel, never to re-emerge. But as is often the case, the explanations are rather more mundane. To test excavation conditions, Brunel dug a small trial section alongside what is now the eastern entrance and the military commandeered this section during World War Two as a safe and fairly secret store for ammunition, records and top brass. Sadly it is not a passage to Narnia!

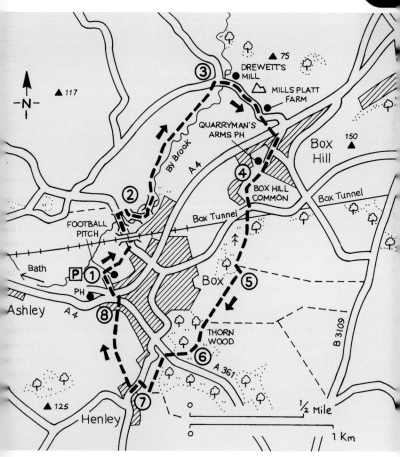

Walk 45 Directions

1 Facing the **recreation ground**, walk to the left-hand side of the football pitch to join a track in the corner close to the railway line. When you reach the lane, turn left, pass beneath the railway, cross a bridge and take the arrowed footpath, to the right, before the second bridge.

Walk 45

② Walk beside the river, cross a footbridge and turn right. Cross a further footbridge and continue to a stile. Walk through water-meadows close to the river, go through a squeeze stile and maintain direction. Shortly, bear left to a squeeze stile in the field corner. Follow the right-hand field edge to a stile and lane.

③ Turn right, then right again at the junction. Cross the river, pass **Drewett's Mill** and steeply ascend the lane. Just past **Mills Platt Farm**, take the arrowed footpath ahead across a stile. Continue steeply uphill to a stile and cross the A4. Ascend steps to a lane and proceed straight on up **Barnetts Hill**. Keep right at the fork, then right again and pass the **Quarryman's Arms**.

④ Keep left at the fork and continue beside **Box Hill Common** to a junction. Take the path straight ahead into woodland. Almost

WHAT TO LOOK FOR

Explore Box and locate the **Blind House** on the main street, one of a dozen in Wiltshire for disturbers of the peace. Look for **Coleridge House**, named after the poet who often broke his journey here on his way to Nether Stowey. Also look for the former **Candle Factory** on the Rudloe road that once produced the candles used during the building of Box Tunnel, and head east along the A4 for the best view of the **tunnel's entrance**.

immediately, fork left and follow the path close to the woodland edge. As it curves right into the beech wood, bear left and follow the path through the gap in the wall and then immediately right at the junction of paths.

⑤ Follow the bridle path to a fork. Keep left, then turn right at the T-junction and take the path left to a stile. Cross a further stile and descend into **Thorn Wood**, following the stepped path to a stile at the bottom.

⑥ Continue through scrub to a stile and turn right beside the fence to a wall stile. Bear right to a further stile, then bear left uphill to a stile and the **A361**. Cross over and follow the drive ahead. Where it curves left by stables, keep ahead along the arrowed path to a house. Bear right up the garden steps to the drive and continue uphill to a T-junction.

⑦ Turn left, then on entering **Henley**, take the path right, across a stile. Follow the field edge to a stile and descend to an allotment and stile. Continue to a stile and gate.

⑧ Follow the drive ahead, bear left at the garage and take the metalled path right, into **Box**. Cross the main road and continue to the **A4**. Turn right, then left down the access road back to **Selwyn Hall**.

WHERE TO EAT AND DRINK

In Box, you will find both the **Queen's Head** and **Bayly's** offer good food and ale in convivial surroundings. Time your walk for opening time at the **Quarryman's Arms** on Box Hill. Enjoy the views across Box from the dining room with a pint of locally-brewed ale, just like the local stone miners once did.

Corsham – a Wealthy Weaving Town

Explore this architectural treasure of a town and the adjacent Corsham Park.

•DISTANCE•	4 miles (6.4km)
•MINIMUM TIME•	2hrs
•ASCENT / GRADIENT•	114ft (35m) ▲ ▲ ▲
•LEVEL OF DIFFICULTY•	🚶 🚶 🚶
•PATHS•	Field paths and country lanes, 10 stiles
•LANDSCAPE•	Town streets, gently undulating parkland, farmland
•SUGGESTED MAP•	aqua3 OS Explorer 156 Chippenham & Bradford on Avon
•START / FINISH•	Grid reference: ST 871704
•DOG FRIENDLINESS•	Can be off lead in Corsham Park
•PARKING•	Long stay car park in Newlands Lane
•PUBLIC TOILETS•	Short stay car park by shopping precinct
•CONTRIBUTOR•	David Hancock

BACKGROUND TO THE WALK

Warm, cream-coloured Bath stone characterises this handsome little market town situated on the southern edge of the Cotswolds. An air of prosperity pervades the streets where the 15th-century Flemish gabled cottages and baroque-pedimented 17th-century Hungerford Almshouses mix with larger Georgian residences. Architectural historian Nikolaus Pevsner wrote: 'Corsham has no match in Wiltshire for the wealth of good houses.' The town owes its inheritance to the once thriving industries of cloth manufacture and stone quarrying during the 17th and 18th centuries.

Architectural Delights

Spend some time exploring the heart of the town before setting off across Corsham Park, as many of the fine stone buildings along the High Street, Church Street and Priory Street have been well preserved. Begin your town stroll at the Heritage Centre in the High Street (No 31), where interactive displays and hands-on exhibits present the stories of the weaving industry and quarrying of the golden Bath stone, which was used to create the architectural legacy of the town. In fact, No 31 once belonged to a prosperous 18th-century clothier, and No 70 (now an electrical shop) was the workhouse providing labour for the cloth industry. The Town Hall was formerly the market hall with one storey and open arches before being converted in 1882. North of the post office you will see the unspoilt line of 17th-century weavers' cottages. Known as the Flemish Buildings, this was the centre of the cloth industry where the Flemish weavers settled following religious persecution in their homeland. In Church Street, note the gabled cottages of the 18th-century weavers, with their ornate porches and a door on the first floor for taking in the raw wool.

Corsham Court – the Methuen Family Home

The finest of the houses is Corsham Court, a splendid Elizabethan mansion built in 1582 on the site of a medieval royal manor. It was bought in 1745 by Paul Methuen, a wealthy clothier and ancestor of the present owner, to house the family's collection of 16th- and 17th-century Italian and Flemish Master paintings and statuary. The house and park you see today are principally the work of 'Capability' Brown, John Nash and Thomas Bellamy. Brown built the gabled wings that house the state rooms and magnificent 72ft (22m) long picture gallery and laid out the park, including the avenues, Gothic bathhouse and the 13-acre (5ha) lake. Round off your walk with a tour of the house. You will see the outstanding collection of over 140 paintings, including pictures by Rubens, Turner, Reynolds and Van Dyck, fine statuary and bronzes, and the famous collection of English furniture, notably pieces by Robert Adam and Thomas Chippendale. You may recognise the house as the backdrop for the film *The Remains of the Day* (1993) starring Anthony Hopkins.

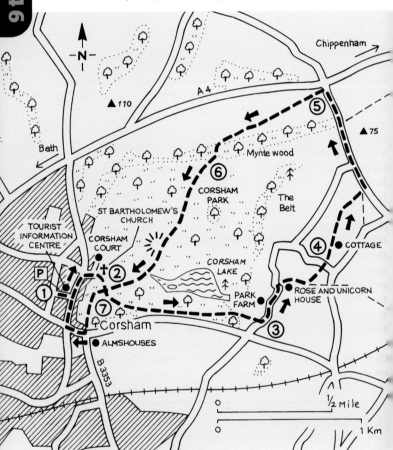

Walk 46 Directions

① Turn left out of the car park, then left again along **Post Office Lane** to reach the **High Street**. Turn left, pass the tourist information centre and turn right into **Church Street**. Pass the impressive entrance to Corsham Court and enter **St Bartholomew's churchyard**.

② Follow the path left to a gate and walk ahead to join the main path across **Corsham Park**. Turn left and walk along the south side of the

Walk 46

park, passing **Corsham Lake**, to reach a stile and gate. Keep straight on along a fenced path beside a track to a kissing gate and proceed across a field to a stile and lane.

③ Turn left, pass **Park Farm**, a splendid stone farmhouse on your left, and shortly take the waymarked footpath right along a drive to pass **Rose and Unicorn House**. Cross a stile and follow the right-hand field edge to a stile, then bear half-left to a stone stile in the field corner. Ignore the path arrowed right and head straight across the field to a further stile and lane.

④ Take the footpath opposite, bearing half-left to a stone stile to the left of a cottage. Maintain direction and pass through a field entrance to follow the path along the left-hand side of a field to a stile in the corner. Turn left along the road for ½ mile (800m) to the **A4**.

⑤ Go through the gate in the wall on your left and follow the worn path right, across the centre of parkland pasture to a metal kissing gate. Proceed ahead to reach a kissing gate on the edge of woodland. Follow the wide path to a further gate and bear half-right to a stile.

⑥ Keep ahead on a worn path across the field and along the field edge to a gate. Continue to a further gate with fine views right to **Corsham Court**. Follow the path right along the field edge, then where it curves right, bear left to join the path beside the churchyard wall to a stile.

⑦ Turn left down the avenue of trees to a gate and the town centre, noting the stone almshouses on your left. Turn right along **Pickwick Road** and then right again along the pedestrianised **High Street**. Turn left back along **Post Office Lane** to the car park.

Lacock – the Birthplace of Photography

Combine a stroll around England's finest medieval village with a riverside walk and a visit to Lacock Abbey, home of photographic pioneer Fox Talbot.

•DISTANCE•	5½ miles (8.8km)
•MINIMUM TIME•	2hrs 30min
•ASCENT / GRADIENT•	426ft (130m) ▲▲▲
•LEVEL OF DIFFICULTY•	🚶🚶 🚶🚶 🚶🚶
•PATHS•	Field paths and tracks; some road walking, 20 stiles
•LANDSCAPE•	River valley, wooded hillside and parkland
•SUGGESTED MAP•	aqua3 OS Explorer 156 Chippenham & Bradford-on-Avon
•START / FINISH•	Grid reference: ST 918681
•DOG FRIENDLINESS•	Can be off lead on riverside pastures if free of cattle
•PARKING•	Free car park on edge of Lacock
•PUBLIC TOILETS•	Adjacent to Stables Tea Room in Lacock village
•CONTRIBUTOR•	David Hancock

BACKGROUND TO THE WALK

Timeless Lacock could stand as the pattern of the perfect English village with its twisting streets, packed with attractive buildings from the 15th to 18th centuries, possessing all the character and atmosphere of medieval England. Half-timbering, lichen grey stone, red-brick and whitewashed façades crowd together and above eye-level, uneven upper storeys, gabled ends and stone roofs blend with charming ease.

With the founding of an abbey in the 13th century, the village grew rich on the medieval wool industry and continued to prosper as an important coaching stop between Marlborough and Bristol until the mid-18th century when, as an estate-owned village, time seemed to stand still for nearly 100 years. Entirely owned and preserved by the National Trust since 1944, Lacock is amongst England's most beautiful villages and is, certainly, one of Wiltshire's most visited. If you're interested in architecture and plan to visit Lacock Abbey allow the whole day and undertake the short stroll.

Fox Talbot and Lacock Abbey

Of all the outstanding buildings in the village Lacock Abbey, on the outskirts, is the most beautiful. It began as an Augustinian nunnery in 1232, but after the Reformation Sir William Sharrington used the remains to build a Tudor mansion, preserving the fine cloister court, sacristy and chapter house, and adding a romantic octagonal tower, a large courtyard and twisting chimney stacks.

The abbey passed to the Talbot family through marriage and they Gothicised the south elevation and added the oriel windows. Surrounded by peaceful water-meadows bordering the River Avon, this was the setting for the experiments of William Henry Fox Talbot (1800–77), which in 1835 led to the creation of the world's first photographic negative. You can see some of Fox Talbot's work and equipment, alongside interesting photographic exhibitions, in the beautifully restored 16th-century barn at the gates to the abbey.

Village Highlights

Architectural gems to note as you wander around Lacock's ancient streets include the timber-framed Sign of the Angel Inn, on Church Street, which retains its medieval layout, a 16th-century doorway and the passage through which horses would pass. Near by, Cruck House, with one of its cruck beams exposed, is a rare example of this 14th-century building method. Further along, you will pass King John's Hunting Lodge, reputed to be even older than the abbey, and St Cyriac's Church which contains the grandiose Renaissance tomb of Sir William Sharrington. In West Street, the George Inn dates back to 1361 and features a huge open fire with a dogwheel which was connected to the spit on the fire and turned by a dog called a Turnspit. Next door to the pub take a quick look at the bus shelter; it was formerly the village smithy.

On the corner of East Street is the magnificent 14th-century tithe barn with fine curved timbers. This was once used to store the rents which were paid to the abbey in kind, such as corn, hides and fleeces. The building later became the market hall as Lacock flourished into a thriving wool trading centre. Finally, don't miss the 18th-century domed lock-up next door. This is known as a 'blind house', since many of its overnight prisoners were drunks. You may recognise Lacock's medieval streets as the backdrop to several television costume dramas, notably Jane Austen's *Pride and Prejudice* (1995) and *Emma* (1996), and Daniel Defoe's rather bawdy *Moll Flanders* (1996).

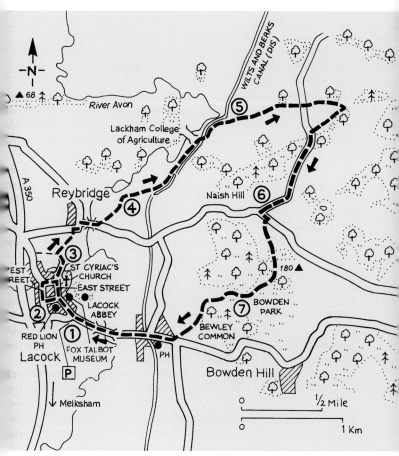

Walk 47 Directions

① From the car park, cross the road and follow the path into **Lacock**. Turn right into **East Street** opposite the **Red Lion** and walk down to **Church Street**. Turn left, then keep left into **West Street** and go left again into **High Street**.

② Walk back down **East Street**. Turn right along **Church Street** and bear left in front of the church to cross a bridge over the **Bide Brook**. Follow the path by the stream then up the lane to the end of the road.

③ Go through the kissing gate on your right and follow the tarmac path across the field to a gate. Pass cottages to a lane, turn right, and then right again to cross the **River Avon**. Climb the stile on your left. Bear diagonally right across the field to a stile and cross the lane and stile opposite. Follow the path to two squeeze stiles and turn left around the field edge.

④ Climb the stile on your left and turn right along the field edge. Follow the path through scrub to a stile and proceed ahead beside the old **Wilts and Berks Canal**. Pass an old bridge, climb a stile into woodland and turn immediately right along a narrow path to a stile. Turn left along the field edge, keep ahead across the next field to a stile and head uphill to a stile.

WHERE TO EAT AND DRINK ⓘ

You are spoilt for choice in Lacock. For snacks and lunches head for the National Trust's **Stable Tea Rooms** or **King John's Hunting Lodge**; for pub lunches try the **Red Lion**, the **George** or the **Carpenters Arms**. For something special try the **Sign of the Angel** restaurant.

---

⑤ Proceed ahead to a gate and cross the next field to a gate. Join a track, cross a metalled farm drive and continue to a gate. Ascend a grassy track to a gate and walk uphill towards a house. Before a gate, turn right across the top of the field to reach double stiles. Bear half right to a gate and ascend the farm drive through woodland, then uphill to a gate. Continue to a lane.

WHILE YOU'RE THERE ⓘ

Just north of Lacock you will find **Lackham Country Attractions**, where historic barns and granaries house an intriguing range of displays depicting Wiltshire agriculture and rural life. There are also walled gardens and a farm park.

---

⑥ Turn left, then cross the stile on the right before a house. Keep to the left-hand field edge, cross a stile and bear diagonally left to a stile in the field corner. Cross the stile ahead into woodland and continue to another stile. Proceed ahead along the field edge to a stile on your right. Bear half left across **Bowden Park**, keeping to the left of a clump of trees, and bear right to a stile beside a gate.

WHAT TO LOOK FOR ⓘ

Look for the print of Fox Talbot's first **photographic negative**, showing the abbeys oriel window, beside the window in the abbey's south gallery. Explore the **cloister court** and see where many scenes from *Harry Potter and the Philosopher's Stone* (2001) were filmed.

---

⑦ Head downhill to a stile and turn left around the field edge to a stile and gate near a house. Follow the path to the drive and follow it left. As tarmac gives way to gravel, bear off right across **Bewley Common** to the road. Turn right and return to **Lacock**.

A Canal and a Church at Bradford-on-Avon

Combine a visit to this enchanting riverside town and its surprising Saxon church, with a canal-side stroll.

•DISTANCE•	3½ miles (5.7km)
•MINIMUM TIME•	1hr 45min
•ASCENT / GRADIENT•	164ft (50m)
•LEVEL OF DIFFICULTY•	
•PATHS•	Tow path, field and woodland paths, metalled lanes
•LANDSCAPE•	Canal, river valley, wooded hillsides, town streets
•SUGGESTED MAP•	aqua3 OS Explorers 142 Shepton Mallet;156 Chippenham & Bradford-on-Avon
•START / FINISH•	Grid reference: ST 824606 (on Explorer 156)
•DOG FRIENDLINESS•	On lead through town
•PARKING•	Bradford-on-Avon Station car park (charge)
•PUBLIC TOILETS•	Station car park
•CONTRIBUTOR•	David Hancock

BACKGROUND TO THE WALK

Set in the wooded Avon Valley, Bradford is one of Wiltshire's loveliest towns, combining historical charm, appealing architecture and dramatic topography. It is often likened to a miniature Bath, the town sharing the same honey-coloured limestone, elegant terraces and steep winding streets that rise sharply away from the river. Historically a 'broad ford' across the Avon, the original Iron-Age settlement was expanded in turn by the Romans and Saxons, the latter giving Bradford its greatest treasure, St Laurence's Church. The Avon was spanned by a fine stone bridge in the 13th century – two of its arches survive in the present 17th-century structure – and by the 1630s Bradford had grown into a powerful centre for the cloth and woollen industries.

Wealthy Wool Town

You will find exploring the riverside and the lanes, alleys and flights of steps up the north slope of the town most rewarding. Beautiful terraces are lined with elegant 18th-century merchants' houses with walled gardens, and charming 17th- and 18th-century weavers' cottages, the best examples being located along Newtown, Middle Rank and Tory terraces. The latter is the highest and affords superb views of the town. The wealth needed to make all this building possible came from the manufacture of woollen cloth. In the early 1700s Daniel Defoe, author of *Robinson Crusoe*, commented 'They told me at Bradford that it was no extra-ordinary thing to have clothiers in that county worth from £10,000 to £40,000 per man.' Bradford's medieval prosperity is reflected in the size of the magnificent 14th-century tithe barn at Barton Farm.

With the development of mechanisation, the wool trade moved from individual houses to large water and steam driven mills alongside the Avon. At the time that the Kennet and Avon Canal was built, in 1810, the town supported around 30 mills and some of these buildings survive, in various degrees of restoration or disrepair, today. With the centre of the wool trade shifting to Yorkshire, the industry declined during the 19th century and the last of the mills closed in 1905. The town is now prosperous once again with tourists and new residents, many of them commuting to Bath, Bristol and even London.

Jewel in the Crown

Down by the river, the tiny, bare Saxon Church of St Laurence is the jewel in Bradford's crown and you really should not miss it! It was founded by St Aldhelm, the Abbot of Malmesbury, in AD 700 and this present structure dates from the 10th century. For centuries its presence was forgotten. The chancel became a house, the nave a school, and the west wall formed part of a factory building. The true origins and purpose of the site were only rediscovered in 1858 and, after careful restoration, it remains one of the best-preserved Saxon churches in England.

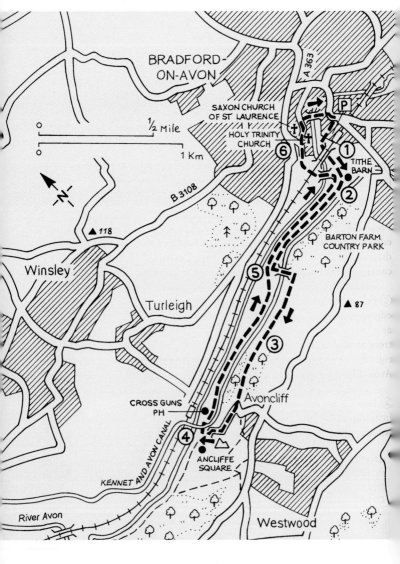

Walk 48 Directions

① Walk to the end of the car park, away from the station, and follow the path left beneath the railway and beside the **River Avon**. Enter **Barton Farm Country Park** and keep to the path across a grassy area to an information board. With the packhorse bridge right, keep ahead to the right of the tithe barn to the **Kennet and Avon Canal**.

WHILE YOU'RE THERE ⓘ

Discover the natural and historical heritage of Bradford with a visit to the town's fascinating **museum**. Linger at **Barton Farm Country Park** to view the craft shops in the former medieval farm buildings, and marvel at the great beams and rafters of Bradford's magnificent, tithe barn, the second largest in Britain.

---

② Turn right along the tow path. Cross the bridge over the canal in ½ mile (800m) and follow the path right to a footbridge and stile. Proceed along the right-hand field edge to a further stile, then bear diagonally left uphill away from the canal to a kissing gate.

③ Follow the path through the edge of woodland. Keep to the path as it bears left uphill through the trees to reach a metalled lane. Turn right and walk steeply downhill to **Avoncliff** and the canal.

④ Don't cross the aqueduct, instead pass the **Mad Hatter Tea Rooms**, descend the steps on your

---

WHAT TO LOOK FOR ⓘ

Note the small, dome-shaped building at the south end of Town Bridge. Called the 'Chapel', it was, in fact, a lock-up or 'blind house' containing two cells with iron bedsteads for prisoners.

---

right and pass beneath the canal. Keep right by the **Cross Guns** and join the tow path towards **Bradford-on-Avon**. Continue for ¾ mile (1.2km) to the bridge passed on your outward route.

⑤ Bear off left downhill along a metalled track and follow it beside the River Avon back into **Barton Farm Country Park**. Cross the packhorse bridge and the railway to **Barton Orchard**.

⑥ Follow the alleyway to **Church Street** and continue ahead to pass the **Holy Trinity Church** and the Saxon **Church of St Laurence**. Cross the footbridge and walk through St Margaret's car park to the road. Turn right, then right again back into the station car park.

WHERE TO EAT AND DRINK ⓘ

In Bradford-on-Avon, try the **Cottage Co-operative Café** behind the tourist information centre, the **Dandy Lion** in Market Street and the **Canal Tavern** or the **Lock Inn Canalside Café** on Frome Road. At Avoncliff, the **Cross Guns** offers traditional pub food and a splendid terraced riverside garden, while lunches and teas are served at the **Mad Hatter Tea Rooms**.

Through the Avon and Frome Valleys

Combine a glorious walk through the beautiful Avon and Frome valleys with a visit to a romantic hillside garden at Iford Manor.

•DISTANCE•	3½ miles (5.7km)
•MINIMUM TIME•	2hrs
•ASCENT / GRADIENT•	170ft (52m) ▲ ▲ ▲
•LEVEL OF DIFFICULTY•	🚶 🚶 🚶
•PATHS•	Riverside, field and woodland paths, metalled lanes, 6 stiles
•LANDSCAPE•	Canal, river valley, wooded hillsides
•SUGGESTED MAP•	aqua3 OS Explorers 142 Shepton Mallet & Mendip Hills East; 156 Chippenham & Bradford-on-Avon
•START / FINISH•	Grid reference: ST 805601 (on Explorer 156)
•DOG FRIENDLINESS•	No real problems
•PARKING•	Limited parking at Avoncliff railway halt
•PUBLIC TOILETS•	None on route
•CONTRIBUTOR•	David Hancock

BACKGROUND TO THE WALK

Virtually every precious ingredient of the ever changing countryside is included in this glorious walk from the Kennet and Avon Canal at Avoncliff to Freshford and the River Frome, and sleepy Iford on the Somerset border. The river scenery by the Avon and the Frome is surprisingly dramatic and, for good measure, there is a Tudor manor house at Iford with beautiful Italianate gardens. If that's not enough to satisfy you, then you can extend your walk along the canal tow path from Avoncliff to elegant Bradford-on-Avon, the most southerly town of the Cotswolds, and return to Avoncliff by train.

Avoncliff Aqueduct

West of Bradford-on-Avon, the meandering River Avon is accompanied by the Kennet and Avon Canal as it passes through the dramatic and steeply wooded hillsides that rise 400ft (122m) above the river, arguably the finest natural landscape in west Wiltshire. Stretching 87 miles (140km) from Bristol to Reading, the Kennet and Avon Canal was built with great skill by the canal engineer John Rennie, opening in 1810 to carry goods to and from London. To negotiate the steep and winding Avon Valley, Rennie had to construct two substantial aqueducts, one of which you can see at Avoncliff. Built in 1804, it is 110yds (100m) long and features three arches, a solid parapet and balustraded ends.

In the Frome Valley

Leaving the canalside, the walk enters the valley of the River Frome. On a steep hillside overlooking lush water-meadows and the confluence of the two rivers stands the attractive village of Freshford. It prospered in the early 19th century through the production of broadcloth and has some handsome stone houses and a popular riverside inn. You've passed into Somerset now, but the scenery is just as fine.

Iford Manor Gardens

Occupying a steep slope on the opposite bank of River Frome, the romantic gardens of Iford Manor, a fine Tudor mansion with a striking classical front added in 1730, are a subtle blend of Italianate layout and English planting. This was the garden created by the distinguished architect and landscape designer, Harold Peto, who lived at Iford from 1899 to 1933. The topography of Iford lent itself to the strong architectural framework of steps, terraces and pools, and the predominant theme of the design is Italian, with plantings of cypress, juniper, box and yew interspersed with stone sarcophagi, urns, marble seats and statues, columns and loggias. You can see the unique and fascinating results of Peto's labours on selected days during the summer months.

Bradford-on-Avon

When you've completed this walk, it is well worth taking a leisurely stroll alongside the Kennet and Avon Canal into the heart of Bradford-on-Avon (▶ Walk 48), where you will find houses of Bath stone, built between the 16th and 18th centuries, rising steeply above the River Avon in a town made prosperous by Dutch weavers. A wander through the town will reveal its splendid 14th-century tithe barn, one of the largest to have been built in England, and the town's most historic landmark, the tiny Saxon Church of St Laurence which dates from about AD 700.

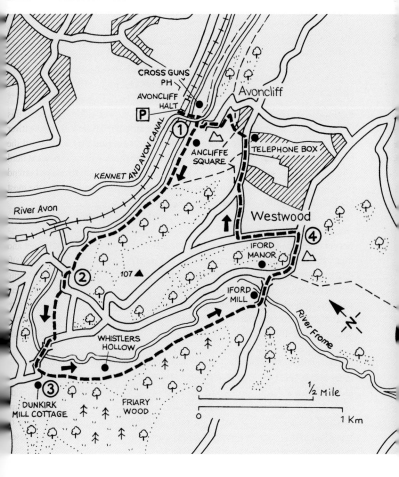

Walk 49

Walk 49 **Directions**

① From **Avoncliff Halt**, cross the aqueduct towards the **Cross Guns** pub. Take the path right and pass beneath the canal. With the **Mad Hatter Tea Rooms** on your left, disregard the tow path signs and keep ahead along the track. As it veers left, maintain your direction through the gate and trees. Go through a gate and soon walk beside the **River Avon** to reach another gate. Pass through woodland to a gate, then head across water-meadows to a lane and the **River Frome** at **Freshford**.

WHAT TO LOOK FOR
Traces of the weaving industry can be found at Avoncliff in the form of **weavers' cottages** and two flock mills (one a ruin the other now converted to a house) that stand upstream either side of the weir below Rennie's fine aqueduct. On your outward route, just beyond the tea rooms at Avoncliff, you'll see the **old workhouse** (Ancliffe Square) which has been tastefully converted into modern apartments.

② Turn left, climb a stile on your right and cross the field to a stile. Maintain direction, towards a derelict factory, to a stile and lane. Turn right, walk beside the river and cross the bridge. Continue uphill and take the bridle path left in front of **Dunkirk Mill Cottage**. Bear right, then take the bridle path left opposite a house.

③ Continue to a gate, keep left down to a track and turn left. Turn right with a yellow arrow, opposite a house called **Whistlers Hollow**, to a stile. Keep left through a field to another stile and walk through **Friary Wood** to a gate. Turn right along the field edge for ½ mile (800m) to a stile and lane. Turn left, pass **Iford Mill** and cross the river bridge to **Iford Manor Gardens**. Bear right and walk steeply uphill to a junction.

④ Turn left along the verge for ¼ mile (400m) and take the bridle path right, signed 'Upper Westwood'. At a lane, turn right through **Upper Westwood**. Turn left opposite the telephone box then, where the lane curves left, take the left of two footpaths ahead. Walk downhill through the edge of woodland. Pass beside a gate, cross a drive and follow the lane left, downhill back to **Avoncliff**.

Extending the Walk
You can combine this walk with Walk 48 which will take you into the historic town of **Bradford-on-Avon**, barely a mile (1.6km) upriver

WHERE TO EAT AND DRINK
At Avoncliff, the **Cross Guns** offers traditional pub food and a splendid terraced riverside garden, while lunches and teas are served at the **Mad Hatter Tea Rooms**. Enjoy a pint at the **Freshford Inn** or home-made teas at the **Peto Gardens** at Iford Manor (summer weekends and bank holidays only).

WHILE YOU'RE THERE
Two miles (3.2km) south east is **Westwood Manor**, a fully furnished 15th-century stone manor with original Gothic and Jacobean windows and fine plasterwork. In Bradford-on-Avon, discover the natural and historical heritage of the town with a visit to the town's fascinating museum. At **Barton Farm Country Park**, view the craft shops in the former medieval farm buildings and marvel at the great beams and rafters of Bradford's magnificent, cathedral-like tithe barn, the second largest in Britain.

A Walk with Good Manors from Holt

Stroll from a rare industrial village to a beautiful moated manor house.

•DISTANCE•	3 miles (4.8km)
•MINIMUM TIME•	1hr 30min
•ASCENT / GRADIENT•	147ft (45m) ▲ ▲ ▲
•LEVEL OF DIFFICULTY•	👟 👟 👟
•PATHS•	Field paths, metalled track, country lanes, 8 stiles
•LANDSCAPE•	Gently undulating farmland
•SUGGESTED MAP•	aqua3 OS Explorer 156 Chippenham & Bradford-on-Avon
•START / FINISH•	Grid reference: ST 861619
•DOG FRIENDLINESS•	Keep dogs under control at all times
•PARKING•	Holt Village Hall car park
•PUBLIC TOILETS•	Only if visiting The Courts or Great Chalfield Manor
•CONTRIBUTOR•	David Hancock

BACKGROUND TO THE WALK

Threaded by the busy B3107 linking Melksham to Bradford-on-Avon, Holt is a rare industrial Wiltshire village with a significant history as a cloth-making and leather-tanning centre. The tannery, founded in the early 18th century, still occupies the main three-storey factory in the appropriately named small industrial area – The Midlands – while bedding manufacture and light engineering now occupy former cloth factories. Holt also enjoyed short-lived fame between 1690 and 1750 as a spa, based on the curative properties of a spring, but its popularity declined in face of competition from nearby Bath. The most attractive part of the village is at Ham Green where elegant 17th- and 18th-century houses stand along three sides of a fine green shaded by horse chestnut trees, and a quiet lane leads to the late Victorian parish church with a Perpendicular tower.

The Courts – Wiltshire's Secret Garden

From the green a walled walk leads to The Courts, a substantial 18th-century house that served, as its name suggests, as the place where the local magistrate sat to adjudicate in the disputes of the cloth weavers from Bradford-on-Avon. Although not open, the house makes an attractive backdrop to 7 acres (2.8ha) of authentic English country garden owned by the National Trust. Hidden away behind high walls and reached through an avenue of pleached limes, you will find a series of garden 'rooms' that are full of charm and a haven of peace away from the busy village street. Stroll along a network of stone paths through formal gardens featuring yew topiary, lawns with colourful herbaceous borders, a lake and lily pond with aquatic and water-tolerant plants, and explore an area given over to wild flowers among an interesting small arboretum of trees and shrubs.

Great Chalfield Manor

You will glimpse the Tudor chimneys and gabled windows of this enchanting manor house as you stride across peaceful field paths a mile (1.6km) or so north west of Holt. Enhanced by a moat and gatehouse, this exquisite group of buildings will certainly live up to your expectations and really must be visited. Built in 1480, during the Wars of the Roses, by Thomas Tropenell, Great Chalfield is one of the most perfect examples of the late medieval English manor house which, together with its immediately adjacent church, mill, great barn and other Elizabethan farm buildings, makes a harmonious and memorable visual group.

Sensitively restored in the early 20th century by Sir Harold Brakspear after two centuries of neglect and disrepair, the manor house is centred on its traditional great hall, which rises to the rafters and is lit by windows, including two beautiful oriels, positioned high in the walls. Join one of the guided tours and you will be able to see the fine vaulting, the chimney place of the hall, the concealed spy-holes in the gallery, designed to allow people to see what was going on in the great hall, and the amusing ornaments, gargoyles and other fascinating details of this fine building.

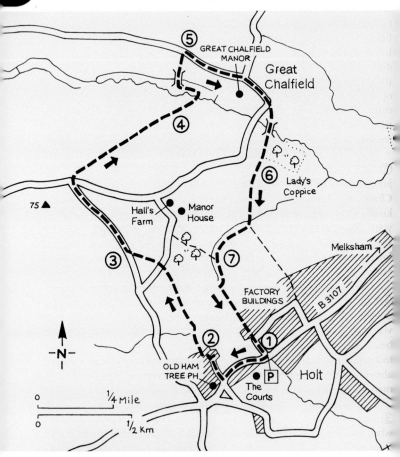

Walk 50 Directions

① Turn left out of the car park and then right along the **B3107** through the village. Just before reaching the

Old Ham Tree pub and village green, turn right along **Crown Corner**. At the end of the lane take the waymarked path left along a drive. Follow the fenced path beside 'Highfields' to a stile.

WHERE TO EAT AND DRINK ⓘ
You will find a choice of pubs in Holt. The 16th-century **Tollgate Inn** offers innovative, freshly produced food on varied menus alongside fine wines and local ales. For more traditional pub food and atmosphere head for the **Old Ham Tree** which overlooks the green.

WHAT TO LOOK FOR ⓘ
A huge **factory** dominates the landscape south of Holt, standing beside the River Avon on the site of a 16th-century cloth mill. The present building dates from 1824 and belongs to Nestlé who manufacture processed foods here. All that remains of **Holt Spa** is an arch, pump handle and stone tablet on one of the factory walls in the industrial estate.

② Keep to the right along the edge of the field, then keep ahead in the next field towards the clump of fir trees. Continue following the worn path to the right, into a further field. Keep left along the field edge to a stile in the top corner. Maintain direction to a ladder stile and cross the metalled drive and stile opposite. Bear diagonally left through the field to a hidden stile in the hedge, level with the clump of trees to your right.

③ Turn right along the lane. At a junction, turn right towards **Great Chalfield** and go through the kissing gate almost immediately on your left. Take the arrowed path right, diagonally across a large field towards **Great Chalfield Manor** visible ahead.

④ Cross a stile and bear half right downhill to a stile. Cross the stream via stepping stones, then a stile and bear diagonally left across the field to a gate. Cross the bridge and keep ahead beside the hedge to a metalled track by a barn.

⑤ Turn right, then right again when you reach the lane, passing in front of **Great Chalfield Manor**. At the sharp right-hand bend, go through the gate ahead and bear right, then half left across the field to cross a footbridge over a stream. Continue straight on up the field beside woodland to a gate in the field corner.

⑥ Follow the left-hand field edge to a gate, then follow the path straight ahead towards a chimney on the skyline. Go through a gate, bear immediately right to a gate in the hedge and turn right along the path around the field edge.

⑦ Ignore the stile on your right and continue to the field corner and a raised path beside water. Go through a gate and turn left along the field edge to a further gate on your left. Join the drive past **Garlands Farm** and pass between small factory buildings to the road and turn right back to the car park.

WHILE YOU'RE THERE ⓘ
Visit **Trowbridge Museum**, located in the town's last working woollen mill, and learn more about the woollen mills and cloth-making industry of the Avon Valley in West Wiltshire.

50 Walks in

The following titles are also available in this series

- Berkshire & Buckinghamshire
- Brecon Beacons & South Wales
- Cambridgeshire & East Midlands
- Cornwall
- Derbyshire
- Devon
- Dorset
- Durham & Northumberland
- Edinburgh & Eastern Scotland
- Essex
- Glasgow & South West Scotland
- Gloucestershire
- Hampshire & Isle of Wight
- Hertfordshire
- Kent
- Lake District
- Lancashire & Cheshire
- London
- Norfolk
- North Yorkshire
- Oxfordshire
- Peak District
- Scotland
- Scottish Highlands & Islands
- Shropshire
- Snowdonia & North Wales
- Somerset
- Staffordshire
- Suffolk
- Surrey
- Sussex
- Warwickshire & West Midlands
- West Yorkshire
- Wiltshire
- Worcestershire & Herefordshire
- Yorkshire Dales

Acknowledgements

AQUA3 AA Publishing and Outcrop Publishing Services would like to thank Chartech for supplying aqua3 maps for this book.
For more information visit their website: www.aqua3.com.

Series management: Outcrop Publishing Services Limited, Cumbria
Series editor: Chris Bagshaw
Copy editor: Pam Stagg **Cartographic editor:** Jenny Skelley
Front cover: AA Photo Library/S Day